D0412056

GUEST HOUSE FOR YOUNG WIDOWS

By Azadeh Moaveni

Guest House for Young Widows

Lipstick Jihad

Iran Awakening (with Shirin Ebadi)

Honeymoon in Tehran

GUEST HOUSE FOR YOUNG WIDOWS

AMONG THE WOMEN OF ISIS

Azadeh Moaveni

SCRIBE
Melbourne • London

Scribe Publications
2 John St, Clerkenwell, London, WC1N 2ES, United Kingdom
18–20 Edward St, Brunswick, Victoria 3056, Australia

This edition published by arrangement with Random House,
a division of Penguin Random House LLC

Published by Scribe 2019

Text design by Susan Turner

Printed and bound in the UK by CPI Group (UK) Ltd, Croydon CR0 4YY

Scribe Publications is committed to the sustainable use of natural resources
and the use of paper products made responsibly from those resources.

9781912854608 (UK edition)
9781925849608 (AU edition)
9781925693010 (e-book)

Catalogue records for this book are available from the
National Library of Australia and the British Library.

For Nader

CONTENTS

CONTENTS

CONTENTS

CONTENTS

PROLOGUE
BETWEEN SEASONS

Spring 2007, Le Kram, Tunis

NOUR DIDN'T CONSIDER HERSELF A PEARL WITHOUT A SHELL, OR A lollipop without a wrapper, or anything other than her thirteen-year-old self, wanting to practice her religion as best she could. She had listened to a sheikh on YouTube argue why the face veil was obligatory for Muslim women, and after listening a further four times, his words played like a ticker tape through her mind. The Quran commanded, in the verse called *Surah al-Noor,* "The Light," that women not display their beauty and ornaments, "except for that which is apparent." And is the face apparent? the sheikh argued. Is there anything less apparent than a face? It seemed to inexorably follow, then, that women wishing to submit to the divine will of God, to be eligible for His blessings and judged by Him approvingly, should cover their faces. The sheikh's words made intuitive sense to Nour: modest covering enrobed women in the core values of Islam itself, in peace, calm, and equality. It dimmed the visible differences between rich women and poor women, dark and fair, beautiful and plain; it was a reminder that God loved all His creations equally.

Nour shared this new belief with her girlfriends one afternoon in the spring of 2007 as they were sitting in the park, Le Kram's nominal neighborhood green space, amid parched palm trees, heaps of garbage, and a decaying swing set covered in rust. The girls agreed it sounded persuasive, and one of them asked, "So who's going first?" Most of them had started covering their hair when their bodies began filling out in the last few years, just a light scarf, and they also had begun praying, as many did in their families and in the neighborhood. Wearing a hijab was ordinary; even though Tunisia's laws banned the headscarf in schools and you could get sent home for wearing one, it was still a commonplace enough infraction. The face veil, the *niqab*, was punchier, more assertive. But the sheikh on YouTube had said one shouldn't be timid about one's Islam, that even though wearing hijab was tough in so many places, "the more we are in number, the stronger our message."

Had Nour been born to an upper-middle-class family in La Marsa, a suburb of the city where liberal Tunisians lived amid Western expatriates and restaurants that served prosciutto and gin, she might have rebelled by piercing her tongue. But she was a daughter of Le Kram, a working-class neighborhood in a country where the state micro-policed people's piety, and putting on the niqab was a natural act of defiance for a teenage girl. That day in the park, as the sunlight caught the glinting sides of the juice packs in the trash heap, she felt a knot of purpose in her stomach. "I'll do it first," she said to her friends. "I'll do it tomorrow."

She already had a niqab from the hijab shop near the pizzeria; she had bought it the previous week after watching videos of the sheikh. She had tried it on in the bathroom at home with the door locked, angling her body in different directions to see what it did to her eyes.

The next morning, she stuffed it into her schoolbag, and said goodbye to her mother as usual. As she neared the school she slipped into a doorway and pinned the niqab—by itself it was a small thing, just a little scrap of fabric that covered her nose and mouth—to her headscarf. The fabric tickled her lips as she breathed against it.

The principal often stood outside the main doors of the school in the morning, greeting pupils as they hurried up the steps. Nour fell in behind some older girls, hoping to pass by without notice, but the principal stopped her.

"Who are you?" she asked, peering at the slim frame obscured by the folds of black. Nour heard, if it wasn't her imagination, a flicker of appreciation in the woman's voice. "I'm going to let you in," the principal said. "But you're going to have to deal with the teachers yourself."

Nour's first class of the day was French, and she took her usual seat in the classroom, assembling her notebook and pens on the wooden desk. The teacher looked at her from across the classroom. She didn't say anything at first, just narrowed her eyes, then approached Nour, stopping to lean on an empty desk a couple of meters away.

"What is this ridiculous thing you're wearing? Do you think God wants you to hang a curtain across your face? I hate God. God isn't some kind, benevolent power, he's cruel." The teacher crossed her arms over her chest, nostrils twitching. To Nour, the things the French teacher was saying were blasphemy. Nour stared ahead at the blackboard, focusing on the strange curve of the teacher's handwriting. "God killed my parents," the French teacher continued. "If I could take revenge against God, I would." The class watched the berating in unprecedented silence. The French teacher finally rose and started the lesson.

Nour's next class was Arabic literature. In Tunisia, teaching of the humanities, especially literature, tended to draw Francophone secularists with a deep antipathy to the religious, whom they viewed as backward and uncultured. When the literature teacher saw Nour, she rose from her seat in surprise and walked over, blocking Nour from reaching her desk.

"You're not sitting in my class with that thing on. Take it off immediately!" she said.

Nour's face went hot, and she refused.

"I said, take it off," the teacher repeated, punctuating each syllable.

Nour wondered if the teacher knew it was her. The literature teacher liked her. Would it matter? "No, I can't, please. It's me, it's Nour." Her voice trembled.

The teacher moved forward and placed a hand on Nour's chest. "Didn't you hear me? I told you to take it off." She was shouting now, her face distorted and ugly with anger.

Nour's heart roared in her ears. She stepped backward, away from the weight of the hand. Students gathered around them, trying to calm the teacher. She pushed them away and planted both of her hands on Nour's chest, shoving hard, as if to topple her.

Nour gasped and stumbled backward. The teacher's arm rose again, as if to strike her, as if to pull the niqab off. One of Nour's friends in the class, a tall girl who sometimes got called the Giraffe, grabbed the teacher's hand. "Please, *ustadha,* please, calm down."

Nour was crying, glad only that no one could see the tears of humiliation under her niqab. By now, the class was openly rioting. Someone had fetched the principal, who came running into the room and ordered the students into the schoolyard. Classes were canceled for the rest of the day.

IN THE MID-TWENTIETH CENTURY AND the decades that followed, men and women led the Middle East's armed opposition groups and insurgencies together. The women who took part often became international celebrities. The Algerian resistance fighter Djamila Bouhired, who opposed French rule of her country in the 1950s, planted a bomb in an Algiers café that killed three people. A French colonial court sentenced her to death and she was tortured in prison. Her trial became an international cause célèbre, prompting a Moroccan princess, tens of British parliamentarians, and Bertrand Russell to plead her case to the president of France, who eventually stayed her execution. Bouhired later married her French defense attorney, who had fallen in love with her during her trial, and became known as "the Arab Joan of Arc." She was featured in *The Battle of Algiers,* along with two other films, posed for Picasso, and was sung about in Persian. When the Palestinian liberation fighter Leila Khaled hijacked an airplane in the summer of 1969, she inspired several rock songs, a character on the television show *Doctor Who,* a feature film, a mural in Belfast, and an art installation called *The Icon,* featuring 3,500 tubes of lipstick. She had to undergo six plastic surgeries to evade her own visibility.

In this age, women like Khaled and Bouhired would certainly be called terrorists. But in the 1960s and 1970s, their popular appeal reflected a worldview that was more understanding of armed struggle. Such opposition, in those years, was seen as an expression of legitimate political aspirations—a symptom of asymmetrical conflict rather than evil ideology. Those decades, leading up to and during the Cold War, were dominated by postcolonial liberation movements that commanded sympathy in the West, and were supported, to varying degrees, by the Soviet Union and the United States itself.

Bouhired and Khaled were striking correctives to prevailing Western attitudes about Middle Eastern women. In Simone de Beauvoir's account of a 1967 trip to Egypt, she was offended to find Egyptian women bound to a "life of repetition," subjugated by men who behaved toward them like "feudalists, colonialists, and racists." A "deadly beauty" from the Middle East who hijacked airplanes in service of her movement's political struggle embodied an unexpected, raw female power. So too did a young Algerian woman who refused to chant "France is our mother," as was rote for students under colonial rule, and screamed "Algeria is our mother!" instead. It was possible, even if not easy, to sympathize with emancipated Middle Eastern women seeking to free their countries from occupiers.

In the decades that followed Bouhired's capture and trial by the French and Khaled's hijacking, the political landscape of the Middle East changed dramatically. The great secular nationalist liberation movements of the post–World War II era that had challenged colonial control saw themselves weakened and subverted. The Palestinians, whose first intifada included many women among its leaders, saw many of their leading figures assassinated by Israel; in Iran, a CIA-supported coup snuffed out a democratic push to nationalize the country's oil industry; in Egypt, defeat in the 1967 war against Israel contributed to sclerosis within the Nasserite movement, and eventually to the entrenchment of authoritarian military rule under Hosni Mubarak, a firm ally of the United States. Across the Middle East, secular movements and leaders fared poorly, whatever they were agitating for, whether the return of occupied land, political freedom, or socioeconomic justice. Enshrined in nationalist and leftist armed struggle or even secular nationalist politics was a belief in liberal universal values and democratic principles, and the assumption that the West—which espoused these ideas—would respond to or tolerate Middle Eastern figures who also upheld them. But over time, it became starkly clear that that would not be the case. Prisons began to swell with Islamists, activists and militants who, disenchanted with the old failed ideologies, turned to religion to inflect their opposition. The torture they often faced accelerated and cemented their radicalism. Politics across much of the region stagnated. In 1979, with markedly little violence, the Iranian revolution did something unthinkable: it dislodged a modern, worldly U.S.-allied government, and propelled to power a Shia cleric, a gloomy medieval figure in black robes who promised his people independence and freedom under the banner of an Islamic republic. This was a defining moment for the Middle East. Where all secular leaders, from cosmopolitan leftists to nationalist democrats, had failed, a cleric had succeeded. And he was propelled to power by crowds filled with women; bare-headed women in skirts, conservative women in headscarves, united in their nationalist belief that Iran must be independent of the United States. The Iranian revolution inspired a new wave of politics in the region; the militant groups, political oppositions, and visions that emerged turned more religious and radical, and with this shift, they also became more firmly the terrain of men.

In the 1980s, in the midst of the Cold War, the United States backed Muslim foreign fighters opposing the Soviets in Afghanistan. That fight drew men from around the world, but women were not invited to join in this religious jihad. The wives of fighters often accompanied their husbands to the front, but in traditional domestic roles. So too with the al-Qaeda movement of Osama bin Laden that grew in its wake, culminating in the 9/11 attacks. When it came to gender roles, al-Qaeda remained starchily orthodox and uninterested in women's involvement. Even as late as 2008, bin Laden's deputy, Ayman al-Zawaheri, maintained that "there are no women in al-Qaeda"; women were simply wives of the *mujaheddin,* "assuming a heroic role in taking care of their homes." Al-Qaeda neither wooed fighters with promises of brides nor beckoned single women to join as members. In 2003, the U.S. invasion of Iraq attracted Arabs from around the region to fight the American occupation, setting off a wave of insurgent violence that would roil the country for years to come. It was here, in the shattered aftermath of liberated Iraq, that a new chapter opened for women's militancy.

Iraqi women were ensnared in both the U.S.-run torture chambers of Abu Ghraib and the brutality of Iraq's criminal justice system; their defiled honor became a rallying cry for al-Qaeda's affiliate in Iraq (a predecessor to the Islamic State in Iraq), and young women themselves began signing up for suicide missions in the Sunni insurgency. This dark interlude remained largely an Iraqi story, an after-wound of the American invasion, but it laid the groundwork for what would later follow. Because so many of the fighters who traveled to Iraq were veterans of previous waves of jihadist violence, it was easy for policymakers and security analysts to cast what was unfolding as more of the same: Middle Eastern terrorism driven by Islam itself. To the Western eye, the dynamics by then were cemented: insurgency was religious, and insurgent leadership, combat, and recruitment were men's work.

You can pick up books on any one of these conflicts, riffle through the index, and not find a single woman. Violence and insurgency were enacted by men, and women blended into the wallpaper of history, believed to be bystanders, passive enablers, sometimes victims. They weren't the ones holding forth on the pulpit, excoriating the West or Arab dictators. They didn't record fatwas on cassette tapes that were smuggled across the world. They didn't carry guns or sit beturbaned and cross-legged on dusty floors with Western journalists. But women were always there in the background: as wives and logisticians, educators and morale boosters, mothers whispering values, politics, and worldviews into the young ears of the next generation. Their roles were indirect. To outside observers, who kept their eyes trained on armed actors on the stage, the women in the wings were invisible.

THE 2010S CHANGED THAT FOREVER. In 2011, a staccato sequence of uprisings across North Africa and the Middle East heralded momentous change. Women galvanized the Arab Spring, often standing at the forefront of protests in Cairo's Tahrir Square, in Bahrain and Yemen, Libya and Tunisia, encouraging and egging on men to confront security forces, demanding political freedom, dignity, and opportunity. Young women like Nour, who had found no place for herself in the old order of Tunisia, formed the backbone of a movement that, more than anything, simply sought the right of all to be included: in school, in politics, in the market of opportunity.

Arab despots moved to crush the protests. And in the tumultuous years of the Arab Spring, these despots found unlikely allies. The West was deeply ambivalent about this sudden wave of change, despite the fact that the United States and Europe had complained for years that authoritarianism was holding back the Arab world's development, allowing women's inequality to fester and fueling radicalism. As Egypt's revolution stumbled to find its feet under the leadership of Islamists—politicians who had been democratically voted into power—President Barack Obama's loyalty shifted toward the country's generals, who were itching to consolidate their control. America's priority, he declared, was stability. In the course of about two years, these hopeful Arab revolutions collapsed one by one, descending into civil wars or suppression by the generals and autocrats who saw that the United States was distracted by other priorities.

Out of this historic interlude of hope and chaos, into the resulting vacuum of instability, the Islamic State emerged. It was sophisticated, organized, and determined to exploit all the grievances, cracks, and disorder the lost revolutions so generously offered. And it had perceptively noted women as a rising political force, even as it proposed a radically patriarchal form of family organization and politics that stripped women of their autonomy.

The Islamic State rose from the recent histories of Syria and Iraq, the specific grievances and fractures of those countries. But from the earliest days, the State told a different, loftier story about itself. It claimed the mantle of leadership for Sunnis around the world, prophesying a final apocalyptic battle between the forces of Islam and the West. It promised the creation of an Islamic homeland, an empire-state where Muslims could live freely and justly under a kingdom of heaven. Echoing the demands of the Arab Spring protests, it seduced tens of thousands of Muslims into traveling to its territory, with assurances of enlightened rule, opportunity, and dignity.

If in 2011 the aspirations of young women across the Arab world had been for freedom, a dream that seemed achingly close before disappearing into the smoke and tear gas of coups and massacres, by 2013, when IS leader Abu Bakr al-Baghdadi declared his caliphate, the future held only more of what Simone de Beauvoir had sniffed at previous generations of Middle Eastern women for accepting: lives of repetition. Conventional wisdom in the West held that nominally secular Arab generals and royal autocrats were "better" for women than political Islamists, but under the rule of such leaders, women faced multiple binds: they had to contend with the patriarchy of their culture, which frowned on women being educated and working; they had to struggle with the structural barriers to accessing work and education in societies like Tunisia that rejected religious women accessing public life—*and at the very same time* could not organize to challenge these norms through politics, because secular dictators didn't allow any politics at all.

These supposedly better-for-women dictators were not opposed to imprisoning women or using sexual violence—gang rapes, virginity checks—to punish women who opposed them. For women who wanted more—more dignity, more public and civic influence, more room to practice their religion—the status quo had no room for them.

It was in this febrile, despairing atmosphere that the Islamic State began unfurling its vision. It was neither authoritarian client state nor pretender to liberal democracy. It was not a conventional nation-state at all, not obliged to follow the dictates of neoliberal capitalism.

In 2013, thousands of women from across the world poured into this promised land. They came from across North Africa and the rest of the Middle East, from Europe, Russia, and Central Asia, the United States and Australia, China and East Asia. Women formed 17 percent of all European travelers to the caliphate. They included educated daughters of diplomats, trainee doctors, teenagers with straight-A averages, as well as low-income drifters and desolate housewives. They swelled the cities under the group's control, settling in the abandoned homes of Syrians and Iraqis who had fled the conflict. They set up makeshift clinics and schools for the Islamic homeland they believed themselves to be building.

Many of these women were trying, in a twisted way, to achieve dignity and freedom through an embrace of a politics that ended up violating both. Perhaps it is difficult, if not impossible, to understand and sympathize with women whose vision of armed struggle deviated so dramatically from the liberation fighters of earlier decades. They embraced an apocalyptic ideology, supported attacks on cafés and places of worship, and seemed to espouse their own subordination, through an ethos of separateness so severe as to forsake any real prospect of justice within its confines.

Perhaps to the outside world, the ending of the story was already written. But the Islamic State's female would-be citizens harbored real expectations, and watched them quickly fall apart. The militants showed themselves to be no better than the tyrants they claimed to oppose; they too used religion as ornament, were obsessed with power, spoils, and territory, ignorant or dismissive of even basic tenets of Islamic justice. Crucifixions and beheadings drew crowds. Their husbands, who had been decent men at home, began to swipe through phone apps for sex slaves.

How regretful were these women? It is exceedingly hard to say. They risked execution by rejecting the Islamic State's rule and trying to escape. If they did escape, they risked death and social stigma afterward if they admitted to having willingly associated with or having believed in the caliphate. Some women rationalized that the atrocities their husbands committed were nothing singular, that their brutality was matched or exceeded by the brutality of the opponents they were up against: Assad's army, the Shia militias controlled by Iran, the Russian air force, the al-Qaeda–linked insurgent groups, the pro-Kurdish autonomy forces supported by the United States. Many women found themselves trapped in a lawless place, strafed nightly by the warplanes of different nations. When their husbands died, there was always a knock at the door shortly afterward, a commander demanding that they remarry, again and again, forever widows.

Though vanquished today as a battlefield force in Syria and Iraq, the Islamic State is still with us: its supporters killed more than 250 people in coordinated bombings on Easter Sunday 2019 in Sri Lanka, and its leader Abu Bakr al-Baghdadi emerged in a video clip that same April, declaring that his group's vision remained alive and vowing to continue its bloody guerrilla war against non-Muslim unbelievers across the world. Affiliates linked to the group continue to wage powerful local insurgencies in disparate corners of the globe, in areas the group insists are its "provinces." Its sectarian hatred has infected a whole generation in the Arab world.

The political fractures from which it arose have not been fixed. History has shown that unless conditions genuinely change, a new insurgency always arises from the ashes of an old one.

If we are to break this cycle, we must contend with the group's shameful, provocative legacy, and understand how it persuaded thousands of women that they could find security or empowerment through joining its ranks.

This book follows thirteen women—some very young, some older; some educated, some not—as they sought lives in, or in support of, the Islamic State. It does not tell a Western story or a Middle Eastern story; it is set across the United Kingdom, Germany, Tunisia, Syria, Turkey, Libya, and Iraq. It charts the different ways women were recruited, inspired, or compelled to join the militants, a process that often ensnared their lovers and relatives, their teachers and neighbors.

The female victims of the Islamic State, specifically the enslaved Yazidi women, have commanded a great deal of attention. No one can deny the extraordinary horror and centrality of their suffering. But along the way, we have been perhaps too caught up in revulsion to fully appreciate the conditions that gave rise to the group's female adherents. If we want to truly understand these conditions, then we must look at the women who joined the group with more nuance and compassion.

As I write this, there are thousands of IS women and children lingering in camps and detention centers across the Middle East— awaiting death sentences, suspended in stateless limbo, or resigned to permanent incarceration. In fetid camps their children are dying in the tens of disease and exposure to the cold. They are no one's priority, the human residue of a conflict that everyone wishes to forget. Their abandonment may be politically expedient in the short term. But it risks stoking another cycle of precisely the same resentments and reactions that led to the group's creation. Not every woman who joined the Islamic State wished to hurt, enslave, or oppress others. Many thought they were saving themselves, or saving others, from unspeakable harm—harm they never could have imagined awaited them in the caliphate.

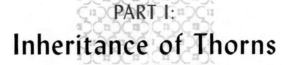

PART I:
Inheritance of Thorns

If I speak wildly in my poems I speak against the police
And if I manage to create a poem it's against the police
I haven't written a single word, a verse, a stanza that isn't against the police
All my prose is against the police

—MIGUEL JAMES

[President Ben Ali] has done a tremendous job in Tunisia and is well respected back home, as well as here in the Arab world.

—U.S. CONGRESSMAN EARL HILLIARD, ON HIS THIRD VISIT TO TUNISIA, 1999

NOUR

Spring 2007, Le Kram, Tunis

AFTER THE NIQAB INCIDENT, NOUR WAS SUSPENDED FROM SCHOOL FOR ten days as teachers and the principal deliberated how to respond to a thirteen-year-old flirting with religion. No one summoned Nour to speak to her about why she had shown up at school wearing a niqab, or whether something was wrong at home. Nour just wanted to be virtuous, to be dutiful to her God and ensure her place in heaven; she was also an adolescent, and it made her feel alive to defy something and play around with her identity. But no one asked precisely why she felt that covering her face was her religious duty. Had they given her the chance to mention the YouTube sheikh, they might have informed her there were opposing and indeed stronger and more valid scholarly views. Instead the principal summoned Nour and her parents to the school and, in the presence of a disgusted-looking policeman, made her sign a pledge to never cover her face or hair again.

IN THE PERIOD THAT STRETCHED from its independence from France in 1956 to the 2011 revolution, Tunisia was said to be a secular country, but the state's approach to religion was not so much secular as simply authoritarian. The state controlled how Tunisians practiced Islam, down to the daily, physical details of their worship—dictating what women could wear, when men could go to the mosque—and it did so with the totalizing scrutiny of a police state. President Habib Bourguiba, who ruled Tunisia after independence, was enamored with the French model of *laïcité*—secularism in public affairs, aimed at bringing about a secular society—and, when he took office, brought Islamic learning and instruction under the full control of the state.

In doing so, he upended centuries of tradition. Tunisia was a country with a deep Islamic heritage stretching back to the late seventh century, when the Arabs wrested control of North Africa from the Byzantine empire. Though the boundaries of the Islamic world shifted continually over time, expanding as far as Spain and Sicily, the region of Tunis remained firmly within the heart of successive Muslim empires. Al-Zaytuna, Tunisia's historic center of religious learning, dated back to 737 CE. When Bourguiba took power, he shut it down. He abolished religious courts, turned imams into civil servants, and bowdlerized religious texts used in schools. He sought to end fasting during Ramadan, arguing that Tunisians couldn't develop without shedding such dogmatic habits; he drank orange juice on national television during the holy month to make his point. Like many of the Middle East's twentieth-century nation-building modernizers, he believed that society needed growth and discipline to modernize and catch up with the West, and that Islam inhibited those qualities.

Zine el-Abidine Ben Ali, who seized power from Bourguiba in 1987, further instrumentalized religion to establish his authority. He allowed radios to start broadcasting the call to prayer, went on the hajj pilgrimage to Mecca, and promoted folksy Sufi festivals, pushing a curated, "moderate" Tunisian Islam that, as an ethos, made full submission to the state a core principle.

In 1989, he allowed candidates of Ennahda, the religious opposition movement, to participate in elections, but when they fared well, Ben Ali tortured and imprisoned them. He also shut down mosques and expanded restrictions on wearing the hijab. Mosques were locked up outside prayer times, and police crept through the streets at first light, making note of who had risen for the dawn prayer.

Despite all this, the state did not manage to turn Tunisians into either state-friendly Sufis or secular proto-Parisiens; the majority remained conservative, traditional Muslims. Under the chokehold of repression, asserting control of one's religiosity became a means of challenging the state. Young women like Nour, who grew up curious about religion, often resorted to watching sheikhs on satellite channels broadcast from the Gulf countries, whose approach to Islam was far more rigid and puritanical than the "Zaytuna" school that had been native to Tunisia for centuries.

Generations of young Tunisians grew up identifying as Muslims, but their worship and religious identity were fraught with political meaning. For many, being religious became a language through which to demand freedom from the state's intrusion into daily life.

WHEN SCHOOL STARTED BACK UP a week later, Nour showed up at breakfast in her pajamas. Her mother told her she was too young to make her own decisions about her future, and that she had better go get dressed. She consented. But the incident had doubled Nour's conviction to wear the niqab, and now, instead of changing surreptitiously by the bakery after she left the house, she put it on openly at home, wore it through the streets, and only took it off outside the school. In the classroom, she felt like a specter, a girl the teachers refused to look at or speak to.

"You should be wearing it too," she told her mother reprovingly. Nour's mother, a housewife with four other children to look after, didn't know what to say to this aggravating teenage daughter. Nour often lectured her mother about taking Islam more seriously. Her mother, it seemed to Nour, had no thought-through position on why she didn't cover her hair, apart from it saving her humiliation on the street and visits to the police station. These were weak positions, Nour thought; not even positions, just a base instinct for self-preservation.

President Bourguiba had famously called the veil "that miserable rag" and banned it from schools and public offices in 1981. There was grainy footage of him pulling the white scarf off a middle-aged woman's head, on the street on the day of the Eid festival at the end of Ramadan; the woman looks startled and embarrassed, and her fingers flutter to pull it back up, but the president pulls it down as if correcting a child, and pats her cheek indulgently. Since 1981, Tunisian women were obliged to go bareheaded in public spaces such as schools, universities, banks, and government buildings.

Like other modernizers in the region, Kemal Atatürk in Turkey and Reza Shah Pahlavi of Iran, Bourguiba didn't explicitly advocate that women abandon Islam, but he made clear that he wanted them to *act* secularly: to mingle bareheaded in mixed company, to dress in modern Western fashion. Along with this, he granted women sweeping rights in voting, marriage, and child custody that rapidly made Tunisian women the most literate, educated, and independent in the Arab world. LIBERATOR OF WOMEN is engraved on Bourguiba's mausoleum, but whether it was liberation for all women or just for some women would become clear in later generations.

Nour's mother, like many in her generation, went along with this model pragmatically, because there were more people than jobs in Tunisia, and she had a family to support. Everyone saw what happened to the families of the resistant women in the neighborhood, the stubborn women who insisted on covering their hair and engaging in religious activism. These families were nervous wrecks, in and out of police stations, living at the brink of poverty, with fathers, husbands, and sons who were imprisoned or in exile for dissident activity. Nour's mother recounted these ghoulish stories often, hoping her daughter's ears would catch some basic truths: the story about the woman who married an Islamist and arrived at the wedding reception to find it swarming with police ripping the headscarves off guests; the stories about nighttime home raids of those suspected of "religious" activity.

She told Nour about a woman three blocks over who was raped by policemen one night during a raid on her house and went mute for a whole year. "A whole year, Nour, she didn't utter a word. Every week, we would ask, 'Has she said anything?' And they always said, 'No, not yet.'"

Nour understood these stories were meant to scare her, but she remained stoic. "If it was easy, it wouldn't be a test then, would it? Allah loves those most whom he tests the hardest." That was true, according to the Quran, but that line had also become a rose-filtered meme popular among teenage Muslim girls.

A few months into her existence as a specter at school, Nour told her parents she'd had enough. "At least finish and get your certificate," her mother said. But Nour could not see how it was possible to learn anything when she felt herself reviled by the teachers. Nothing entered her head anyway, not how to graph an atom or the qualities of a hypotenuse. What was the point?

She quit school in 2009. Now, instead, she spent her mornings at home helping her mother clean and cook. After lunch she read the Quran. The neighborhood mosque had a prayer room where girls could meet to talk and discuss religion, and it was here that the imam's wife befriended her.

Nour liked the imam's wife's spirited laugh and genuine conversation, the small lessons she gave that illuminated aspects of the religion—lessons about the mindset to bring to prayer and the importance of charity, and how it would ennoble a person. She told Nour stories about the prophets, about Moses and Jesus, and most of all, stories about the Prophet Muhammad's qualities. The Prophet said: "Guard yourself from the Hellfire even with half a date in charity. If he cannot find it, then with a kind word." Nour could manage half a date, and feeling like she could help others, even when she herself had so little, was heartening. She wasn't as powerless as she thought. When the imam's wife invited other women over for a circle of discussion, Nour was often too shy to say very much herself. But she listened avidly and took it all in.

ASMA

Summer 2009, Raqqa, Syria

IT WAS ONE OF THOSE PERFECT, SUN-KISSED DAYS WHEN THE SKY ABOVE
Raqqa was the color of Herati turquoise, the baklava at the sweet shop
tasted like brittle layers of heaven, and Asma almost thought she could
be happy in this provincial city, if she had Hisham at her side and all
their days passed like this one.

They started with coffee in the morning at Negative Café, where
Hisham had been trying to take her for weeks, after she'd complained
Raqqa had no modern coffee shops. It was all right—white leather
chairs, walls collaged with black-and-white photos, as if someone had
been told to imagine 1950s Paris—but she smiled prettily to show she
appreciated his effort. She felt the eyes of the other women survey her
as they walked out. She would have liked it if the others had been
dressed more fashionably; it would have given her something to look
at and think about. To Asma, it wasn't especially satisfying to be the
best-dressed woman in the room; it just meant you were in the wrong
room.

They walked around the ruins of Qasr al-Banat, the Castle of the
Ladies, the structures that the Abbasid caliph Harun al-Rashid built
when he moved his capital from Baghdad to Raqqa in the twelfth
century. They smoked on the steps and swatted away flies as the midday heat grew stifling. Hisham suggested swimming by the Old Bridge,
but really the suggestion was that *he* could swim, because she wasn't
about to wade into the Euphrates with all her clothes on.

Asma was trying to be enthusiastic about Raqqa, her new city, because she loved Hisham and also desired him. He was slender, with black hair that curled, honey-colored eyes, and an appealingly hooked nose. His parents were well off, by Raqqa standards, and he had a privileged-boy personality: prankish, easily bored, fluidly moving between decorous and louche. But Raqqa itself she found disappointingly dull. Asma had grown up in Damascus and had only moved to the city (was it even a city, she thought, or a town?) in her late teens, when her parents decided to return to her mother's hometown. She missed the buzz and glamour of the capital: the pool parties, the five-star hotels, the tourists and language students from across the world, the modern restaurants, the sheer cosmopolitanism of the place. Damascus felt connected to the pulse of the twenty-first century, while Raqqa, for all that it was a religiously mixed, easygoing enough, river town, felt exactly no more than that.

Asma was studying marketing at al-Hasakah University, a forty-five-minute bus ride to the northeast of Raqqa. She spent most of her free hours reading and online, watching, learning, yearning to be part of the outside world. She wanted to know what everyone in the West was reading, eating, wearing, listening to, thinking. Marketing, she'd felt, would be a good path to lead her outward, hopefully far out of Raqqa, out of Syria, into the broader world. She wanted to interact with foreigners, maybe even work in tourism, or tourism marketing, anything global. Her shelves were lined with books—by Dan Brown, Victor Hugo, Hemingway, the Egyptian writer-philosopher Taha Hussein. She was on Facebook and Instagram, listened to Coldplay, and, like women the world over, felt there was something ineffably unappealing about Angelina Jolie. She read in English as much as she could, and began using English for certain terms that seemed to demand it: *relaxation, money, power*. They just had a different ring in English. She felt herself to be a modern young woman with aspirations, and that's why Hisham's suggestion that she start wearing the hijab rankled so bitterly.

It was one evening after they'd had burgers for dinner and were sitting in the car, talking, at the end of a quiet cul-de-sac in an affluent neighborhood with villas that Asma liked gazing into. Hisham laced his fingers through hers and said, "A man has different expectations from a wife than a girlfriend. Why should your beauty be available to everyone?" He spoke about how precious she was to him, how he wanted to possess some part of her others did not.

This was the first time he'd mentioned it, and she couldn't believe he was saying these things. They had spent time at the beach together, her in a yellow bikini, in short skirts, tank tops, everything easy and relaxed. Her brothers didn't care, her father didn't care, and she thought her boyfriend hadn't either.

"You do have special access to a special part of me," she replied. "My heart."

He said he wanted some *visible* part of her all to himself.

Was it because he doubted her chasteness? Was it his parents?

"If you want to marry me, you have to cover," he said flatly.

"Hisham, faith is here," she said, tapping her fingers against her heart. "It's not here"—she ran her hands through her hair, then down her body. "You loved me first without hijab. Why, now, do you say I have to put it on?"

He shrugged. "I can't change that part of me that wants that. It's fixed."

LINA

Summer 2000, Weinheim, Germany

"So what? German or French, friend or enemy, he's first and fore-
most a man and I'm a woman. He's good to me, kind, attentive. . . .
That's good enough for me. I'm not looking for anything else. Our
lives are complicated enough with all these wars and bombings.
Between a man and a woman, none of that's important. I couldn't
care less if the man I fancy is English or black—I'd still offer myself to him if I got the opportunity."
—IRÈNE NÉMIROVSKY, *Suite Française,* 1942

LINA SOMETIMES WEPT SO COPIOUSLY INTO THE RICE SHE STUFFED
into the vine leaves that she wondered whether they didn't grow salty
or bitter from her tears, and whether the customers who ate them
weren't made ill by her sorrow. Life in Weinheim, a small town near
Heidelberg, had always been difficult. Then her Lebanese in-laws had
moved to the city from Beirut, and their presence was so tormenting
that she found herself wistful for the old times. At least then she'd not
been so physically exhausted.

Lina had three young children and was married to a man she ab-
horred; he had small eyes, a snouty nose, and a bloated face. He had
a girlfriend and frequented discos; he did not pray or read the Quran
or acknowledge God in the slightest. The long German winters—the
season of low, pale gray skies that often stretched from September all
the way to June—sharpened Lina's depression. Lina and her husband
had moved from Beirut to Weinheim in the early 1990s. The first year

after their arrival, when she went for long walks around the town, growing familiar with its winding streets and crooked, gabled old buildings, she came across a Lebanese cedar planted in the gardens of an old palace. Its trunk stretched at least two meters wide and it had towering limbs and roots that, she imagined, pushed deep into the earth. Lina looked at it admiringly, accepting she was a less successful transplant.

Lina's in-laws, in the spirit of Lebanese entrepreneurs the world over, followed the couple to Weinheim a few years later, confident in their ability to identify what sort of business their new locale lacked, and to launch that business themselves with verve and competence. There were no Lebanese restaurants in the area, and setting up a restaurant seemed the obvious choice. Her father-in-law prepared the shawarma meat—this was the task of a man—but it fell upon Lina to help her mother-in-law cook the rest of the fare. Often she woke before dawn to ready the dishes expected of her: stuffed vine leaves, roasted eggplant dip, thyme pastries. She cooked these things so often that she grew to hate eating them. They tasted like labor.

Lina's husband worked at the restaurant, and he usually took the food she had prepared with him when he left in the mornings. But her shift didn't end then. Her mother-in-law expected her to help with the cleaning and housework at her apartment. In Beirut, where the in-laws had lived previously, household help was readily affordable. For the price of a fancy sandwich, one could hire a local Lebanese or a South Asian woman to do the cleaning. Much of middle-class Beirut was composed of women whose manicured hands hadn't touched a toilet brush in decades.

But in Weinheim, there was no such supply of cheap labor. Or there was, and it was called Lina. On days she didn't go over right away, when her own housework and cooking piled up, or her shoulders and fingers clenched up from fatigue, or she simply wanted to spend an hour watching television, the phone call always came after lunch. Her mother-in-law's withering, sing-songy voice, "*Shou*, Lina? Where *were* you today?"

Lina knew she was a faint-mannered woman; her milky-blue eyes and barely audible voice meant that people were perpetually asking her to speak up. But despite her own softness, she felt like the man in her marriage. Her husband couldn't (wouldn't?) stand up to his parents; he couldn't get them to stop summoning Lina to clean, to give her one less dish to cook for the restaurant; he couldn't ask for time off for himself. It was only after the birth of their third child that Lina told him enough was enough, he could ask for one day. When he was home, he did the bare minimum, and then spent all his time and money going out. She washed his discarded shirts that smelled of other women's perfume; she economized so that they could get by with what he shared with her each month, after he'd subtracted the sizable amount he needed for his extracurricular life. The hours he spent at home steadily decreased until eventually he only came back to sleep. The only signs of him were the boxers he left in the bathroom, and the stub of the cigarette he smoked with his morning Nescafé. Sometimes, when she was on one of her now infrequent walks through the small town, she thought perhaps there was nothing greater to expect from a marriage born of desperation.

When Lina was six years old, her German mother and Lebanese father parted acrimoniously. Her father kidnapped her and took her from her native Germany back to Lebanon, not because he especially wanted her, but because he wanted to punish his German ex-wife. The six-year-old girl was suddenly motherless and plunged into Arabic, a new language she barely knew. Her father remarried quickly.

It was clear to Lina that her stepmother was jealous of any claim on her new husband's attention. When her father read her German stories at bedtime or they sang German songs together, her stepmother banged doors or blared the television. In Lebanon they moved house so many times that Lina had to keep repeating the same grade, because they never stayed in one place long enough for her to take the final exam. When her father was at work, her stepmother was frosty and sometimes shouted at her, heaping the young girl with chores. Most nights Lina fell asleep crying, listening to the lives of other people in the building. In the sticky summer heat, everyone kept their windows open for the breeze, and the neighbors' voices wafted up and down. She knew that the couple upstairs quarreled over their wastrel son; that the family downstairs was pooling money to send their daughter to art school. She sometimes wished she were that girl's sister and belonged to that family, so tender were they with one another, coming home with little surprises, inventing pet names.

When she was fourteen, her father announced that Lina would be marrying her cousin. Nobody asked her whether she liked his snout-nosed face or unhurried gait, or whether she even wanted to get married. But her father wasn't marrying her off because he thought it would fulfill any special dreams or help her ascend to a better station. He simply wanted to be rid of her. And Lina saw no other prospect of leaving that house, where the air was heavy with her stepmother's displeasure and her father's resigned sighs.

They married, and moved to Weinheim almost immediately after. Lina was fifteen and enrolled in the seventh grade. Her German slowly started coming back. She looked forward to the hours in the schoolroom—so orderly and clean, the teachers' behavior so soothingly reliable. But after a couple of weeks, after she missed a period and felt her stomach churning in the mornings, she realized she was pregnant. Too ashamed to show up at school with a swelling stomach, she stayed at home instead, watching hours of German television. Her mind was nimble with languages. She had learned some English in Lebanon, in those on-again, off-again spells at various schools. She felt some satisfaction when her ears discerned English words from the torrent of language on the television. It was like some kind of private puzzle she was actually good at.

Islam had always been Lina's sustenance. When she was ten, she saw the Prophet Muhammad in a dream. She kept the memory of that encounter like a talisman, something to reach for when she felt especially alone. The dream made her pull the Quran off the shelf and try to decipher its passages; its plot, the path it set out for God's creations, became her plot. In her early twenties, as she contemplated leaving the husband with whom she had three children but not an actual relationship, Lina grew more religious. She found herself praying and reaching for the Quran even more during those bleak winter days, when the sky was a steel dome. The Germans passing her on the sidewalk looked straight through her, as though her hijab did not simply cover her hair but cloaked her in invisibility.

She felt as though she were playacting, detachedly going through the motions of her tasks as a homemaker, mother, restaurant worker. She raised the subject of divorce with her husband five or six times. He reacted so violently—calling her an animal, a disgrace—that she locked herself in the bedroom afterward and waited months before broaching it again. She discussed her unhappiness with her family and in-laws, who were inconveniently tangled together; her husband was her first cousin, which made her mother-in-law also her aunt. No one was willing to acknowledge the abuse she faced, and they all dismissed her idea. "Are you crazy? You have kids, you can't get divorced," her mother-in-law said with finality.

One night late in 2009, after her three children were in bed, Lina sat by the telephone with a pad of paper. She had scrawled the numbers of three imams she found online, who were available for phone consultations. She said the same thing to each one: "My life is a farce. My husband doesn't pray or respect Islam. He drinks alcohol. He goes with other women."

In response, they uniformly said the same thing. According to the principles of Islamic law, her husband was committing *zina*, adultery, the most grave of sins. Not only did she have the right to ask for divorce, she shouldn't even be living with him in the interim. The voices of these imams, saying words that were correct and firm, confirmed her belief that only religious men had decency and backbone. She attributed her husband's fecklessness and abuse to his lack of faith.

She packed her bag silently. She knew she couldn't take her children. Where would she take them? Who would support them? Their father found it easy to mistreat her, but he was decent enough to the children; she had no genuine fear of leaving them in his care.

She had lived her whole life dedicated to the service of others. It was time to save herself.

Spring 2010, Beirut, Lebanon

In the years since she had left the city, her father and stepmother had moved into an upscale building near the Martyrs' Cemetery off Tariq al-Jadideh, a predominantly Sunni neighborhood named for the long overpass road that led to the airport. During the ride in from the air-port, Lina saw that Beirut had been transformed.

The downtown that she remembered as gutted by the civil war of the 1980s—its graceful, arched buildings had been empty shells, streets strewn with bombed-out rubble, empty lots like gaping teeth—was now a knife-edged, glittery re-creation of its former self. The old buildings were now the golden color of spun sugar and housed Prada, Dior, and other boutiques. There were restaurants with tanned young men in white slacks waiting outside to valet-park cars. Lina gaped at every street they passed, at the city that looked familiar and utterly alien at once. She thought she recognized the juice stand near their old street, the one her father would sometimes take her to in the eve-nings when she was a little girl, for a fruit cocktail topped with clotted cream and honey. Despite the infusions of glamour and wealth, Beirut was still one of those cities where the streets permanently bore the flags and billboards of an unresolved political story: the same old im-ages of warlords from rival religious clans, militias, or power dynasties vying for control of the statelet, each beholden to some greater re-gional power with its own agenda.

The apartment building was imposing. She felt nervous as she walked through the lobby, lined with exotic potted ferns that reflected infinitely in the mirrored walls. The elevator glided up silently. When her father opened the apartment door and saw her standing there, he froze, a look of dismay flashing across his face.

"Have you lost your mind?" He gestured at her all-enveloping black robe and headscarf. Few women dressed that way in this neighbor-hood, which was inhabited by people, Lina assumed, who aspired to bank jobs for their children and weddings in prominent hotels rather than investing in the spiritual labor that might guarantee a better hereafter. But whatever she thought of his godlessness, he was still her father, and still capable of hurting her. She dug her teeth into her tongue to hold back tears. He stood there, one arm holding the door, as if reluctant to admit her. He didn't reach to hug her, or ask how she was. It was his wife's voice from inside that recalled them both. "Come in," he said at last, standing aside and patting her awkwardly on the back a few times.

The scene repeated itself in the kitchen, where her stepmother was making coffee. "Sweetheart, *why?*" she said, sweeping her hands up and down at Lina's frame. Her stepmother's lips were inflated and cartoonish, and she wore skinny jeans, white sneakers, and a tight T-shirt. A teenager's outfit, thought Lina. Photos of the couple on holiday lined the wall, one of them featuring her stepmother in a bikini. The three of them sat together at the table in the kitchen. Her father wore a pained expression and kept looking out the window. "Listen, take this black stuff off," he said. "Go back to Germany and start wearing modern clothes. Find a boyfriend. I'm okay with it, even if the others aren't." He was referring, she assumed, to his sister, her mother-in-law, who forbade divorce.

Lina stared at her hands on the table; she should have known better than to come. The gulf that separated belief and disbelief was impossible to cross. How easily her father spoke of her finding a boyfriend, becoming a loose woman. They didn't understand her decision to dress like this. They didn't understand how faith soothed her. She wanted to be in God's good graces, to dress like the wives of the Prophet, peace be upon him. To them it was foolish, but Lina truly believed in Judgment Day. She truly believed in the Hellfire that awaited those who displeased God, and she was willing, indeed eager, to do anything in this life that would earn His mercy.

As her father kept crossing and uncrossing his legs, Lina could sense how desperate he was for her to leave his house, to leave Beirut and go back to being someone else's problem. She collected her bags and, the next evening, took a taxi to the airport.

The sun was setting, bathing the city in luminous peach light. Lina had wished to stay here a while, to walk along the promenade near the sea, among the old houses with their arched, jewel-toned windows standing in charged conversation with the aggressive luxury high-rises. She knew she was prone to depression, and had to fight all the time to keep herself from its grasping fingers. She had hoped her mood would be lightened by the light and warmth of spring and autumn in Beirut, seasons that scarcely existed in Germany. She had hoped to walk the streets of the neighborhood doing her grocery shopping, stopping for a chat at the produce stand or the local corner shop.

In Beirut, people who did not know each other still interacted with great warmth. Lina's clothes would not create an immediate disincentive to conversation or a barrier to being seen as someone employable, likable, human. She could sit in cafés frequented by pious men and women, where people drank spiced coffee and strawberry juice and enjoyed the frantic glimmering of the sun on the Mediterranean.

But there was to be no such chapter in her life. God had not willed it for her, and He knew best.

UPON ARRIVAL AT THE FRANKFURT airport, Lina found a policewoman and explained to her that she had nowhere to go and that her ex-husband, the last time she saw him, had tried to kill her. This was not something she liked to dwell on; the memory made her pulse quicken. But it was true, and pertinent information as she sought the state's aid in finding a place to live.

The airport policewomen were kindly. They took Lina to a women's shelter with unobtrusive staff, who showed her the communal bathroom and her own private bedroom. She was so tired she could only murmur "Thank you," but tried to express gratitude with her eyes. For the first two days, she stayed in bed, anticipating problems. Surely it could not be so simple to be allowed to stay in her own private room. Surely they would ask her to leave, or ask her to stop wearing her Islamic clothes. But nothing of the sort happened. She was surprised and grateful to find the staff at the women's center respectful and welcoming. They even helped her find work. Eventually a small studio flat opened up at the shelter. It had a living room and a kitchenette, where Lina could make tea and light meals for herself.

After a few months, she heard from an Arab woman staying in the same shelter about a job opportunity—one that would, crucially, allow Lina to wear her hijab and niqab. A Moroccan man in Frankfurt ran a company that offered caregiving services to the ill and elderly. Lina began working for the Moroccan in December, during an especially rainy winter when the clouds would not relent. Her job was to go to the homes of elderly women, do some light cleaning, give them baths and dispense medications. The women were lonely, and grateful for the company. They did not stiffen at her appearance, or at least, not after the first couple of visits.

Lina felt compassion for them, because in their depression and isolation, she saw a reflection of her own condition. It was fine to pause her work and pray the noon or afternoon prayers, and she was grateful to God for this opportunity to earn money and practice her religion. But eventually the work dwindled. The Moroccan complained he wasn't getting enough new clients due to the fact of his being Moroccan. Lina didn't know about that; she just needed work.

She found a second job as a school janitor, working on the weekends. The problem here was that she had to work alongside another cleaner, a man, and she worried about wearing her niqab around him. Germans could be touchy about the niqab. But she came up with an ingenious solution: a doctor's mask. "The cleaning products are really toxic," she explained, and the man nodded, uninterested. It was striking how much it mattered to others exactly what you were covering your face with. On the best days, the man didn't show up and she handled the cleaning by herself, free in her isolation.

THE DAYS PILED UP. LINA, still living in the shelter, stopped cooking real meals for herself and subsisted on boiled chicken and potatoes: sick-person food. She stopped looking up at the night sky, stopped noticing whether the moon was round or crescent. The smell of the elderly women's rooms—a sour, curdled smell—seeped into her mind, along with images of their fungal nails and cloudy glaucoma eyes and the sound of their confused mumblings. She never spoke to her children. Sometimes she even had difficulty remembering the sound of their voices. When someone died, at least that grief had stages and might eventually abate; this kind of grief was ever present, an ache, like a ringing in the ears. She was afraid that if she called her children, her ex-husband would find out that she was in Germany. She knew that he would search for her and try to harm her.

She feared that even here in Germany, had she tried to divorce him in court, she might not be protected. Just a couple of years earlier, in 2007, a German judge had refused to grant a German Moroccan woman a quick divorce from an abusive husband, on grounds that the couple were Muslims and that, as such, the woman did not qualify for the hardship criteria required for a fast split. The judge interpreted a verse of the Quran—one that has been contentiously debated by Muslims for centuries—to argue that both God and custom permitted a Muslim man to beat his wife. The case caused great public uproar, especially among German Muslims, who felt the judge had inexplicably sided with a rebarbative, fringe reading of their faith. How any German judge felt qualified to read and interpret the Quran was unclear to Lina. There was no example of the Prophet ever beating his wives; indeed the Prophet's forbearance, his playfulness, his storied understanding, offered a model of conduct that wives over the ages had nudged their husbands to follow.

The thought came to her one night, previously unconsidered, that her ex-husband might have remarried. What if his new wife treated her children harshly, as Lina had been treated by her own stepmother? The idea panicked her. Her pulse went staccato fast and she felt breathless and jumpy, as though there were butterflies beating their wings under her skin. She took one sleeping pill, which usually helped when sleep eluded her. She loved nothing so much as sleeping and spent most of her days off in bed, not even bothering to change out of her pajamas.

It was hard for her to see a way out. Later that night, she took several more sleeping pills. She decided that nothing would be sweeter than not having to wake up at all.

WHEN LINA AWOKE MANY HOURS later with a metallic taste in her mouth, shoulders stiff, in a pool of her own vomit, she recognized that God had given her another chance. For the Muslim who takes her own life, Hellfire is a ceaseless reexperiencing of the means of her death; Lina had been spared this.

Each morning after that, she stared into the bathroom mirror and reminded herself that God did not impose on any of His creations more than they could bear. She hardened her heart against the yearning she felt for her children. Her life depended on not seeing their father. She prayed every night to have a chance to see them later in life and explain her story, such that they could eventually understand and forgive her.

She was solitary by nature, but started going to the mosque because she was self-aware enough to know that being so utterly alone was making her sick. Having left her children, she felt that it was her duty to try to be at least a little happy, and attending Friday prayers each week lifted her mood. There was the intimacy of her sleeve being tugged as the women lined up in tight rows for prayer; the feeling that, for even just that quarter of an hour, there was one specific spot designated for her; within the collective of women kneeling down in unison, as one body, submitting to God.

Afterward, in the courtyard of the mosque, as she greeted brothers and sisters she had gotten to know, she was often asked if she was open to getting married. These questions made her blush deeply and she invented a fiancé in order to fend them off. This imaginary fiancé began to take definite shape in her mind. It was then that Lina acknowledged to herself how badly she wished to remarry, to have more children, to visit her father in Beirut in triumph—to show him she had made a success of things the second time around, and that with her faith, she was in every way superior to him.

EMMA

2007, Frankfurt, Germany

We was young and we was dumb, but we had heart.
—TUPAC SHAKUR, 2003

EMMA'S MOTHER WAS A NATIVE-BORN GERMAN, A SEAMSTRESS WHO worked odd jobs to support her two young daughters. Her personal life was chaotic and brought pain to her daughters, but as an adult and a convert to Islam, Emma was reluctant to linger over the details, because Islam counsels respect for one's parents, regardless of how abusive or negligent they might have been. Before she met Emma's father, who was from Spain, her mother had been married to a Moroccan man. She did not manage to divorce him promptly, so Emma bore the absent Moroccan ex-husband's last name.

In later years, Emma thought perhaps this had foretold her destiny, her very surname evoking the ghostly presence of a Muslim man who should have been taking care of her but was not. Emma and her sister's actual father abandoned the family soon after her sister's birth and returned to his native Spain. Her mother viewed her experiences at the hands of these various men as a reflection of general male brokenness, rather than her habit of choosing broken men. Emma grew up hearing variations on "All men are dogs," lines that she associated with her mother's haplessness but that filtered into her consciousness as possible wisdom nonetheless.

Theirs was not a household filled with the finer elements of German child-rearing that other residents of Frankfurt enjoyed: wooden building blocks, vintage editions of Grimm's fairy tales, and cartoons featuring intellectual farm animals. It was a meager childhood. Sometimes, depressed and exhausted, Emma's mother even forgot basic things, like the colorful, candy-filled cones—like tall, inverted dunce caps—that children were expected to bring on the first day of school.

When her mother moved Emma and her sister to the city in the early 1990s, Turkish immigrants lived among the white native Germans in their working-class district in Frankfurt.

The Turkish families in the neighborhood, nearly all Muslims, lived under a uniform level of strain. Their cramped, shabby flats didn't get enough sunlight, permanently smelling of damp from drying clothes; their paychecks didn't stretch easily to cover all the things a family needed. Everyone shopped at discount supermarkets; no one went on holiday.

But when Emma visited the homes of her Turkish school friends, it was like stepping into an alternative world. To her, all Muslim families were alike in their happiness. The apartments were small, but the interiors were orderly and clean, with pride extending to protect even modest furniture with plastic doilies or sofa covers, and always on the table a glass bowl of hard sweets or raisins. These families were almost living on top of one another, constantly in and out of each other's houses; no one felt obliged to call first before coming over, and no day passed without a visitor. Whatever was cooking for dinner could accommodate an unexpected guest. Very little food was wasted, because there was always an auntie on hand to do something with it. If parents worked night shifts in taxis or restaurants, there were relatives or friends to put children to bed and ready them for the next school day. For the Turkish immigrant kids of Frankfurt, being raised by a whole klatch blunted the effects of poverty, keeping it from bleeding into neglect.

By the time she was a teenager, Emma, along with most of her Muslim friends, was tracked into *Hauptschule,* a low-level school for children destined to work vocationally. The German state believed it could determine which children had the aptitude to enter the academic education system and which were best served (or alternatively, which best served the state) by entering a vocational stream that would end in apprenticeship and a life of, ideally, skilled labor. The *Hauptschule* track held no promise of securing for Emma the one material possession she had come to covet in life—a BMW 6 series, with its sleek lines and glint of power—but spending time in the homes of her Turkish friends showed her that family, with lots of children, was a wealth of its own.

She preferred spending time at her friends' small and busy houses. In fact, though she was native to Germany, she felt much more like her Turkish friends in general; she enjoyed their warm manners, the music they liked, the open, natural acknowledgment of men's and women's different but complementary duties. She liked the way each family kept folded-up mattresses and bedding in the corner in case of impromptu sleepovers. Only one thing set her apart from them: she was not Muslim.

Many of her friends weren't especially devout, but Islam was an intimate part of their identities, values, and social rituals, and it was hard to disentangle culture from religion. Tending to family, behaving with warmth and pleasantness, even the act of smiling itself: these were formally articulated Muslim values. Emma learned this as she started reading about Islam in her late teens. "No one smiled more than the messenger of God," Imam Ali said about the Prophet Muhammad.

Emma wanted to be a part of it. She wanted a share of the belonging and the warmth. When she was nineteen, she converted to Islam. At first, she did not wear the hijab. Some of her friends wore it and some didn't, reflecting the range of attitudes among second-generation Muslim girls, from the cheerfully practical—concerned with career ladders and fitting in, confident that their *iman,* their faith, was in their hearts—to those who wanted those things too, but wanted to please Allah most of all.

One weekend afternoon in early autumn in the late 2000s, Emma and her girlfriends were walking through one of the central squares in Frankfurt, where Turkish Kurds who supported the Kurdish separatist PKK movement back home in Turkey liked to gather. They hoisted placards with the mustachioed face of their leader and bleated their horns, in solidarity with fellow Kurds. German matrons in blazers walked past with bags of groceries, eyeing the commotion. On the far side of the square, Emma and her friends stopped at an Islamic *dawah* (preaching) stall, manned by people her friends knew. The imam smiled at Emma and handed her a "Have you considered Islam?" leaflet. She felt a flash of irritation. "I'm already Muslim, thanks be to God."

"*Alhamdulillah*," he repeated, smiling. "But why no hijab, sister?"

She explained that her family wasn't Muslim and she was trying to ease them into her new identity. "Do you really think that's a good excuse?" the imam asked. Among the stacks of leaflets on the table, he handed her a pink one, about the virtues of hijab. It featured a serene pink ocean with a partially obscured pearl in a half shell, radiating light.

"I'd like to. I will one day, I just don't know when," Emma replied.

"If you pray to Allah for help, He will make it easier for you. There are so many reasons to start now. When you don't wear a hijab, you discourage other Muslim women from wearing it. Also, wearing hijab makes you a message. Imagine you are Muslim walking around this square and you see a woman in hijab and you feel happy! . . . You think to yourself, 'Look, there are Muslims here!' You become a happy signal."

A happy signal—Emma had never *not* wanted to be a happy signal. Even though the imam's words were pressing and intent, his tone was soft and his pale blue eyes smiled. Emma liked talking to him. She liked the feeling he gave her: that her actions mattered; that if she listened he would not stop looking at her; that their exchange was light but consequential; that it was perhaps the most important conversation going on in the whole of the leaf-strewn *Platz*. The imam had abundant charisma. He was clearly the right kind of guy to be running a *dawah* stall.

"By not wearing it," he continued, "you also make things harder for other Muslim women. They see you not wearing it and it plants doubt in their mind . . . they think to themselves, 'If others don't wear it, why should I?'"

"Thanks for your *naseeha*," Emma said to the sheikh as they were leaving, wanting him to know that she knew the word for sincere Islamic advice. He wished her good luck in her efforts. She thought of how she might recount the conversation to her mother. Surely her mother would say, "That is very controlling behavior," because that is how she thought of Muslim men; but in that moment, Emma did not feel controlled or admonished. She felt cared for; she felt the loneliness inside her slowly being chipped away.

That night, she sat crossed-legged on the couch at home, lit a cigarette, and studied the leaflet.

Women are taught from early childhood that their worth is proportional to their attractiveness.

The definition of beauty is ever changing; waifish is good, waifish is bad, athletic is good, sorry, athletic is bad. Women are not going to achieve equality by putting their bodies on display, as some people would like to have you believe. That would make us only party to our own objectification.

Wearing the hijab has given me freedom from constant attention to my physical self. Because my appearance is not subject to public scrutiny, my beauty, or perhaps my lack of it, has been removed from the realm of what can legitimately be discussed.

In the Western world, the hijab has come to symbolize either forced silence, or a radical, unconscionable militancy. Actually, it's neither. It is simply a woman's assertion that judgment of her physical person is to play no role whatsoever in social interaction. Its purpose is to give back to women ultimate control of their own bodies.

And we do not lay on any soul a burden except to the extent of its ability (al-Quran, 23:62).

Despite its saccharine fuchsia cover, despite the cliché metaphor of the pearl ensconced in its shell, despite knowing she partly just wished to please the blue-eyed imam, Emma did not find a single thing in the leaflet to disagree with.

AT HOME, EMMA'S NEW IDENTITY as a Muslim discomfited her mother and sister. They didn't try to dissuade her, but they made their opinion clear: it was a disloyal, diminishing, wrong-minded choice. As though the path her mother had chosen, under the shade of a diffident German Christianity, had brought her any measure of success in the realms of men, children, and work.

To Emma's mind, most Germans were fairly racist at their core; if they weren't outright racists, they lived in such overt petrification at the idea of people different from them that, for all intents and purposes, they might as well have been racist. As in most cities and towns where Turks had settled, in Frankfurt, native Germans' discomfort with foreigners played itself out in petty squabbles over the aesthetics of shared public space.

A pensioner in Emma's building who resented the strange smell of her downstairs Turkish neighbors' cooking would berate the family for failing to keep their window-ledge plants in bloom. The upkeep of hedgerows, gardens, and lawns became a battleground through which Germans expressed anxieties that they could not communicate more directly: their dislike of having to live alongside foreigners, of having to tolerate their different customs, manners, appearance, and food smells. They were reluctant to concede that if their modern economy required the labor of foreigners with names like Ahmet and Fatima, Ahmet and Fatima would build places of worship and eventually want access to higher education, better job opportunities, and citizenship; that they would bear children and those children would inherit their culture; that inevitably, the singular German identity defined by whiteness, rigid social mores, and norms would need to exist alongside a very different identity, a German-Turkish-Muslim identity that laid equal claim to being "authentically German."

The pensioner was relentless in her torment of the Turkish family. She objected to the mother vacuuming on Sundays, because proper Germans did not vacuum on Sundays, the day of rest. Didn't the foreigners realize this? She thumped on the floor with her mop when this occurred and posted sharp notices in the communal hallways. Occasionally she would drop litter from her balcony onto their ground-floor garden, and then knock on their door to inform them they were failing to keep the garden tidy.

Like many who were young when the German state began accelerating its guest worker program in the 1960s, the pensioner had internalized the government's early position that the foreigners were there to fill a void in the labor market and then would eventually go home. As Germany struggled to rebuild itself and reenter European trade networks in the aftermath of World War II, the foreign guest workers filled the jobs native Germans didn't especially want: construction, mining, metal industries. Initially, German law handled this imported labor as a pure human transaction and regulated the workers' transience: they had to leave after two years of labor and were barred from bringing their families. Eventually that changed, in successive stages. Workers were permitted to stay longer, bring spouses, and become citizens. But the attitudes that had underwritten this slow process—native Germans' reluctance to live among strangers and their fears about the dilution of a national identity based on whiteness—endured.

By 1980, the population of foreigners in Germany had increased eightfold. Social prejudice and intense occupational discrimination was growing, though it was rarely discussed or acknowledged by the state. Though many Eastern and Mediterranean Europeans had moved to Germany, employers and German society at large reserved special xenophobic disapproval for Turkish foreigners, who were nonwhite and Muslim. The derogatory term for nonwhite, nonnative, non-Western Germans was *Ausländer,* and it was gaining ground.

By 2013, Turks constituted 4 percent of the German population, around four million people. They were systematically turned down for professional, skilled jobs, and tended to live in neighborhoods like the one in which Emma grew up. Educated, second-generation German Turks with higher aspirations sometimes moved to European capitals like London or Paris to seek employment by a German multinational company. From there, they could return to Germany and slide into a decent position as just another expat hire. For the hiring of management positions and other desirable rungs of employment, German employers tended to shun their Turkish-origin citizens, who in turn developed bitter grudges against the country that refused to acknowledge them. Equally frustrating and baffling were the parochial rules that governed public space, rules that seemed arbitrary and purposely obtuse, designed to give those of Turkish origin the sense they were never doing anything right.

Emma's mother, though a native German herself, didn't have a reflexive dislike for foreigners, but she did respond to Emma's new identity with indifference tinged with denial. She refused to call her by her new Muslim name, Dunya. Emma had chosen Dunya because it sounded different. It meant "world" in Arabic, and she hoped it would portend an opening of horizons for her.

At eighteen, Emma/Dunya moved into a small flat she shared with one of her close friends, a modest little place with a wood-paneled kitchen untouched since the 1970s and a bathroom with a tea-rose pink bathtub. It was housing for vulnerable young people, supported by the state. Being on her own, away from her mother and sister, made experimenting with Islam easier. It also made smoking pot easier. She started wearing the hijab, something she had been reluctant to do while living with them.

Everything about Islam was fascinating; it was a novelty that did not seem incongruent with the rest of her life, which she spent watching romcoms with her girlfriends, listening to R&B, and debating the relative merits of Arabic pop stars, agreeing that Samira Said was the hottest singer, despite Haifa Wehbe's devilish hip swirling and Elissa's elegant sluttiness. Dunya and her friends experimented with ranges of mascara and kohl, and Dunya found herself feeling almost Arab herself, or Turkish, or Muslim, something certainly not German, whose women were proud to be plain as oatmeal and sneered at femininity and makeup.

Fitful Quiet

Across much of the Arab world, the early winter of 2010 passes
unremarkably, like so many seasons of so many years past. Each
country endures long-running economic and political troubles and
popular discontent, but the status quo feels permanent, presided over
by dictators-for-life who demand the obedience of their people: Zine
el-Abidine Ben Ali in Tunisia, Hosni Mubarak in Egypt, Bashar
al-Assad in Syria, Hamad bin Isa al-Khalifa in Bahrain.

Iraq is once again restive, as it has been regularly since the
American invasion in 2003. The Shia-led government in Baghdad is
discriminating against the country's Sunnis, threatening to rekindle
the Sunni insurgency that was only quieted in 2007 after a surge of
U.S. troops and an "Awakening" movement that drew prominent Sunni
tribesmen and families away from the militants. Though many factors
contributed to the reduction in violence in Iraq, top U.S. generals
declared the surge a victory, and said the tide of the battle had finally
been turned.

Those Sunni insurgents formed a group called al-Qaeda in Iraq in
2004, and then rebranded as the Islamic State in Iraq (ISI) in 2006,
under different leadership. The group's prospects have waned in
recent years as the Iraqi government has sought to govern more
equitably and inclusively, but they track the mounting dismay of Iraqi
Sunnis with watchful eyes, waiting for an opportunity to harness their
extremist aims to a community's legitimate grievances.

NOUR

January 2011, Le Kram, Tunis

SUNLIGHT POURED INTO THE ROOM AS HER LITTLE SISTER YANKED open the curtains and slapped at Nour's bare feet, which were poking out from under the blanket. "Get up!" she hissed. "The quarter is exploding! We're allowed to go as far as the end of the street as long as you come."

A few weeks earlier, Nour's quiet life in Tunis as a high school dropout, a girl who had chosen her faith over the discomfort of pretending to be secular at school, had been abruptly interrupted. On December 17, 2010, in Sidi Bouzid, a provincial town in Tunisia's parched, jobless heartland, a young fruit seller who supported five members of his family by selling produce from his cart challenged a policewoman. She was demanding a bribe, but he offered to pay a small fine instead. The policewoman confiscated his electronic scales and slapped him in the face before a crowd. The fruit seller was humiliated, but most of all, he needed his scales back. He remonstrated at the local municipality office, but no one would see him. With a bucket of gasoline in hand, he stood in full view of the street and screamed out, "How do you expect me to earn a living?" and lit himself on fire.

His desperate, simple act of protest resonated with those in Tunisia who had also endured the state's needless molestation at the most intimate level. Demonstrations broke out in the streets of Sidi Bouzid and then quickly spread across the country.

The protests reached the capital city of Tunis in January 2011. Nour's neighborhood, Le Kram, was the first to erupt. Le Kram sat perched just below Carthage, the district that was home to the presidential palace and lined by palatial villas, overlooking the Mediterranean from a gentle cliff near ancient Roman ruins. Le Kram was the lone working-class quarter situated near this seat of power. In the late 1970s, as President Bourguiba sought to modernize the port district of La Goulette, he expelled poor families from the area and dumped them into Kram. Many squatted in homes abandoned by Tunisian Jews who had left in the 1950s and 1960s, after the founding of Israel. The families set their clocks in these vacant homes, waiting for the requisite fifteen years a property had to be empty in order to claim it as one's own.

Kram looks different from many of the capital's narrow, crowded slum districts; its streets are wide and tree-lined, reminiscent of better days. But closer in, among the fraying buildings, the signs of Kram's restiveness are evident: heaps of garbage the municipality fails to collect, graffiti that revolves around the despair of young men with too little to do, convulsed by anti-police rage and soccer mania.

Since the 1970s, Le Kram had produced ministers and assassins, Communists and Islamists, pimps and poets—men and women who didn't feel as though they belonged to modern Tunisia, and who dedicated their lives to redressing or venting that feeling. It was a *shaabi* neighborhood, working class and of the people, a place you went when you had to go underground. Le Kram had a rich history of swinging the country's politics. When Bourguiba cut bread subsidies in 1984, Kram was the first district in the capital city to revolt. A sepia news photo from the time shows a Kram woman in a traditional white veil standing down an army tank in the streets. The day after Kram rioted, Bourguiba reinstated the subsidy.

That day in January 2011, Nour got dressed, her little sister almost levitating with impatience. Outside, neighbors stood at their front doors or leaned out their windows, speaking quickly. The lady next door was in her housedress, telling everyone that local protesters had torched the police station and were now heading toward the headquarters of President Ben Ali's political party. Nour blinked at this news. The police station in Kram was the largest in all of greater Tunis. She grabbed her sister's hand and they ran.

Out on the main thoroughfare, there was no traffic, and people were congregating in the middle of the road. Plumes of black smoke rose from the tram stop, billowing behind a line of fir trees. A man cycled past with one hand on his handlebars, swerving to look over and behind. Another staggered about, pumping a two-finger V in the air, slurring the two demands of the revolution, *"Hurriya"* and *"Karama,"* freedom and dignity. The baker's muffins, usually finished by this hour, piled against the glass, unsold and forgotten amid the chaos.

Kram contained a multitude of political currents—there were Islamists of many persuasions, trade unionists, Communists—but in the early months of 2011, all were united in a seething revolt against the Ben Ali regime. Jamal, a young man in his early twenties, was a devoted Communist, but when he talked about Kram, about what they did that day and the days that followed, he spoke in a collective "we." "All of us felt like we didn't belong," he said. "Everyone wanted to leave. Every political problem that existed in Tunisia? We had it."

On January 13, Jamal stood alongside the Salafis that his leftist group sometimes rumbled with. Together, they watched the police headquarters burn, their affiliations subsumed in the battle between the neighborhood and the police, who felt more than ever like an occupation force. By night, as the fire of burning tires glowed orange, the air fluttered with singed papers and the mosquitoes hurled themselves toward the light. At least nine Kram protesters were killed that day. The police abandoned their charred station and vacated the area. The neighborhood had won.

THAT AUGUST, DURING THE FIRST Eid celebration of Ramadan after the revolution, Nour and her mother walked to the mosque for Friday prayer, down a residential street lined with palm trees and bougainvillea. Never in fifty years had anyone in Kram seen so many women en route to pray publicly.

Nour saw women she knew converging from all directions. There were so many women that it was mayhem trying to get inside, into the small women's prayer room. After Ramadan that year, the mosque built a separate women's entrance, the first since its establishment many years before.

In January 2011, President Ben Ali boarded a plane to exile (he reportedly wobbled on the tarmac, teary at leaving his pillaged country, only to be upbraided by his wife: "Get on, imbecile. All my life I've had to deal with your screw-ups."). After the collapse of the regime, the neighborhood changed quickly. It started policing itself through newly formed groups like the Leagues for the Protection of the Revolution. Local Salafis trained together and patrolled in groups that sometimes crossed the line into vigilantism, roughing up drug dealers, delinquents, and thieves.

In Tunisia, the Salafis were relative newcomers, both religiously and politically. The term *Salafi* refers to followers of a strain of puritan, revivalist Islam that originated in the eighteenth and nineteenth centuries, in the lands that eventually became Saudi Arabia. The founders of the Salafi movement believed that contemporary Islam had strayed from the true path of the Prophet Muhammad, and moved to create a stripped-down, back-to-fundamentals Islam. For this, they called themselves after the *salaf,* the term for the pious early followers of the Prophet. Salafism grew and evolved over time in Saudi Arabia, fusing with the young state's emerging national ideology and becoming crucial to the ruling al-Saud family's claim to legitimacy. Salafism contained various strands, some apolitical, others more activist. Various scholars and religious dissidents from around the Arab world took refuge in Saudi Arabia over the years, injecting the Salafi scene with orthodox theologians from other parts of the Muslim world.

At its doctrinal core, Salafism mostly overlaps with orthodox Sunni Islam. It mainly diverges in its harsh anathematizing of its enemies, or those deemed outside the fold of Islam. The overzealous tendency of making *takfir,* or excommunicating, those whom the Salafis oppose is what makes Salafism so intolerant and potentially flammable. Because Salafism coexisted with, indeed underpinned, Saudi Arabia's transnational activities during the 1970s and beyond— through its support for the jihad in Afghanistan against the Soviets; through its soft-power investments in exporting ideas across the Muslim world via books, imam training, the building of mosques and religious centers—it eventually grew into a complex global movement with many different manifestations. Sometimes it existed quietly in European cities where it made people more pious and apart, but still peaceful; sometimes it took root in restive ghettos and banlieues, offering a language of division and militancy to Muslim youth who already felt aggrieved, alienated, and isolated by European society.

In the 1980s, when the Soviet Union invaded Afghanistan, the United States funded the Arab mujaheddin who traveled to fight the Soviet occupiers. Those jihadists were also very much favored sons of the Saudi state, but they turned against the Saudi ruling family after the first Gulf War of 1991, when American military bases cropped up across the Saudi Kingdom. To the disquiet of many Saudis, Osama bin Laden among them, these military bases never went away. The virulent opposition to this American presence in the Gulf peninsula eventually coalesced into al-Qaeda, a group that described its growing political militancy as a jihad.

Throughout the 1990s, the al-Qaeda project of Salafi jihad remained marginal and underground across most of the Middle East; it gained traction in the mid-2000s, after the 9/11 attacks provoked American invasions in Afghanistan and Iraq. The broader War on Terror was like truth kindling to the al-Qaeda remnants who claimed the United States was at war with Islam: a years-long campaign operating across large swaths of the world, involving torture, black sites, and many civilian deaths, in the name of fighting terrorism. Those resisting the U.S. occupation in Iraq looked for religious ideas and symbolism to galvanize support for their insurgency; those within the Sunni community found ready material in the al-Qaeda vision, while Shia Iraqis formed their own sect-based militias to fight the Americans. The aimless insurgent veterans of the Afghan war had been searching for the next front, the ideal just war. The Iraqi insurgency offered them exactly that. It drew fighters from far and wide, from Jordan and Syria, from Saudi and Tunisia.

Before the Arab Spring of 2011, the Salafis had little influence or public presence in North Africa. In Tunisia, religious political activism mostly coalesced around Ennahda, a party that was Islamist in identity and outlook but pragmatic and willing to work within the electoral process.

While the Ennahda represented the interests of a socially conservative middle class during the years of President Ben Ali's reign, the Salafis appealed to a younger generation of lower- and middle-class Tunisians, especially in urban areas. Their followers tended to be socially marginalized (though often university-educated), and drawn to an ideology that felt appropriately radical and antiestablishment in the time of the Arab Spring.

But within the Salafi movement, there was division and disagreement. Two main strains competed: one that saw itself as a local social project with revolutionary aims, seeking to prepare society for a gradual move toward religious governance by teaching and activism; and a second strain, with an apocalyptic worldview more receptive to transnational jihadism and absolutism. This second strain recognized only themselves as true Muslims, and labeled everyone else (even other Muslims) as *kuffar,* or unbelievers. It tended to draw older-generation Salafis who had fought in Afghanistan against the Soviets and in Iraq following the U.S. invasion.

This first and more moderate group stepped into the space that opened after the revolution, eager to participate in civic life through charity work and religious teaching, and to be recognized as a normal civic actor. While this group believed, as a matter of core principle, that Muslims should be ruled by Sharia law, they did not advocate imposing this through violent means, nor were they necessarily jihadists. But to liberal Tunisians—the teachers who were skeptical of Nour wearing her niqab or even a hijab, those who wanted public and government spaces to be staunchly secular—the two strains of the Salafi movement were indistinguishable. The stereotype of the second strain—bogeymen with long beards, body odor, and tasteless Afghan-style tunics who wanted to drape the capital in black flags and ban yoga—was the predominant one. To liberal Westernized Tunisians, the appeal of Salafism after the revolution seemed bewildering and disturbing, carrying with it a threat of socially conservative, majoritarian rule.

But in Kram itself, many regarded Salafis as neighborhood guys, not shadowy, Saudi-funded "foreign" figures. Communists like Jamal viewed the Salafis' local efforts with skepticism, but not alarm. "Once the neighborhood policed itself, things really improved," he said.

Jamal, despite being fond of Charles Bukowski, believed Tunisian society had an "over-masculinity" problem that applied to everyone, not just Salafis, an amplified machismo that resulted from being kept permanently under the state's boot. The neighborhood thugs who embraced Salafism often imported their brutish behavior with them and assigned it a moral compass: harassing girls who wore short skirts, roughing up stores that sold alcohol, even if they themselves had until recently been drinkers. In the aftermath of the uprising that unseated the Ben Ali regime, Salafism gave these men an outlet to vent long-standing social and political frustrations. Childhood angst, urban thug life, acute marginalization, and political and class grievances all fused together in a new Salafi identity.

"When the local guys see a policeman beat up an old woman for wearing hijab, they develop a complex against Ben Ali," Jamal explained. "But also a complex against the West, which supports him. They want to take revenge, and that means against the West. Every Ben Ali policeman has created four Salafis."

IN THE SUMMER OF 2011, Nour could walk through Kram at dusk feeling more secure, without scanning for policemen who might hassle her for wearing her niqab, or some amped-up junkie who might suddenly lunge for her ankles. Her neighborhood was safer than it had been before the revolution.

In the wake of the Arab Spring, neighborhoods across Tunisia formed local brigades that came to be called Leagues for the Protection of the Revolution. At first, these brigades protected residents from looting and vandalism after the collapse of the police force. Later, they grew into hubs of political activity, where organizers strategized on the local level, to ensure that old regime figures—from mafia bosses to local officials—did not creep back into political influence post-revolution. That, at least, was the original vision. With time, the Leagues began to function as political enforcers for the factions that found themselves facing off post-2011.

In Kram, the local version of this league was called the Revolutionary Men of Kram, and it included activists of varying backgrounds. Emad, an activist in his fifties who looked more like a French academic, dressed as he was in white jeans, a black leather jacket, and aviator Ray-Bans, described it this way: "When the regime fell, it didn't mean that we were just going to cling to the mosque. We had a lot to do. Everyone in Kram was on the same page. Everyone wanted to work on employment, dignity, and to make the youth feel like they had some stake in the state."

Nour was ready for this, to start expanding her horizons, to find a place for herself in this new Tunisia. One evening in that summer of 2011, she went to visit with the imam's wife. Their house was small and spare: a living room with a foam sofa, a chipped lacquer coffee table, and a plate embossed with *Allah* in calligraphy hanging on the wall.

Nour sat at the kitchen table as the imam's wife prepared dinner and their toddler eyed the electrical socket in the corner. "I've been talking about you," the older woman said. A Tunisian man who had been living in France had recently come back home, and asked the imam to find him a wife. "I said I knew just the girl for him," the imam's wife said. "A good girl, very religious, devoted, she would make a perfect wife."

Nour was young and had plenty of time to marry, but given that she hadn't finished high school and lacked any skills or the liberal dressing habits that might allow her to find work in a shop, marriage was a promising prospect. She could get out of her parents' house. She could finally assume an identity beyond failed student and perpetual daughter. She asked the imam's wife to tell her more about this man.

Karim came to Nour's house the next day. He was thirty-three, fifteen years older than Nour, but he was attractive, with black hair and steady coffee-bean eyes. There was kindness in the way he stooped down to speak to her younger brother and sister, pulling a bouncy ball out of his pockets for each of them. She and Karim sat with her parents in the living room, drinking tea as they all searched for things to talk about: he told them about his parents back in Ben Gardane, a town near the Libyan border, and the challenges of living in France, where he had worked for some years as a waiter, trying to save up enough money to do something better than that.

Karim had dreamed of going to France his whole life, but upon arrival, he said he had felt smaller and more fenced in than he ever had in Tunisia. Floating from restaurant to restaurant, often washing dishes, not even waiting on tables, he started to despair. It was hard to get by, let alone save money. During his time in France, he started becoming more religious, which made work tricky, because he no longer wished to work in restaurants that served alcohol. This, in Paris, left him with poor options: greasy shawarma joints or a possible new career in what he called "commerce."

Nour didn't know exactly what "commerce" meant, but by day six (Karim was now coming to the house every day), she accepted it as honorable and correct that Karim had left France—a country that had never wanted the best for Tunisia or its citizens anyway—and returned home, where he could start over. She grew accustomed to seeing him in the living room with her family, to the sound of his voice, to a male presence that radiated warmth and made her feel, simply because he was there for her, more mature. On the seventh day, she accepted his proposal. Karim said he needed to go back to France to wrap up his affairs. Upon his return three months later, they married.

THAT FALL, THE YEAR AFTER the revolution, they still had hope. Nour and Karim slept on a roll-out mattress in a room at her parents' house, which they shared with her two younger siblings. This was scarcely ideal. Her little brother mewed in the night and they often awoke to both children peering down at them with cartoon-wide eyes, willing them to get up and play. But it was better than the alternative: living with his parents.

Nour hung her hijab and clothes on the same rusty nail she had used since that fateful day at high school in 2007. Karim was looking for work, any kind of work at all, so they could move out and get their own place, but ultimately he aimed for a proper job. Something that would enable him to have two children and feed and educate them well, so that someday their children could live on the other side of the wall of inequality that he, Nour, and everyone they knew had been scrambling against from childhood.

Some days Karim was out until evening, meeting contacts in street cafés, tracing friends' networks for someone who might be able to get him a government job. In Tunisia, a state sector job was a golden ticket: a steady salary for life, a measure of social status. Nour learned to gauge from Karim's expression and the cast of his shoulders whether she should ask how the day went. Some days she let herself imagine that it was good news: that he had found something, that he would be starting the next week, that he would tell her to start searching for a flat, and everything would change.

It hardly seemed too much to expect from the new Tunisia. The revolution spread to other parts of the Arab world—first to Egypt, then later to Libya, Yemen, Syria, and Bahrain—but in all of these countries, upheaval only led to more intense repression, civil war, or outright collapse. Tunisia was the sole country to emerge steady enough to hold elections and withstand their result.

In late 2011, in the first free elections in Tunisia's history, the Islamist party Ennahda swept by a wide margin. The party's leader, Rachid Ghannouchi, back from decades of exile in London, promised that "Tunisia was for everyone." Ennahda members who had suffered torture under the previous regime now served in the government alongside politicians from the old regime who had overseen those abuses. The fruit-seller martyr Bouazizi got his own postage stamp.

Nour was energized. There were things to do. The mosques in Kram bustled with activity, and religiously tinged social activism was gaining ground both locally and nationally. In the past, even charity work was dangerous; the state viewed it as gateway behavior that led to Ennahda or Islamist sympathies. But now the atmosphere was open and freewheeling. It was acceptable to exude an aura of Muslimness. Popular personalities like Rikoba, a singer who led the crowd during soccer matches, grew a beard and meshed his revolutionary anthems with Islamic *nasheed*s, or devotional songs. He posted clips on You-

Tube, standing beside a young man with a black Salafist bandanna, saying to a journalist, "Why don't you speak to my friend here, this young Salafist? He's a good guy!"

In Kram, the women's group that Nour attended affixed themselves to Ansar al-Sharia, the post-revolution Salafi group launched by Abu Iyadh, the most senior religious militant who had been imprisoned by the Ben Ali government and released after the revolution. Ansar al-Sharia grew by about 1,000 percent between April 2011, the year it held its first annual conference, and April 2012, when the same event drew almost ten thousand young Tunisians. It was early days in the political market of the new Tunisia, and everyone, from Ennahda to Ansar al-Sharia, wanted to draw on the widest possible constituency. Ansar al-Sharia operated skillfully in the new climate, with a robust Facebook presence; in a two-month span, the group held sixty-five events in about thirty locations across the country. A young Tunisian graduate student who wrote his thesis on Ansar al-Sharia described it as "charity work on an industrial scale." The founder of the group said, "We want to reach the hearts of people, not hurt them," although he did little to intervene when Salafis went too far and harassed people for drinking alcohol or dressing immodestly.

From the outside, the group's appeal to young women like Nour was bewildering. Salafi attitudes toward women were extremely strict: no free mixing of genders; full Islamic dress, often including the niqab. Somehow the group managed, within these strictures, to create a sense of solidarity across genders. While, for women, the secular space within liberal Tunisian society was emancipated but archetypically Western and objectified, Ansar al-Sharia encouraged women to study, work, and function in society, albeit on the other side of a cloak of separateness. The Tunisian graduate student described women in Ansar al-Sharia as feeling not constrained but empowered; the group was very respectful of the women within its own boundaries. It made no pretense of espousing Western-style feminist equality, but it advocated women's access to education, and participation in civic life through charitable and religious activities. This was, to a young woman like Nour, the more resonant message.

Women conducted their own *dawah* circles, where they invited new members to study and understand Islam, and were active in running Ansar al-Sharia's social media accounts. The conversations and buzz of activity, though religious in nature, often focused on practical concerns, such as how to build a halal tourism industry in Tunisia. It was one of the fastest-growing types of tourism in the world, as demand surged for resorts that did not serve alcohol, offered private or separate swimming areas for women and families, and encouraged modest dress. Many young Salafis thought it would be ideal for Tunisia, which—with its long Mediterranean coastline of sandy beaches, palm-tree-lined ancient ruins, and whitewashed desert towns—relied heavily on tourism for national income.

The more cautious young Salafis tried to fuse Ansar al-Sharia's magnetic, antiestablishment energy to a more considered approach that emphasized working practically within the system. Karim's friend Walid was of this persuasion. Nour admired Walid; it was hard not to. He came from a middle-class family from Ben Gardane; his father was a successful landowner and Walid was well educated, a graduate in economics with family connections that had enabled him to find a government job. He wore polo shirts in bright colors and white sneakers. He was tall and broad-shouldered, and he looked equally capable of playing tennis and beating the shit out of someone. Walid was objectively handsome, but what Nour found especially attractive about him was that he was a "good family" militant, an Islamist out of pure belief, not because he was born destitute in some urban slum.

Walid had an intellectual's grasp of the origins of Salafi jihadism. He could parse its theoretical and political evolution from the earliest writings of Sayyid Qutb, the Egyptian militant-ideologue who advocated radical resistance to the nationalist authoritarianism of Nasser, through to Abdullah Azzam, the Palestinian jihadist theologian and co-founder of al-Qaeda, who insisted that defensive jihad placed strict safeguards around civilian casualties. Walid had listened to their arguments as a teenager on cassette tapes and videos, impressed by their plans to bring justice to society. Crony capitalism, he grew to believe—the kind practiced by Ben Ali and supported by the West, especially France—not only failed to bring Tunisians jobs and dignity, but it also robbed them of spiritual comfort. As long as powerful forces in the West imposed such secular autocrats on Tunisia, the people stood no genuine chance of overthrowing their oppressors, he thought. Because it was, in the end, hard to overthrow a regime that was bolstered—through direct aid, military help, intelligence sharing, and training—by wealthy Western nations. This postcolonial distrust of Western interference also happened to be part of al-Qaeda's strategic vision. Though Walid faulted bin Laden for many things, he agreed that bringing about change in autocratic Muslim countries required weakening the will of Western nations to back them.

Fighting the Americans in Iraq, to Walid, was clearly just, an anti-imperial war. But in Tunisia, he saw no need for any violence. After years of secular indoctrination, it would take time and patience to persuade Tunisians to give the Islamist vision a fair hearing, to see it as a possible way of ensuring independence, social justice, and the core demands of the revolution.

Walid sometimes teased Nour, who listened gamely to his discussions with Karim but tended to filter the ideas through posts she read on Facebook, distilled to an easily absorbable level. Like many young people in Tunis, she spent hours on social media. She flicked through the video of a song by the rapper Weld El 15, *"Boulicia Kleb"* ("Cops Are Dogs"). If there was any one sentiment the youth of Tunisia shared in 2012, it was probably this song. She read a post from two local doctors, both women, who said they were working longer hours so they could donate a third of their salary each month to the Ansar al-Sharia movement.

While Karim looked for a job, Nour continued to soothe him with words of patience, but recently her reserves had been waning. When Karim had asked to marry her, he had mentioned the existence of an ex-wife, a Tunisian woman with whom he had had a daughter a few years before moving to France; he had made it sound tidy and long resolved. And perhaps it had been while he lived abroad, but now that he was back in Tunisia, the ex-wife was showing up in their lives. Nour took this gracefully, welcoming the little girl when she came to visit Karim, braiding her hair and taking her for ice cream along the seaside corniche. The ex-wife rang Karim almost every day, demanding to know when he would start giving them money. But Karim had nothing more than the occasional shift driving a taxi. When he explained this to his ex-wife, she shrieked that she couldn't spin money out of air, either, and threatened to report him to the police as an extremist if he didn't sort things out.

His mobile phone vibrated at all hours with calls from an unidentified number. His body stiffened when he saw the caller; sometimes he ignored it, and sometimes he answered in a clipped voice. The conversations made the lines around his eyes deepen. Eventually he told Nour it was the police calling, asking to see him, asking him about men he knew from France. Karim told Nour that back in France, the police had also been monitoring him.

Nour's mother finally asked her why the police were bothering him. "His religion. It's his religion that causes him trouble," she said.

ASMA

January 2011, Raqqa, Syria

FOR MUCH OF THAT JANUARY, AND EVEN INTO EARLY FEBRUARY, ASMA imagined, as she stepped off the bus that took her back and forth between her university and central Raqqa, that the distant rumblings of revolt would never reach them. The Arab Spring had quickly spread from Tunisia to Egypt and Yemen, with smaller protests in Jordan and Oman, but the Assad family had ruled Syria her entire life, all nineteen years of it, and they seemed as rooted in the country's firmament as the pine trees that lined the coastal mountains. Enormous statues of Hafez al-Assad loomed over so many urban squares, Hafez with his preternaturally long forehead, arm outstretched and beckoning, as if to say, "Welcome to Syria, my personal home!"

The Assad family were Alawites, a minority religious sect in the area of the Levant that came to be known as Syria, after the fall of the Ottoman Empire. France administered Syria after the Ottoman dissolution, and during this time, it encouraged Alawite participation in its military with the conventional imperial aim: dividing the local citizenry by exacerbating natural fault lines. It was the first time in centuries that the Muslims of the Levant had been ruled by European Christians, and Sunni Muslim dismay and resistance was fierce. The new colonial borders drawn by the French blocked Sunni traders and merchants from access to their traditional Ottoman trade markets and seaports. For the Alawites, who were primarily peasants living in rural areas, the new arrangements offered a quick, unexpected path to power. Hafez al-Assad, the father of Bashar, took power following a coup in 1970. Rural Alawites slowly urbanized, while traditionally wealthy, conservative Sunnis in cities like Aleppo and Homs saw their influence and fortunes wane.

By the early 1980s, the Muslim Brotherhood emerged as what one historian called the "natural spokesman" of the Sunni community, whose social interests, particularly among landed, trading, and manufacturing classes, suffered under Assad's secular, nationalist-socialist project. The Brotherhood released a declaration in 1980 that was scarcely concerned with Islam or ideology at all, but advocated a different economic program that would aid a broader swath of constituencies and promote political and civil liberties. It was, as ever, a demand for better governance: more equitable economic policies, less patronage, a less stifling political environment. Though the Muslim Brotherhood exists in the Western imagination as an extremist movement driven by ideology, its historical roots in the Syria of the 1970s and 1980s grew out of political advocacy for an underrepresented group.

Hafez al-Assad, by that time, had cultivated a vivid personality cult that overlaid his oppressive rule: he was "father," the "leader forever," the "gallant knight," even the country's "premier pharmacist." In that era, just as today, the divides in Syria could be mapped as Alawi versus Sunni—but not without blurring many lines, because there were also contentions that fractured along economic and social interests, and geographic and commercial ones. Before the 1970s, there was no perception of a grand sectarian conflict in Syria, because no one considered the Alawites to be Muslims; Sunnis and Shias alike considered them heretics, outside the fold of the faith. But Assad wished to endow his narrow, minority rule with religious legitimacy and to incorporate Islam into his national mythology. He sought to recast the Alawites not as an impious and singular religious tribe of its own, but as Shia-esque Muslims. He offered protection and patronage to Shia clerics who were willing to anoint them as such; the prominent Lebanese Shia cleric Musa al-Sadr offered the gelatinous term "partners in distress," hinting that Alawites and Shi'ites shared contemporary political concerns, if not theological roots.

In February 1982, the Sunnis of Hama, through the Muslim

Brotherhood, rebelled against the rule of Hafez al-Assad. The city of Hama had around 200,000 inhabitants. Assad dispatched 12,000 troops and sealed off the city, tanks rolling through the streets and helicopter gunships roaming the skies. In the course of three weeks, government forces killed between 5,000 and 20,000 citizens.

Nearly every family lost at least one member. There were so many bodies lying in the streets that the city began attracting packs of wild dogs, who would gnaw at corpses and attack people searching for their relatives' bodies. Asma wasn't born yet, but her parents were living in the capital city of Damascus. By that time, Assad had catered success-fully enough to the interests of the capital's middle class, including its Sunnis, that their concerns no longer overlapped so neatly with those of Sunnis in other towns and cities.

Hama. To this day, to anyone from the Middle East, the name of the town is one of those coffin words, like "Srebrenica," synonymous with atrocity on the widest scale. "It is difficult to explain the sudden disappearance of a large city, especially one located on the main high-way between Damascus and Aleppo," wrote a historian shortly after the massacre.

Assad and his Ba'ath Party, once they had mopped up the uprising, warned Syrians against the "beastly" Muslim Brotherhood that had "sold itself to the devil." In a speech following the uprising, Assad des-ignated those who had rebelled against the government as extremists.

> They are butchering children, women, and old people in the
> name of Islam. They are wiping out entire families in the name
> of Islam. They extend their hand to the foreigner and his agents
> and to the pro-U.S. puppet regimes on our borders. They extend
> their hands to them to receive funds and arms to double-cross
> their homeland and to kill fellow citizens. . . . They carried out
> every act banned by God. . . . They are apostates. We are the
> ones who defend Islam, religion, and the homeland.

The chokehold of repression remained a constant in Syria during the decades that followed, as power passed from Hafez to his son Bashar. But now it was February 2011, just a few weeks after the revolt in Tunisia, and Arabs across the region were transfixed, emboldened to think that their dictators too might be held to account. In Dara'a, a southern town near the border with Jordan, a group of youths scrawled graffiti on the walls of a local school. "It's your turn, Doctor," they wrote playfully, addressing Bashar al-Assad, an ophthalmologist by training, riffing the rhyme in Arabic, *"Ejak el door, ya Doctor."*

But when they were arrested by police, their mocking graffiti turned into something like prophecy. By late March, word got out that the youth were tortured in prison. That Friday, after the noon prayer, demonstrators protested angrily in the streets of Dara'a, demanding their release. The police shot indiscriminately into the crowd, killing several people. Within a month, the protests spread to dozens of towns and cities across Syria, flaring regularly after Friday prayers and growing into the most sustained, serious challenge to the Assad family's rule since the rebellion of Hama in 1982.

Bashar responded like his father. Though the protesters' initial demands were for reforms, he shrugged off their grievances and refused to offer any concessions, moving to crush the challenge with violent force. Like his father, he used his first televised address to call the protesters "extremists" and warned that without him, Syria would fall to jihadists. Many Syrians, including prominent and middle-class Sunnis in Damascus itself, feared this prospect.

The regime's military laid siege to Dara'a and began killing protesters who poured into the streets, sometimes more than a hundred a week. Large cities like Homs grew restive, and a tweet circulated: "Homs 2011 = Hama 1982, but slowly slowly."

The revolution was slow to come to Raqqa. Asma continued to board the bus each day for her marketing classes at al-Hasaka, leaning her head against the window, engrossed in her phone: texting her boyfriend, scrolling through her Facebook feed. Slowly, the uprising that had initially seemed so distant began to inch closer. Asma's classes at the university were canceled, with no date given for when they might resume. Eventually there were marches through the center of the city, the citizens of Raqqa finally shouting what Syrians had already been calling for across the country: *"The people want the fall of the regime!"*

But even as news of massacres and heavy fighting reached the city, as refugees from cities in the west began appearing, as the city's young men started to sign up with the most popular anti-Assad groups in the area—mostly Jabhat al-Nusra—the fabric of life seemed mostly intact. Within two to three days, the Free Syrian Army and Jabhat al-Nusra worked together to liberate the city.

Revolution

The Arab uprising of 2011, optimistically called the Arab Spring, have disrupted the political alignment that has organized the Middle East for more than half a century: the implicit bargain between Arab client state dictators and the West, whereby authoritarians rely on the United States, France, and Britain for political backing, aid, and military protection, and pay it all back through investments in Western economies and tens of billions of dollars in arms purchases, buoying the defense industries of those nations.

In Syria, in the course of little more than a year, what began as a peaceful protest grows into an armed rebellion against the government of President Bashar al-Assad.

Assad moves swiftly to portray the protesters as extremist Islamists and warns the country of their violent, sectarian intentions. To make this story come true, his security forces target peaceful activists, detaining thousands in prisons where they are tortured and raped. He releases scores of Islamists and hardened jihadists from prison, allowing them free rein to group and organize.

Defectors from the Syrian military form the Free Syrian Army, while the released jihadists intermingle with more religious and militant strains of the emerging opposition. Abu Bakr al-Baghdadi, who runs the Islamic State in Iraq (ISI), spies an opportunity and dispatches a senior operative to open a front in Syria. This new effort is called Jabhat al-Nusra, the Nusra Front, and attracts both freshly released local militants and Muslim fighters from abroad. Al-Qaeda leader Ayman al-Zawahiri, the successor of Osama bin Laden, issues a statement lauding the Syrian resistance and urging Muslims from around the region to travel to Syria's "fields of jihad."

In February 2012, the *Sunday Times* journalist Marie Colvin and French photographer Remi Ochlik die when Assad's military forces shell a media center in Homs.

In May, around one hundred people are killed in the Houla region of Syria, nearly half of them children. Shadowy death squads dispatched by the regime, called the *shabiha,* who wear civilian clothing and white sneakers, are believed responsible.

Western governments call on Assad to step down, and impose sanctions. Key regional states—Qatar, Turkey, Saudi Arabia—cut ties, and begin to fund and support Assad's opponents. Russia and Iran, Syria's closest allies in the region, stand staunchly behind him; Tehran sends advisers and starts backing militias working with the Syrian military.

President Obama authorizes the CIA and other agencies to arm and finance the Syrian rebels. Much of this effort is coordinated by the Saudis, who view the opposition to Assad as a sectarian Sunni uprising, and an opportunity to mobilize Sunnis against both the Shia-dominated governments in Iraq and Iran, their great regional foe and a Shia power. President Obama warns that any use of chemical weapons is a "red line" that will bear enormous consequences and "change my calculus" on U.S. intervention.

In 2012, the United Nations dispatches Kofi Annan to broker a cease-fire. He resigns after just five months, saying that the refusal to include Iran in negotiations defeats any possibility, already slim, of a political settlement.

The Syrian civil war becomes a proxy war, involving several regional powers and also the United States.

RAHMA AND GHOUFRAN

June 2012, Sousse, Tunisia

RAHMA CLIMBED THE STAIRS TO THE ROOFTOP, HOLDING THE BONY, bedraggled alley cat by the neck scruff. The dead cat had been lying on the side of the road near the bakery where her mother worked an afternoon shift. Thirteen-year-old Rahma had grabbed it and stuffed it in her backpack.

On all sides Sousse stretched out into the distance, a horizon of low-slung concrete-block houses, huddled together along narrow, rutted streets that became rivers of mud in the rain. Sousse was a city perched on the Mediterranean coast, about a two-hour drive south of the capital, Tunis. The old quarter had an antique medina where the tourists sometimes wandered. But apart from the luxury hotels splayed along the beach, enclaves where nearly naked Brits and Germans lay on deck chairs amid palm trees, much of the city was squat and strewn with rubbish, lined with fast-food joints with cheap metal doors and closed storefronts. Some of its streets were wide, some narrow, the buildings a mishmash of varying styles, as though the city had developed as a series of afterthoughts.

Rahma lived with her mother, Olfa, three sisters, and one brother in a small two-room flat in a grimy, trash-strewn neighborhood. Their father, Olfa's ex-husband, was a drunk who lived in a nearby town and didn't have the money or inclination to help them. Olfa worked multiple jobs and was away for long hours, trying to earn enough to cover the electricity and rent. When she returned home, she was usually exhausted and prone to screaming at her children for minor infractions or squabbles. Olfa was keen for her daughters to grow up with proper morals and modesty, even though she wasn't around to oversee their movements the way a less work-burdened mother might be. At school, other children looked down on them for their poverty and fatherlessness and for their secondhand clothes.

That June day it was quiet up on the roof, except for the rumble of Rahma's stomach. Some days there wasn't very much food in the house, and today was one of those days. Rahma thought of her sister Ghoufran downstairs in the flat, watching their younger brother and sister on her own, and resolved to make quick work of the dead cat. The roof contained little but the makeshift corrugated-tin shack where Rahma did her dissections. She had a small table lined with various-sized knives. She started at the base of the neck, slitting a clean line down to the tail, and started edging the knife in sideways, separating the dirty pelt from the muscle underneath. Rahma specialized in this, skinning the neighborhood's dead animals. Ghoufran, who at fourteen was just a year older, called the shed on the roof "the butcher shop," but to Rahma, it wasn't butchery. Something about the precision, the deconstruction of a cat or a bird into its smaller component parts, calmed Rahma. When she was on the roof working on an animal, nothing else existed.

The night before, Rahma told her mother that she was suspended from school for two days for shouting back at the chemistry teacher. It had begun when two girls had mocked her during recess for not having a father. "Who knows if your mother even knew who he was," one of them said. At this, Rahma pounced on her. She was suspended for shouting at the teacher in the aftermath of the fight. Rahma was a strong-willed girl. On other occasions, she had gotten herself into trouble for sticking up for weaker girls who were bullied for their looks, their poverty, their families.

Olfa was a thickset woman in her mid-forties with a freckled, flat nose and bright brown eyes that hinted at both temper and playfulness. Life hadn't allotted her the freedom to develop hobbies or pastimes, and she spent most of her waking hours working in a tin-roofed bakery and then waiting tables in a restaurant. She constantly did sums in her head, making sure she would earn enough each week across her shifts. Many evenings, when she got back from the long evening shift at the restaurant, Olfa lay on the sofa rubbing cream onto her puffy ankles. She tried to convince Rahma to be sensible. "Why do you always have to be the voice of defense? Would that girl have done the same for you?" Olfa wondered, as she did countless times, why God had seen fit to give her such a challenging daughter. "There's always going to be someone treated badly in front of you, Rahma," she said. "You don't have to always get involved."

That summer evening, Rahma held up the cat's right paw and inspected it. There seemed to be a piece of metal, like a nail without its head, stuck in it. She prized it out and finished the cat off. The animal looked even skinnier without its fur, sinewy and pink-fleshed. Rahma tossed the knife to the side and walked back out onto the roof, wondering what dinner they could make for the younger children.

THE DAWAH TENT AT THE head of their street went up quickly. Since the revolution the previous year, the local imams often set up preaching tents around the city, hoping to expose the good people of Sousse to the religious learning they had been denied during the Ben Ali years. The tent was filled with tables covered with pamphlets and Qurans, and stands that promoted various charity activities.

It wasn't often, indeed exactly never, that a free event pitched up on their barren side street. Ghoufran asked Olfa if she could visit the tent, explaining that she was just curious to see what was going on. As her children had grown older, Olfa had started leaving them on their own; she had taken to locking the children in for the night when she left for her restaurant shift. Olfa said it was all right, and left the key with her thirteen-year-old daughter.

After evening prayer, when the heat receded with the scorching sun, Ghoufran approached the tent. A young man in a clipped beard and white *thobe,* the long robe worn by men in the Gulf, greeted her and summoned one of the women to look after her. This woman wore a full black abaya but her face, freckled and smiling, was uncovered.

The woman led her to a corner inside the tent where women were sitting in chairs arranged in a circle. Ghoufran took a seat and listened to the woman addressing the circle, talking about the straight path God has laid out for them, how by submitting to His will and dedicating themselves to living purely, they would be eligible for blessings not just in this life, which was fleeting, but in the forever of hereafter. God, the woman said, had infinite wisdom; though changing their lifestyle would be difficult, though they might alienate their families, if they trusted deeply what they would receive in return would be nothing less than the purest tranquility, the most settled of hearts.

This all sounded exquisite to Ghoufran. She had never heard Islam described in this fulsome, compelling way: as a salve to sorrows, an eternal puzzle for her curious mind, a tether she could reach for when she felt lost. These women talked of the justice Islam offered women. They described the attributes of the Prophet, peace be upon him, and how he revered women; how he chose for himself an independent, accomplished woman as his wife, and remained devoted to her until the day she died. After the talk, one woman pulled Ghoufran aside and handed her what she called *shari'i* clothes, a soft black abaya and a headscarf. Ghoufran was a teenager and often fretted over her clothes: their sameness or their fadedness or their lack of resemblance to what other girls wore. But in that moment, slipping into the abaya and headscarf, those anxieties were erased. Wearing the abaya felt like laying her head against someone's chest.

When Ghoufran got home, Rahma looked up from the television and burst out laughing at her older sister. There was an Adele video playing on the television—Ghoufran loved Adele—but she took the remote and turned it off.

Of the two sisters, Ghoufran was the conventionally more beautiful. She was creamy-skinned, with full lips, soft almond eyes, and a narrow European nose. Rahma was small-boned and darker, her eyes walnut brown and set too far apart. They had both inherited Olfa's undeniable charisma, a trait that subjected Olfa to some rude whispers in the neighborhood, because a woman like Olfa, who worked nights and whose eyes could laugh like that, she must be up to no good.

Ghoufran wore her abaya to breakfast the next morning. Olfa raised her eyebrows. "The girls handed it out yesterday," Ghoufran said to her mother, "the ones who are going to teach me about Sharia."

Olfa saw no reason to oppose this. She welcomed her daughters' dressing more conservatively; perhaps if they looked more severe, as Ghoufran did that morning, if their beauty was toned down by the stark black abaya, the rapper and rocker types that they sometimes talked to would stay away.

"Ghoufran looks like a ghoul!" Rahma snorted.

"You shut up. Maybe you should try it out, instead of just mocking. It might be good for you," Ghoufran said.

Though she tried, Ghoufran couldn't persuade Rahma to come with her to the *dawah* tent. The prayer circle women had started coming to the house to visit and talk with Ghoufran, but Rahma only gave them sullen looks and disappeared into the bedroom to blare rock music at high volume.

A few days later it was a man, one of the sheikh's assistants, who stopped Rahma in the street. "Why are you wearing those clothes?" he demanded, blocking Rahma's way as she tried to step past him. With her father out of the picture, no man had ever concerned himself with Rahma's dress, her well-being, the state of her soul, or even, frankly, her basic health. The rocker guys and the break-dancers mostly wanted to flirt with her. But this man, the sheikh's assistant—in the half hour he spoke to her that day, his gaze never once strayed from the level of her head. Rahma never told anyone exactly what he said to her, but she came back into the house sobbing, full of loathing and fury at herself.

Such feelings were not unfamiliar. Growing up, she'd always felt she was bad, always doing something wrong. Her mother often shouted at Rahma for wearing the wrong things, or for socializing on the street after dark, even though they had no one to watch them in the evenings. Olfa didn't like Rahma talking to young men, but Rahma earned their school-supply money by dancing in Fadi's wedding band, and how were they supposed to be in Fadi's wedding band without talking to Fadi?

SALAFISM CHANGED THEM BOTH, LIKE a tint that brought out their temperaments in starker relief. Ghoufran became cheerier and more loving, tending to Olfa and chattering openly about the things she was learning. But Rahma took Salafi ideology and used it to become the family bully, criticizing Olfa and the younger girls for doing everything wrong—for not waking up for the dawn prayer, for wearing tight clothes, watching *haram* television, listening to *haram* music. Rahma tried to force her youngest sister, then nine, to start covering her hair. When she didn't listen, Rahma refused to sit next to her at mealtimes. Here Olfa intervened and threatened to slap her if Rahma continued calling her nine-year-old sister *kafira*, an unbeliever.

Olfa, at first, did not grasp the seriousness of what was transpiring with her daughters. The women from the mosque were now coming over every single day. Even the sheikh himself was coming. He would sit down on the faded couch and draw his *thobe* around him imperiously, and admonish Olfa: "The girls tell me you've instructed them to come straight home after prayer. Sister, I've explained to you, they need to attend classes as well; this is where their real learning takes place. I respectfully ask that you don't stop them."

As long as it was within reason, Olfa didn't have any problem with her daughters' becoming more religious. It was the "within reason" part that was hard to parse, because Olfa had completed only up to a secondary education, and her understanding of religion was extremely basic. Her interpretation of the Salafism her daughters had taken up was that, while stultifying and severe, it promoted chastity and good Islamic morals. For a single mother who worked most waking hours in order to avoid all-out destitution for her family of five, severity was a better problem to have than looseness.

A couple of weeks later, as Olfa was preparing for her evening shift at the restaurant, Rahma handed her a long cloak and told her she needed to start dressing properly. "What you wear right now, it's not *shari'i*," she said, pointing to Olfa's sequined tank top, navy trousers, and fitted pink cardigan.

"I've been dressing like this for years, and I like it like this," Olfa replied, wrapping a red scarf over her hair.

Rahma's eyes welled up with tears. She didn't want to be separated from her mother in the afterlife, and the bar for heaven was high. "You think I'm just being horrible," Rahma said. "But how are you going to make it to *jannah*, going out like this?"

As she walked to the restaurant, Olfa considered what to do about her daughters. Recently they had graduated into positions of minor local influence within Sousse's budding Salafi community. Because marriage was an essential part of a Muslim life—the Quran made it clear that marriage was intended to "give ease"—Ghoufran was tasked with matchmaking for those in their circle. It was her job to identify young men and women in the area who were inclined to marry and help make suitable connections. Sociable and romantic, keen to be beautiful and proper, the Jane Bennet of the family, this work fit Ghoufran very well indeed.

The tough and strong-willed Rahma had the role of advocate and mediator. She would turn up at schools or private homes and argue on behalf of girls in the movement who were clashing with their parents, or who were barred from school for wearing the niqab. Olfa couldn't help but think this work suited Rahma well: Rahma could never keep her mouth shut, always rushing headlong into conflicts at school, if only as a way of easing her own pain.

Olfa's working life was a one-woman case study in the challenges of the Sousse labor market: there was little work, and the little to be had was strenuous, ill-paid, and impermanent. That her girls received some modest payment for such labors—Ghoufran's matchmaking, Rahma's mediating—was almost as inconceivable as their being whisked away to a ball by a pumpkin coach. This was working-class Sousse: there were no coding classes or after-school chess clubs, no avenues for poor teenagers to improve themselves. To be invited to participate in local charity work, raising money for refugees fleeing the conflict in neighboring Libya, or soliciting donations for religious celebrations—in Sousse, this was the only thing that might pass for civic engagement. It was better to have something positive to do in the community, to gain some measure of social status and confidence, rather than sit at home watching Justin Bieber videos, as Rahma and Ghoufran might have been doing otherwise.

NOUR

IN PREVIOUS YEARS, BEFORE THE REVOLUTION, WHEN SHE HAD DROPPED out of school and had nothing much to do with her time, Nour had found it easy to slumber through the summer weather with long afternoon naps. That seemed like a different life; now, she almost had too much to do—attending meetings of her women's group at the mosque, going to charity events, keeping up with all the Facebook activity that drove much of the Salafi movement. Karim's friend Walid was also busy, between his job and his own political meetings. It was just Karim himself who seemed out of sync with them, still dragging himself out looking for work, scrolling through his mobile phone contacts for the hundredth time, as though willing some helpful, connected imaginary friend into existence. She sometimes winced when she came home and found him on the sofa, in almost the same position she'd left him.

What unfolded next, on a warm Friday in September, would change all three of their prospects. At a mosque in central Tunis, Abu Iyadh, the leader of Ansar al-Sharia, gave an impassioned sermon denouncing an amateur YouTube video that mocked the Prophet Muhammad. His supporters swarmed on the mosque terrace outside. There were buses idling on the street, waiting to drive the men across the city to the hulking compound of the U.S. embassy, in protest of the California man who had made the video.

Later that day, the protesters breached the embassy gates. They hung the black Salafi flag from the building and torched the nearby American school. Smoke rose from the buildings. *"Obama, Obama, we are all Osamas!"* they chanted at one point. A few looters came out of the embassy carrying computers under their arms. Police fought to keep the protesters back and the president sent the presidential guards, who killed two and injured nearly thirty protesters. The video, and the ensuing protests, had led to bloodshed across the region: four days prior, militants affiliated with Ansar al-Sharia in Libya had attacked a U.S. diplomatic compound in Benghazi, killing the ambassador and three other Americans.

Stoking anger at the United States was easy. At the end of 2010, WikiLeaks had released U.S. diplomatic cables that described the corruption of the "sclerotic" Ben Ali regime in granular detail. American diplomats acknowledged that the country was "troubled," yet underscored Ben Ali's importance as an "ally" in fighting terrorism. The American ambassador recounted a dinner invitation to the home of the president's son-in-law. The mansion's infinity pool was filled through a lion's head, Roman columns lined the terrace, and frescoes adorned the ceiling; the son-in-law kept a pet tiger called Pasha, who consumed four chickens a day. Human food arrived on planes, from Paris. The Western-backed regime was so brazen that the son-in-law felt at ease telling a French newspaper, "I've got Ferraris, limousines, but nothing gives me a hard-on, not even my wife, like a boat. It's like an uncut diamond."

But while many Tunisians might have sympathized with the protesters' resentment of the United States—the cables noted Tunisians' deep anger at the U.S. invasion of Iraq—the public mood was not receptive to violent confrontation. Ennahda, the Islamist party elected after the revolution, sought to allay people's fears; its leader Rachid Ghannouchi said that "with time, such extremism will vanish." This view was born of his long years in Islamist movements, witnessing countless young hotheads mellow with time through long-term engagement with politics. Political scientists call this approach the "inclusion moderation hypothesis," which holds that the more a society democratizes and allows radical groups to participate politically, the more such groups are inclined to soften their rhetoric and behavior. But despite Ghannouchi's attempts at mollification, the media, Tunisian and Western alike, fed the public's panicked reaction to this display of violence. (Tunisian media remained largely under the control of old-regime supporters, and Western reporters tended to speak to English- or French-speaking politicians and secular activists, rather than young women like Nour, when they wrote about the Salafist movement.)

Ennahda, at that moment, was bogged down in a dispute over Tunisia's new constitution. The committee writing the constitution was deciding whether to criminalize blasphemy, which meant outlawing the defamation of God or Islam. This value was shared by many of the party's supporters, but unacceptable to its secular coalition partners. Ennahda's chief objective was to become a normal political party, acceptable to the international community and tolerated by its political rivals. Becoming politically "normalized" required Ennahda to distance itself from religious ideas and contentions, but the expectations of its constituency, and its very identity as an Islamist party, required religious engagement. In the end, facing ferocious pushback from secular parties and civil society groups, Ennahda abandoned most of its legislative aims; it dropped any reference to Sharia as a source of law; its leadership rejected a proposed law that would have forbidden former members of the ruling party under Ben Ali to run for parliament. It did not concede so much as relent entirely.

And in the eyes of the Ennahda party, this willingness to compromise seemed eminently sensible, given what was unfolding around them, both domestically and in the nearby region. In Egypt, in a coup that was backed by Saudi Arabia and the United Arab Emirates, military officers had recently overthrown the democratically elected Islamist government of Mohammed Morsi; the army and security forces killed approximately a thousand protesters in a single day. The West largely yawned. The Arab Spring, for all its froth and glory, was already a receding memory; the regional Arab powers and their Western backers seemed most at home with authoritarian order, not democratic tumult.

But if slowness and caution made sense to Ennahda, to the young radicals of the Tunisian revolution, it was a betrayal. If a religious po-

The Revolution Loses Its Innocence

By early summer of 2012, the armed opposition has defeated the Assad government in several cities across Syria. The group known as the moderate rebels, the Free Syrian Army, battles the Nusra Front for control of Raqqa. In March 2013, the city falls to the Syrian opposition.

In April, a disagreement cleaves the Islamist rebels. Abu Bakr al-Baghdadi claims that Nusra is an offshoot of ISI and declares both groups will be subsumed into one, which he calls, for the first time, the Islamic State in Iraq and Syria. A day and a half later, the leader of the Nusra Front rejects this: Nusra is its own brand, he insists, focused on the fighting in Syria and loyal to al-Qaeda central.

There are sincere disagreements between them over tactics and degree of hostility to non-Sunnis, but no one knows whether the split is genuinely ideological or intra-jihadi politicking. The world struggles to understand how these rivalries and divisions should shape its response to Syria's war.

In August, a sarin gas attack on Ghouta, a suburb of Damascus, kills 1,500 civilians, including more than 400 children. Videos flood the internet of foaming and twitching bodies, sprawled in basements and on hospital floors. A United Nations investigation establishes the use of sarin, but has not received a Security Council mandate to assign blame to any party. Obama does not launch immediate strikes, but turns to the U.S. Congress. By October, Assad admits to possessing chemical weapons and agrees to dismantle his armory.

The American aid worker Kayla Mueller travels to Aleppo to accompany her boyfriend on a mission for Doctors Without Borders, and is abducted.

In December, the U.S. State Department launches "Think Again, Turn Away" across social media platforms popular with ISIS followers, in an attempt to challenge the group's appeal with "counternarratives." The account bumbles into numerous unwinnable exchanges with online jihadists about U.S. military abuse of prisoners at Abu Ghraib. It accidentally trolls prominent religious figures who oppose ISIS. It is shut down after a few short months, its online archive wiped from the public record.

LINA

LINA, THOUGH NOW COMFORTABLY ENSCONCED IN THE WOMEN'S SHELter after leaving her husband, still didn't have a television, nor did she buy newspapers. Most often she heard the news while she was working. Her elderly patients liked having the radio on.

But her life changed dramatically when she opened a Facebook account. Suddenly she could see who was doing and saying what, without feeling the pressure to participate. After some weeks, she tentatively posted a quote from the Quran. With a small delight, Lina—a shy, quiet woman her whole life—watched people liking her post. One day that winter, she came across a post from a man called Abu Salah al-Almani. He was, like her, Frankfurt-based, and he was asking if there were any good Muslim women open to getting married and emigrating abroad. The post included a contact number.

At first, she was too shy to make contact on her own behalf. She messaged Abu Salah and said she knew a Muslim sister who was interested in marriage. Could he please share some more information that she could pass on? Abu Salah seemed genuine, and obliged. He sent pictures of a man called Jafer, who had traveled to Syria to join a group that was working to build a new Islamic society, an Islamic state. Jafer was born and raised in Germany, but of Turkish origin, a man who had recently converted to Sunni Islam. His face was open like a palm, with thick eyebrows and an aquiline nose. Lina and Jafer corresponded and then eventually spoke on the phone.

Over several weeks, they talked about life and marriage, their expectations and temperaments. Jafer seemed kind and, most important, devout—nothing like her first husband, who was lazy and unreligious, but even more than that, immoral and cruel. Lina wanted a brand-new life and a new husband, all under the shadow of God's blessing.

Jafer described what life was like in the new Islamic State, how the authorities were trying to take over local municipalities, establish schools, and provide the kind of fair governance people had been missing. Traveling to a war zone to secure a new life did not seem an extreme decision. Lina had grown up in Lebanon in the 1980s during the civil war; conflict and instability were not unfamiliar to her. She was not one of those people who refused to go back until the bombs stopped. Would she be happier in a new life with an upstanding, devoted, faithful husband, in a fractious atmosphere—or alone in a women's shelter in Frankfurt? The choice seemed obvious to her.

EMMA/DUNYA

Spring 2012, Frankfurt, Germany

IN EARLY 2012, WHEN SHE WAS TWENTY-THREE AND FLOATING THROUGH life trying to find herself as a young Muslim woman in Germany, Dunya met Selim.

He was friends with one of her friends' brothers, and they encountered each other one night at a kabob shop in Frankfurt. He was Turkish-born and handsome, with a strong jaw and sweet eyes. She felt something fizz in her stomach when he spoke to her. They talked for a long time under the fluorescent glare of the restaurant; the tomato-red Formica tables might as well have been linen-draped and candlelit. Selim was funny and as readily silly as she was, and they developed an easy banter. Dunya didn't like to reveal details about those early heady days. "In Islam these things remain private between a husband and wife," she said sniffily when asked. (Like many converts or second-generation young Muslims in Europe who had grown up viewing the Islam of elders or parents as lazy, too soft, and "cultural," Dunya often spoke about a singular "real Islam," as though such a thing could exist.) But it was clear she was in love with Selim, whose only flaw, she said, was his habit of waking her up in the night by eating potato chips in bed.

Selim was not especially practicing, but she pressed for them to get an Islamic marriage contract, a *nikah,* before developing their relationship. They couldn't afford their own place, so sometimes Selim stayed over at her flat, and sometimes they lived together at the home of his friend. Several months into their relationship, in the autumn of

2012, according to Dunya, Selim began to grow more religious. He started spending time with a group of Salafi brothers at the mosque; he asked her to start wearing the niqab instead of just the normal headscarf. His piety grew oppressive at times, like when he decided to uphold a puritanical prohibition on birthdays. Dunya found this very sad. It was just one day to celebrate oneself during the year; did it have to be such a problem? But to Selim, birthdays became impermissibly *haram*. She started buying more cake around their respective birthdays, so that she could pretend the cake just happened to be on hand.

Later that year, a few weeks after their *nikah,* Selim arranged a dinner at a restaurant, at which Dunya would meet his mother. It was a gray, drizzling day. People walked to the subways and buses with their heads down. It was so grim that Dunya changed her WhatsApp picture to an image of a bungalow on stilts over turquoise waters. She considered bringing a gift for Selim's mother, but decided it would only be appropriate once she'd been invited to their home. Selim's mother had shoulder-length hair, with ash highlights, a wide, open face, and wore sensible loafers. She was strikingly short, enough that Dunya snuck a text message to one of her girlfriends after they sat down. "Cute. Pokemon."

She seemed like one of those tireless Turkish mothers Dunya had grown up watching at her friends' houses in Frankfurt, a woman who would cook stuffed bell peppers, keep the floors mopped, and serve everyone tea in slim-waisted cups; competent, never hesitating, never letting the sons lift a finger; slightly a martyr and prone to mysterious, attention-seeking ailments as a result. Selim's mother asked questions about Dunya's parents and looked pained to hear that her father lived in Spain and rarely visited. She clearly would have preferred a Turkish daughter-in-law, one who shared her language, who came from an intact clan known to them, who could be relied upon to keep Selim integrated into the family, and who held the promise of wishing to learn to stuff peppers. When the dinner was over, they exchanged the limpest of handshakes, not even a double kiss, and Dunya texted one of her girlfriends, "😬."

Selim's parents had done reasonably well for themselves and appeared content to be living in Germany. Or at least Dunya intuited that his mother was content, and because his mother was the one who ran things in their household, the husband and sons elected not to express any discontent. Selim's father worked as a security guard at a train station. He would sometimes tell his sons that he would rather move back home, to Turkey. Dunya, like any woman who feels judged and rejected by her mother-in-law, began to project onto Selim's parents a family dynamic that merged with her own pique: the mother overruled everyone, determined how everyone would feel about life in Germany, about faith, about everything.

But Selim's mother also had real reasons to be alarmed by her son's behavior, the long robes he wore, the Arabic expressions he was lacing into his conversation, his newfound piety. Once she found some musk, the kind the Salafi perfume sellers sold outside mosques the world over, in his room. When he came home that evening, his mother waved the vial in his face, screaming, "What's this? Why are you trying to smell like a fucking Arab?"

Because Dunya had entered Selim's life around the same time that his behavior began to shift, his mother was convinced she was radicalizing her son. Exactly who was encouraging whom remains contested. Dunya maintains that Selim was the one growing more devout, that he asked her to start covering more of herself. Others tell a different story.

The first time she was invited to visit his family home, she arrived wearing the niqab. His mother looked at her in stupefied horror. "What do you know of Islam? Maybe you misunderstand. Why do you believe this is wanted of you?" Dunya did not see much point in arguing. Selim's mother was a typical Kemalist, the type of Turk who worshipped Mustafa Kemal Atatürk, the twentieth-century modernizer who ended the Ottoman caliphate and founded the secular Turkish state. Selim's mother considered herself a Muslim, as well as a devoted Turkish nationalist and a strong believer in the secular nation-state. (This, to Dunya's mind, was disbelief and compromise. Real Muslims didn't believe in the nation-state, and they certainly didn't venerate secular politicians above the faith.) And yet, unfairly, Dunya felt that Selim's mother discounted everything she said on the grounds that she hadn't been born a Muslim and wasn't Turkish. Selim's mother claimed a cultural authority over Islamic knowledge, even though she didn't cover her hair and never prayed. In that moment, Dunya's mother-in-law seemed to her like Atatürk and Hitler rolled into one authoritarian, thimble-sized figure.

After this first visit where Dunya wore the niqab, Selim's mother barred her from the house. She told her son that she'd heard worrisome things about Dunya from others, that she was ill-behaved, not a decent girl. When he refused to break up with her, she asked him to leave the house.

This enraged Dunya. She felt she was destined to struggle with mothers; mothers always found in her something to oppose rather than nurture. She imagined his mother poisoning Selim against her, whispering malicious gossip in his ear. It was with this open domestic warfare in the backdrop that the couple started talking about traveling to Syria. "When your mother is a dragon, it's not hard to leave," Dunya said.

The State Emerges

In January 2014, President Obama calls ISIS the "JV team" of the jihadist sphere. The casual remark is meant to underscore how al-Qaeda, as a transnational movement, remains a greater security threat to the United States than ISIS.

In June, in the space of a week, ISIS fighters capture Mosul, the second-largest city in Iraq, along with Tikrit and Tal Afar. Mosul, population two million, falls in four days. ISIS fighters encircle Baghdad, coming within twenty-five miles of the city and close to the airport. "This is not a terrorism problem anymore," says a think-tank expert in Washington. "This is an army on the move in Iraq and Syria, and they are taking terrain."

At the very end of June, on the first day of Ramadan, Abu Bakr al-Baghdadi makes his first public appearance to give Friday prayers at the historic Grand Mosque in Mosul. He declares the establishment of an Islamic caliphate and invokes the ancient distinction between the Land of Islam and everywhere outside its borders: the Land of Disbelief.

"Rush O Muslims to your state. Yes, it is your state. Rush, because Syria is not for the Syrians, and Iraq is not for the Iraqis. The earth is Allah's," he says. "Soon, by Allah's permission, a day will come when the Muslim will walk everywhere as a master, having honor, being revered, with his head raised high and his dignity preserved."

"The picture is no longer scary. It has become close to a nightmare scenario," says a spokesman for the Kurdistan regional government, in northern Iraq.

U.S. military commanders start talking about ground troops. By August, it takes a combination of U.S. warplanes, Kurdish forces, and Shia militias backed by Iran to repel a major ISIS advance into northern Iraq. Iran dispatches military advisers and logisticians to support both Iraqi and Kurdish forces; both Washington and Tehran downplay that their militaries are acting in unexpected alignment.

EMMA/DUNYA

Summer 2014, Frankfurt, Germany

"This message is to the free women of Mesopotamia in particular, and the women of the 'Muslim Ummah' in general: Where are you from this holy jihad? What have you contributed to this Ummah? Do you not fear God? Do you raise your children to be slaughtered by tyrants? Have you accepted submissiveness and shunned jihad?"

—ABU MUSAB AL-ZARQAWI, from "Religion Shall Not Lack While I Am Alive," 2005

A MERE EIGHT DAYS PASSED BETWEEN THE DAY SELIM CAME HOME AND started talking about emigrating to Syria, and the day they boarded a flight to Istanbul. Selim had spent the evening at the house of a friend, one of the Salafi brothers; they had watched Al Jazeera the whole night, absorbing images of Syrian children and women being pulled from rubble. When he got home, he sat on the floor, as though the gravity of it all required him to be closer to the ground, and told Dunya that Bashar al-Assad's regime was killing Muslims and that he needed to help. He showed her the images on the screen of his mobile. There was a woman cradling a toddler with half its face blown off.

"Stop it," she said, pushing his hand away. But he wouldn't stop. His argumentation those days was a constant flow of disjointed, crude persuasion; how they could not stand idle while fellow Muslims were being hurt in this way; how once an Islamic caliphate had been established, it was *everyone's* religious duty, *her* religious duty, to leave the

Land of Disbelief and migrate there. Dunya tried to talk him out of this vision. "Is there no other way to help?" she asked. No, he said. Going to Syria was the only way.

These views were central to a radical political and eschatological worldview that Dunya at times seemed to uphold, and at other times to reject. Like many converts, she had watched the YouTube sermons of the globally popular Yemeni American imam Anwar al-Awlaki. He offered rich, thoughtful guidance on everything from daily health practices, to Ramadan fasting, to the qualities and habits of sound marriages. Awlaki was good to listen to, no matter if you were new to Islam or had years of practice and study. His voice was appealing, he was witty and articulate, and he refracted stories about early Islam and the lives of the Prophets into discussions that seemed contemporary and relevant.

In the early 2000s, Awlaki was the imam at a large mosque in Falls Church, Virginia, and widely known as a moderate willing to engage with the wider community, even the government—he attended a lunch event at the Pentagon and preached on Capitol Hill. In the wake of 9/11, he declared, "There is no way that the people who did this could be Muslim, and if they claim to be Muslim, then they have perverted the religion."

In the year that followed, the FBI conducted raids across the area of northern Virginia that fell within Awlaki's congregation. Awlaki was sharply critical of how the agents had behaved, holding guns to the heads of women and children and handcuffing them for long periods. But he leveled his criticism as a civil rights concern and evoked the historical struggle of African Americans to organize and defend their communities. When he criticized U.S. foreign policy in the Middle East, the emerging War on Terror, and the FBI's heavy-handed tactics, he stayed carefully within a framework of legal rights and an ethic of nonviolence, an ethic he applied as stringently to states as to armed groups. In October 2001 he maintained, "The fact that the U.S. has administered the death and homicide of over one million civilians in Iraq, the fact that the U.S. is supporting the deaths and killing of thousands of Palestinians, does not justify the killing of one U.S. civilian in New York City or Washington, D.C. And the deaths of six thousand civilians in New York and Washington, D.C., does not justify the death of one civilian in Afghanistan."

Some terrorism experts cite such views—which morally equate deliberate, state-inflicted military violence against civilians with attacks like 9/11—as evidence that Awlaki was an extremist from the outset. But, if anything, such views were not uncommon among many Muslims and even non-Muslim Middle Easterners. What happened to Anwar al-Awlaki next is a dark story, largely unknown to his thousands of online admirers from across the world.

As the FBI picked up intelligence that at least two of the 9/11 hijackers had prayed at Awlaki's mosque, they began monitoring him closely. In the course of their surveillance, they picked up evidence of alleged meetings between Awlaki and prostitutes, the disclosure of which would have destroyed his reputation and ruined his life as a respected imam. Awlaki later told associates he had been set up, that the FBI had fabricated evidence against him.

In March 2002, following a series of seemingly indiscriminate and aggressive FBI raids on the homes of Muslims in northern Virginia, Awlaki delivered an angry, blunt sermon, warning that American Muslims were becoming second-class citizens under the law: "So this is not now a war on terrorism. We need to all be clear about this. This is a war against Muslims. It is a war against Muslims and Islam. Not only is it happening worldwide, but it is happening right here in America, that is claiming to be fighting this war for the sake of freedom while it's infringing on the freedom of its own citizens, just because they're Muslim."

In the spring of 2002, Awlaki left America for London and never returned. Those who portray him as a silver-tongued extremist argue that he left the United States because he feared the FBI would go public with its alleged prostitute dossier. Others believe that politics reshaped him and propelled him out—that he found the post-9/11 realities in the United States, the expanding legal harassment of Muslims, and the invasion of Afghanistan irreconcilable with his moderate theology. He spent two years in London, his views growing more strident, and then traveled on to his native Yemen. In 2006, local Yemeni authorities arrested Awlaki and, according to a *New York Times* journalist, kept him detained at the behest of the U.S. government. During the year and a half that he was in prison in Yemen, Awlaki was tortured.

It was after he left prison that his views fundamentally began to shift. His empathy for American civilians waned. Upon his release, he said that FBI agents were present and involved during his interrogations, that they were aware of the abuse. He dropped his warnings against targeting civilians and started calling for violence against the United States within the context of a global jihad. He articulated his new position in a 2010 lecture called "A Call to Jihad," against the backdrop of what he described as a mounting and expanding campaign of American violence across Muslim lands.

> What we see from America is the invasion of countries; we see Abu Ghraib, Bagram, and Guantanamo Bay; we see cruise missiles and cluster bombs; and we have just seen in Yemen the death of the twenty-three children and seventeen women. We cannot stand idly in the face of such aggression, and we will fight back and incite others to do the same. I for one was born in the U.S. I lived in the U.S. for twenty-one years. America was my home. I was a preacher of Islam involved in nonviolent Islamic activism. However, with the American invasion of Iraq and continued U.S. aggression against Muslims, I could not reconcile between living in the U.S. and being a Muslim. And I eventually came to the conclusion that jihad against America is binding upon myself just as it is binding on every other able Muslim.

In the words of one scholar, Awlaki's "radicalization is consistent with the historical pattern of activists adopting a belief in terrorism when political action fails to bring about change." It also fit the pattern of Islamist or Muslim activists emerging from prison, where they endured intensive torture, with a radically altered position on the use of violence against civilians.

This is not to say that torture mechanically reshapes all individuals to make them capable of greater cruelty. But scholars of psychopathology, like the great Simon Baron-Cohen, have found strong links that show enduring trauma can cause a person to lose empathy. To lose empathy is to view other human beings as objects, which is necessary to the infliction of cruelty and violence upon them. Baron-Cohen's research shows that torturing a person, rendering him an object, a vessel out of which intelligence can be extracted, radically dulls that person's ability to focus on another person's interests at the same time as his own.

The thousands of Muslims who had watched him online did not know what befell Sheikh Anwar in a Yemeni prison cell. They did not know that he was detained on the demand of the United States, and they did not see what he endured. All they saw was that this adored, admired imam had shifted his views from religious tolerance and co-existence, to an ambivalence around violence deployed in self-defense, to armed militancy targeting American civilians. He pulled many young people along because he already had them on board. After his time in prison, Awlaki went on to inspire so many high-profile terror attacks that President Obama felt justified in authorizing his killing by drone strike, the first assassination of a U.S. citizen without trial since the Civil War. Even now, "the Awlaki problem" is shorthand for the challenge presented by his legacy as a thinker, a militant, and a martyr. Tech companies eventually worked with governments to scrub his presence from the internet, but his lingering appeal to a new generation of Muslims raised a troubling question no one really wished to grapple with: was Anwar al-Awlaki the source of militancy, or were his voice and biography, so complex and deeply human, just an articulation of its causes?

Dunya understood the compelling logic of Sheikh Anwar. It was hard not to see his point of view, which he had arrived at—he said it himself—reluctantly. She was also capable of understanding how it could simultaneously be true that Anwar al-Awlaki was right about everything and yet, that it was a terrible decision to go to Syria and join the Islamic State.

Dunya could reconcile these seemingly conflicting positions, but Selim could not. She did not so much believe that Selim had been brainwashed, but that he was one of those people who has to believe in only one truth. At the same time, he was her husband, she adored him, and she did not for one second think that they could ever be apart. And there were other ways in which she sold the idea to herself: as the adventure of a dutiful wife acceding to her husband's wishes; a journey to a place she had never been—Syria, so near Beirut, the stomping ground of the Arabic pop stars she admired; a gun-slinging foray to fight against a dictator who was undeniably murdering his own people.

She told her family they were going to live for a while in Turkey. She packed quickly, throwing things into a single suitcase: clothes, toiletries, makeup, the essential things she couldn't go anywhere without, like extra-long-lash mascara and a mild facial soap. She bought extra batteries and some flashlights before they flew to Istanbul. She had no idea if they would be useful, but it seemed like they might be.

SABIRA

October 2013, Walthamstow, Northeast London

THE WHOLE FAMILY HAD GATHERED AT THEIR GRANDMOTHER'S HOUSE for lunch on Saturdays since forever, since childhood. The place filled with the odors of cooking and the shouts of children playing and the sorts of discussions sisters and mothers had in kitchens: ailments, negligent husbands, broodings about the acquisitions and goings-on of more distant branches of the family.

Sabira had known for two weeks now that her brother Soheil was planning to go to Syria, and the knowledge had made her panicked and watchful. She had found out from her mother, in whom Soheil had confided. Her poor mum hadn't known what to do. She felt a glimmer of pride that her son *wanted* to go, but she would have preferred to leave it at that: a noble impulse that he then got talked out of by his father, ideally, though his father wasn't around. In the end she told her daughter Sabira, in the bathroom one night as they were brushing their teeth, because she was upset and had to tell someone.

When you were a single mother and had ceded authority to your too-young son, simply because he was a man-to-be, it was almost impossible to claim it back. Ever since her husband had left, she had allowed Soheil to take care of so many household things. His resulting sense of dominance, of knowing well enough for himself, meant that his mum couldn't change his mind anymore. But what did Soheil, barely eighteen, actually know of life?

To his younger sister Sabira, he tried to play the role of their absent father, which was a confused role in the best of circumstances:

the conservative Pakistani British father encouraging his daughter to go out into society, while also overseeing her morals and proper behavior (*Go to university! Study hard! Don't talk to boys!*). Grown men tended to navigate this role poorly, let alone a teenage boy. Soheil did his best to become the man of the house. He took the meter readings for the gas bills, he built the ready-to-assemble furniture, he took his mother to the doctor. He told Sabira to wear the niqab. He studied hard and put his total faith in Allah.

Sabira was fifteen, accustomed to doing as he said in exchange for her older brother's friendship and loyal protection. When he decided he was going to Syria, explaining that it was his religious duty as a Muslim, that it would be an honor to dedicate his life to the defense of innocents being killed, she raised her objections with him only once.

"Are you sure?" she'd asked. "How will we see you again?"

He smiled at her fondly, as if to say *I love you.* But aloud he said, "I'm never coming back."

He was implacable. Like the story was already written in his head.

Sabira didn't make any dire pronouncements or try to change his mind. Instead she started rubbing lotion onto her hands obsessively, a mild alternative to nail-biting. There was no obvious reason to think that this Saturday, the day for cooking and family and gathering, was different from any other. Soheil hadn't done any extra laundry; she hadn't caught him packing a bag. But they were close enough that she could read his moods. That Saturday, he looked at everything a split second too long. She took extra pictures of him during and after the family lunch, as they played hide-and-seek with the cousins. When he finally said to her, "I'm going to go now," it felt like some kind of joke, an unreal scene that they would laugh at later. He hugged her and then hugged their mum, glanced around the living room that had been the backdrop to their whole childhood, and turned to walk out the door.

It was early winter, the time of year when it was already dark at four-thirty. The street lamps made the PVC window frames glow starkly white against the brick houses, and the wind blew tufts of brown leaves around the pavement. Sabira pulled a sweater on and sat on the steps, watching her brother leave. She kept her eyes open, refusing to blink, until he was all the way down the street, a small dark figure in the distance, turning the corner.

IT HAD ALL STARTED WITH a leaflet. Soheil Rasheed (age seventeen, a normal Pakistani kid from North London, fond of trampolining, cycling, boxing, Shaolin kung fu, going to the gym, action movies, and smoking shisha with his little sister Sabira; by multiple accounts one of the nicest young men in the neighborhood; bright and openhearted, polite to elders, perennially attractive to girls) was one day walking down the high street of his neighborhood when he noticed some brothers running a *dawah* preaching stall and stopped to pick up a leaflet. His older cousin Nadim, who was with him, picked one up too.

For Soheil it was the end of Year 11, a turning point at the end of secondary school. He looked forward to starting professional training, in mechanical engineering. In recent years, London had poured money into its urban schools, raising standards and results dramatically. This sapped funding for schools across the rest of Britain, but turned many secondary schools in working-class districts of London into high-achieving, competitive institutions. Though their neighborhood was soaked in drugs and stabbings, and the obvious path out of poverty for most young people seemed to involve drug dealing or petty fraud, Soheil and Sabira received the kind of education that gave them skills and aspirations. They had a sharp sense of the opportunities and rights they were entitled to as British citizens, as citizens of Europe and the world; certainly a sharper sense than their parents had ever had. Soheil graduated with a high-level vocational diploma that positioned him to go on to a promising apprenticeship or university, if he wished it. Both branches of the family ran successful businesses that he might have joined. "We weren't from some family of no hope," Sabira said. "We had a lot to give back."

The brothers who offered Soheil the leaflet were from a local cell of al-Muhajiroun, a small extremist group of disruptive loudmouths. They invited him to attend a talk that evening, they took his mobile number, and from that day on, they encircled him. They had events going several nights a week: talks, brothers' soccer, *dawah* stalls, demonstrations, meetings. Soheil was suddenly with these men all the time. When he was at home, he listened to talks on the internet and watched videos of Syria, which made him fiery and intense. He often asked Sabira to sit and watch as well, which bothered her at first, but Soheil was Sabira's older brother, and she wasn't about to tell him what to do. And, actually, the videos made her feel the same way. It was impossible to watch them and not feel any response—not to feel outraged, and moved to action. When Soheil suggested she start attending the al-Muhajiroun sisters' circles, she agreed.

Their neighborhood of Walthamstow had the highest density of Muslim residents of any area of Britain. The borough was home to between sixty-five thousand and seventy-five thousand Muslims and about fifteen mosques. The main thoroughfares of Walthamstow were lined with halal restaurants, barbershops with names like Lahore or Kashmir Hairdressers, travel agents specializing in the hajj pilgrimage tours, and dessert cafés, a social mainstay of young Muslims. There was an Islamic bookshop that carried stern-minded, English-language books, many printed in Saudi Arabia. The largest local mosque, on Lea Bridge Road, was where most of the city council's decisions were actually made. The councillors handed down political influence among families, their networks of patronage transferred seamlessly from rural Pakistani villages to this dense London neighborhood.

This mosque shared a building with a community center and gym run by a community youth organization called the Active Change Foundation. For many years, the foundation had received government funding to counter the appeal of radicalism in the area; it offered young people a place to hang out, with gaming consoles and pool tables, but like many such groups, it also worked closely with the police and security services. The group's primary aim, many local residents came to believe, was surveilling the community. The foundation's youth workers and the al-Muhajiroun guys knew and mutually despised each other. They argued with one another after local talks and religious events, they challenged each other's religious learning (or even their basic right to self-identify as Muslims), and they sometimes battled over the lives and souls of young men from the neighborhood.

Soheil was one such battle. Muhajiroun followers were actively working to recruit him, though if you were to ask them, they didn't view their efforts as recruitment per se. They sincerely believed in their political cause and were just trying to educate him, to awaken him as to how extreme the War on Terror had become in its targeting of Muslims.

In the spring of 2013, Soheil watched ISIS propaganda videos that told him Muslims could not live in peace in the West, in the Land of Disbelief; that they were fundamentally unwelcome, that they should hasten to join the group as it strove to create a caliphate where Muslims could live under Islamic laws, as they were meant to. This tactic was acknowledged openly by groups like al-Muhajiroun and ISIS. They spoke of targeting the "gray zone," the space in which Muslims coexisted peacefully in Western societies. The erosion of the gray zone was the primary way ISIS sought to draw recruits to Syria from the West. With time, it would also become a tactic of conservative British politicians seeking to win votes and popularity by inflaming public sentiment against Muslims.

In this effort, both ISIS and right-wing politicians had a devoted partner—much of the British media was equally eager to show that Muslims were an awkward fit in Europe, that they were a threat to the existing social order and could only hope to assimilate by renouncing their religion altogether. Newspapers published a steady stream of coverage that encouraged people to think that the Muslims they lived among were a fifth column, lurking extremists with terrorist sympathies plotting to impose "Sharia law" and sneak halal food into the supermarkets. Studies showed that the message got across: 31 percent of young people in the UK believed that Muslims were taking over the country; 56 percent believed that Islam, as a religion, posed a threat to Western liberal democracy.

About a ten-minute walk down the high street stood another gym, with separate men's and women's workout spaces, run by two brothers who gained notoriety when they, along with their families, were barred from boarding a flight to Los Angeles for a Disneyland holiday. The *Daily Mail,* one of Britain's most popular tabloids, ran a photo of the family home in Walthamstow with a column that read, "Just because

Britain's border security is a Mickey Mouse operation, you can't blame America for not letting this lot travel to Disneyland—I wouldn't either." The *Mail* alleged that the family were extremists, based on a link to a Facebook account that ended up being unrelated to them. The newspaper later apologized and paid the family compensation, but this hardly undid the social harm or discouraged such reckless reporting in the future. It had become commonplace for both tabloids and mainstream newspapers to publish false stories about Muslims with impunity; the coverage sold well and the country's liberal and conservative commentators reliably echoed the message.

Academic research showed and warned that mainstream media coverage of Muslims was fueling hate crimes and creating a climate of extreme hostility. Why did the newspapers carry on with such relish? Some argued that the media's dehumanization of Muslims wasn't just a reflection of the bias of media proprietors, but also vital to foreign and security policy in an increasingly diverse Britain. A leaked report by the Ministry of Defence in 2014 acknowledged that the government would find it more difficult to conduct military interventions in countries where UK citizens or their families originated. It was a rare acknowledgment of how complicated it was becoming for Britain to pursue strategic policies—support for the U.S. War on Terror and Israel's occupation of Palestinian land, the ongoing troop presence in Afghanistan, lucrative arms sales to Saudi Arabia, and complicity in the Saudi war in Yemen that resulted in thousands of civilian deaths— that British Muslims opposed. The media, this argument held, was structurally essential to British foreign policy: the public needed to believe that Islam was the greatest social and security threat to modern Britain. If Muslims were dehumanized, it was easier to repress and silence their political objections to such policies, easier to justify the human toll of the invasions and campaigns waged globally in the name of fighting extremism.

The belief couldn't just exist on an abstract level. It needed to become a part of people's daily lives, persuading them that the Muslims down the street were traveling to Disneyland with nefarious aims. Tabloids routinely found ways to portray Islam as a religion of sexual violence, spotlighting marginal characters from across the world—figures that virtually no British Muslim had ever heard of—and running screaming headlines like "Islamic Scholar 'Says Allah Allows Muslim Men to RAPE Non-Muslim Women to Humiliate Them.'" Or "Egyptian Lawyer Says Raping Women Who Wear Ripped Jeans Is a Man's 'National Duty.'"

The British press ranked last in all of Europe in a 2017 poll by the European Broadcasting Union that measured how truthful citizens perceived their media to be. In domestic polling, the right-wing tabloids regularly came last in rankings of trustworthiness. But people kept on buying the papers nonetheless.

SABIRA REMEMBERED A BRILLIANT BOY she had gone to school with. Faisal was ahead of the class by bounds, the top in every subject, attracting the attention of the teachers, who noticed his exceptional intelligence. But his parents ran a restaurant and they pulled Faisal out of school at age sixteen, to wait tables. He would have been a straight shot through university exams to Oxford or Cambridge, but instead he would spend his life running a restaurant. First-generation Pakistani parents were well attuned to the struggles of making a decent living in a changing, unequal economy that had an oversupply of unskilled labor; they often coped, like Faisal's parents, by prodding their kids as quickly as possible into wage-earning of some kind, rather than enduring longer, costlier stretches of higher education.

This approach was driven by hard work and a real aspiration for prosperity, but often ended up leading Asian Muslim kids down fitful, scheme-pocked paths that secured little real opportunity. A BBC television documentary in 2018 queried why Asian Muslims seemed to fare so poorly compared to Asians of other religious backgrounds, like Punjabi Sikhs or Hindu Gujaratis. Why was it that these other Asian kids performed better at university exams and slid into early home ownership? Was it possible, the BBC presenter even suggested, that Hindus and Sikhs were receptive to drinking beer at the pub, and this openness to social drinking helped them assimilate and access opportunity better? Was it possible, in effect, that what was holding British Muslims back was their Muslimness? These conversations tended to glide over the way racism in the United Kingdom had matured, shifting from crude prejudice against anyone brown as a generic "Paki," to a more targeted discrimination against Muslim people of color.

Walthamstow embodied all these challenges. It was an ordinary, slightly grimy northeast London village-suburb, but it was a microcosm of everything that British authorities faced in dealing with the threat of radicalism. More than one violent plot had been hatched by men who lived in the rows of terraced houses and attended the local mosques, including the 2006 plot to bring down an airliner with liquid explosives.

Walthamstow was the launching ground for al-Muhajiroun, and contained its densest network of cells. The group was led by a man called Anjem Choudary. He had no religious credentials or scholarly standing, but relished saying incendiary things that reliably put him on television or in the newspaper. He craved and thrived on attention. His media prominence grew in seemingly inverse proportion to his standing among British Muslims; the more they viewed him as destructive, self-promoting, and divisive, the more frequently he appeared on television. Even while mainstream and respected Muslim figures in Britain—journalists, lawmakers, academics, and activists— openly rejected Choudary, even while mosques across the country banned him from their premises, his notoriety never diminished.

In a way, Choudary was the ideal straw man for the newspapers. With his jaunty smile and crass bigotry, he instantly discredited the notion that Muslim radicalism had any rational political context. He wanted to slap "Sharia Zone" stickers around East London; he organized morality street patrols that, in fact, no one attended but his own small band of followers. All he lacked was an evil cackle. In 2010, a journalist wrote memorably in *The Spectator* that "Anjem Choudary . . . is one of those thick-as-mince gobby little chancers who could only possibly come from Britain." This was patently true, and yet—and yet—he was wanted, needed by the media: the loser Tartuffe figure from Walthamstow, who decried Britain as the corrupt Land of Disbelief, but sponged off its benefits system to support his large family.

Walthamstow had a high volume of Muslims, and many sympathized with the core political views that animated groups like al-Muhajiroun. The majority of those sympathizers certainly did not condone violence against civilians. But certain underlying truths were easy to empathize with: the belief that the West, through its War on Terror, was waging neo-imperial wars in majority Muslim lands; that with each year the war's geographic scope and brutality, its secret torture sites and drone strikes and targeting of civilians, grew more extreme; that through support for Israel and Arab tyrants, it enabled Muslim underdevelopment and suffering on a vast scale.

There was a gap between agreeing with these truths intellectually and acting on them in a violent fashion. It was a slim, fateful gap that the majority felt condemned to and capable of living within. But for some, the gap felt so slight that it was easy to bridge. It was easy to lure an impressionable young person to the other side. ISIS called that gap the gray zone of complicity and sought to crush it. The tabloids called it "creeping Sharia"; a prominent neocon thinker called it "the strange death of Europe." Walter Benjamin called it the "state of emergency" that had become, for the oppressed, "not the exception but the rule." British Muslims just called it life.

This was one of the reasons why it was especially hard for immigrant Muslim parents to spot deviance in their children's behavior. Watching their kids behave more piously made many happy; it meant, actually, they could relax a little bit; there was less danger of their children losing their values and straying from the faith. They weren't culturally primed to see more conservative behavior as worrisome.

And as for the political views about the overarching tensions between Muslims and Western state violence, they were widely held. And because so many thousands of the community's young men carried those *very same* attitudes, held the *very same* identities, but had some internal compass keeping them away from violence, it was extraordinarily hard for a parent to notice when conventional views suddenly became subversive. It was extraordinarily hard to know when a child's internal compass was no longer functioning.

But Walthamstow arguably had bigger problems than extremism. The neighborhood was awash with drugs and knife crime. Soheil, like most boys, had learned to avoid certain barbershops that were hubs for drug dealing, where the barbers' eyes were glazed over. Dealing drugs was a fast way to rise in the standings of the neighborhood, and the Muslim kids who took this route assuaged their guilty consciences by pulling up to the mosque in their Porsches and passing the imam wads of cash for charity.

The respectable path to a decent life was hard, because even in the 2010s, the old prejudices and systematic discrimination remained alive. A 2017 BBC survey found that an applicant called "Adam" was offered three times as many job interviews as an applicant with an identical CV and skill set called "Mohammed." Half of Muslim households in London lived in poverty. Muslim students didn't get into good enough universities, and didn't emerge from good universities with strong degrees.

Indeed, when it came to British Muslims, the challenges were arguably more socioeconomic than religious; the vast majority of Muslim immigrants to Britain from Pakistan, India, and Bangladesh arrived from villages, bringing the norms of rural farming life with them. Had they stayed in Pakistan and moved to cities, being exposed to education and work in a language they already spoke, the women in these families might have arguably secured greater independence and decision making than they did in Britain. Two generations after arrival, British Muslim women often remained less educated and less likely to work than women from British Indian families of Hindu or Sikh background, who had emigrated from urban centers and were already better educated.

This social disparity was also evident in the academic achievement of second-generation Pakistani and Bangladeshi kids, who tended to perform poorly compared to second-generation Indian kids from Hindu families. In modern Britain, what came to be seen as a problem of "oppressive Muslim culture" leading to lower attainment was more a reflection of socioeconomic migration patterns: a need for more education development, and opportunity rather than a problem of faith.

• • •

THE POLICE CAME ON MONDAY night, two days after Soheil had left. Sabira was in her bedroom when she heard the banging at the door. In the kitchen, her mother was sitting at the table, an untouched cup of tea beside her. There were two officers, a man with glasses and a fat upper lip, and a woman who looked around their living room and announced that they would need to search the house.

But it was too late by then anyway. Soheil had already texted his mum to say he was in Turkey and about to cross the border into Syria. The hardest part, at first, was figuring out what to say to the rest of the family when they asked where he was. Early on, Sabira made excuses for him. "Soheil's busy." "Soheil's at the gym." "Soheil's at work." Eventually, they had to tell the truth.

Winter came as it always did, a sudden early descending of darkness that compressed the day's prayers into a short succession. Some mornings Sabira woke up for the dawn prayer and crept past her mother's bedroom, deliberating whether to wake her or to let her sleep. Her mother alternated between proud stoicism and blank-eyed despondency. She spent whole days wrapped in a blanket, preparing bland meals that tasted of resignation. There was pride to be felt, certainly, for a son who had chosen to donate his life to God in the protection of others; but there would have been pride as well in a son who stayed by his mother's side, working to grow prosperous and start a family, creating a shade under which she could have sheltered. Their mother felt selfish when she had such thoughts. Perhaps that was not the path that God had set out for him. Who was she, to question His wisdom?

It was shocking, his sudden absence, and distressing, because he would never come back. But it was the early days of the Syrian civil war, back when it was a clearer conflict with good and bad sides. Sabira felt no shame about her brother's decision. More than anything, she felt abandoned, now for the second time. Their father had left when she was eight, when the fighting at home with their mother had gotten too intense and he said vaguely that there were "important things" he had to do elsewhere. He was a gentle man who worked as a postal clerk, though he had ambitions of doing something else. Once he left, her mother began cursing him, and Sabira realized the only real adult in the house was gone. Soheil had filled their absent father's role unconsciously, always caring, always solicitous.

She continued attending the Muhajiroun women's circles, because they felt like a thread tying her to Soheil, but she felt increasingly detached from their talk. The women sat in a circle, speaking in a rough, black-and-white way about the West and its conflicts. Sabira filtered out the politics. She was fifteen, and those politics had stolen her brother. She wanted only to be a good Muslim, to have as much trust in Allah and his plan, as much *tawakul*, as Soheil had. Most of all, she aspired to his level of spiritual clarity. But the version of Islam the ladies at Muhajiroun were dispensing at the meetings felt like a death sentence.

Sabira and her cousin spoke about it one evening as they were walking through Bethnal Green, where they had gone to have dessert and look through the abayas at a local boutique. There was a new collection out, with high-waisted robes in regency colors like dusty rose pink and powder blue. There was so much beauty and purpose in the world, she felt, so much room to serve Allah and also gain some earthly happiness. The extreme views of the women's circle allowed for none of these possibilities. "What are they trying to do, get blood out of a stone? If you want to do everything as they say, it strips you of everything, the possibility of studying or working. Talking to men is 'free mixing.' What is there left to do but just stay at home?"

She and Soheil were in touch a lot. They chatted on Telegram and he eventually managed to get back onto Facebook. He sent her pictures of himself playing in the snow and swimming in the Euphrates. She peered at the images for long minutes, noticing how much thinner he seemed, his cheeks gaunt. Sometimes he asked in advance if the family could be together, and they would Skype him from the living room at their grandmother's. It was always just a few short minutes, but Sabira was happy to see his face, to hear his voice. She didn't know what to say, so he did most of the talking. "Sabira, you have to come," he said. "You can stay with us, and we can get Mum, the whole family to come. Try and save up some money, get yourself to Turkey."

"It's never gonna happen," she said. She explained she had just applied for a job, was waiting to start work. He tilted his head and smiled at her. "You'll be happy here, you'll see."

Not long into the new year, Sabira's cousin Nadim left for Syria. Soon it seemed everyone knew someone who had gone. A well-off local businessman's daughter. The bookseller's son. Joining the caliphate was like an infectious fever dream, spreading among the neighborhood's youth.

Edging Toward Baghdad

ISIS lays siege to the northern Iraqi town of Sinjar, home to the Yazidi religious minority and strategically located near the crossroads of Syria, Iraq, and Turkey. The Yazidi heartland has been caught up in regional and national rivalries since the 2003 overthrow of Saddam Hussein, and the minority group suffers discrimination under successive rulers.

As ever, ISIS proves to be the most extreme. The fighters launch a genocidal campaign of massacres and kidnappings, taking Yazidi women and girls as sex slaves. Thousands of Yazidi families are stranded on Mount Sinjar; the United States, together with Kurdish forces it now relies on as ground troops, organizes rescue corridors.

In an important victory that could shift the militants' power on the battlefield, fighters capture the Mosul Dam, which controls the flow of water to the city and to millions of Iraqis living downstream along the Tigris River.

They come within fifteen miles of Erbil, one of the two capitals of Iraqi Kurdistan, and again advance toward Baghdad. It is only a flurry of U.S. air strikes, backed by Kurdish forces and Iran-led militias, that prevents Erbil from falling. It becomes apparent that the only thing holding ISIS back is U.S. military might from the skies.

PART II:
Gone Girls

The girls took into their own hands decisions better left to God. They became too powerful to live among us, too self-concerned, too visionary, too blind.

—Jeffrey Eugenides, *The Virgin Suicides*

They're calling me a terrorist
Like they don't know who the terror is
When they put it on me, I tell them this
I'm all about peace and love. . . .

—Lowkey (the British rapper Kareem Dennis), "Terrorist"

SHARMEENA, KADIZA, AMIRA, AND SHAMIMA

December 2014, East London

IT WAS A TRUTH UNIVERSALLY ACKNOWLEDGED THAT ALL YOUNG WOMEN traveling from Britain to the Islamic State needed to go shopping first, and in that strange winter when girls started to go missing, Westfield Stratford, a sprawling mall in East London, emerged as a favorite final destination before the journey.

It was almost dark as the four teenage girls got off the Jubilee line. They had come straight from school, Bethnal Green Academy, where they excelled in their studies and were admired by teachers and fellow students alike as examples of fine young women: intelligent and well-spoken, joyful and vivacious. They were all fifteen or sixteen and best friends, passionately close as only adolescent girls can be, and so protective of their group friendship that they often tweeted warnings about the danger of keeping secrets. It was early December and the mall was draped in glowing stars and lacy angels, teeming with women carrying bags of Christmas shopping. The four girls walked past the trendy steak place with the halal menu they would now never try, past the champagne bar where the bag-laden women took refuge, past an advertisement for the film *American Sniper* ("The Most Lethal Sniper in U.S. Military History").

Sharmeena needed a new mobile phone and some winter clothes, because it was already snowing in Syria, the clothes she'd ordered online from Forever 21 had not arrived, and she was leaving the next day. Button-nosed, with a soft, round face and steely eyes, Sharmeena was the fast-talking, opinionated personality in their group. Her friends watched her face carefully for reactions, the flicking lights behind her eyes that meant she was deliberating, the few moments it would take for her small mouth to open and tell them they were being either ridiculous or perceptive. Everything that came next, everything that followed, turned on her, for Sharmeena was the first among them to walk through real darkness.

A year prior, Sharmeena's beloved mother had been diagnosed with lung cancer, and died after six months of illness. Sharmeena was stunned it could happen that quickly, how a mother, still a young woman in her thirties, who seemed radiant and perfectly sound, could speed-decay from the inside. She became skeletal and wheezy in a few short months, at the end barely able to speak, coughing up her insides through a tube that her daughter held to her mouth. Sharmeena had grown up with her mother, grandmother, and maternal uncle in a small council flat in Bethnal Green, a neighborhood in East London. The plan was always for her father, who was back in Bangladesh, to join them once he saved enough money, but in 2012 the UK government imposed a new income threshold for spouses coming to Britain that was beyond what her mother made, and so her father lingered in Bangladesh. Sharmeena knew him only as a faint, questioning voice on the phone: *How is school? Are you being good?* When he eventually made it to London, she was already a teenager. He was convincingly her father: her face was precisely mapped on his. But she scarcely knew him.

After her mother died, her father secured a council flat in Shoreditch, but he worked long evening shifts as a waiter, returning home well past midnight. Often Sharmeena stayed at her grandmother's instead. When her mother was alive, it hadn't mattered so much that they lived, like so many immigrant families, not in a nuclear unit but with extended family. But now that her mother was gone, Sharmeena felt orphaned, as though she had no proper place anywhere. She started spending time nearly every day at the mosque, the one in East London in the backstreets of Whitechapel, a short walk from home. It had a separate building for women, with a spacious, softly lit, warm prayer area on the second floor. Stepping inside instantly soothed her. She often didn't realize her body was clenched and that she was holding her breath until she knelt down and put her forehead to the inviting turquoise carpet. She felt such release that she stayed in that position for long moments.

Sometimes, after evening prayer, Sharmeena would linger at the mosque and read a book, delaying the return to the home where her mother's absence filled all the space. Other women from the neighborhood did the same. There weren't that many places for young Muslim girls from conservative families to go to in East London that were socially acceptable to their parents. To meet your girlfriends regularly at a dessert café was excessive, bound to elicit a "Weren't you just there yesterday?" and the suspicion that your true motivation was boys, not waffles. The mosque was an immaculate, incontestable destination.

Walking past one of the cobblestoned roads that led down to the back entrance of the mosque, Sharmeena passed an apartment building, one of the high-ceilinged factory conversions that made this former garment district so attractive to young professionals. She looked up to see if the three Bangladeshi sisters were at their perch. Life at home was harder for young Muslim girls born into the conservative Asian families of the East End; mothers and families cosseted boys, spared them chores, let them roam outside freely. But girls, they were expected to come home straight after school, stay pure, stay demure. Sharmeena didn't know their names, but the Bangladeshi girls were always leaning out the window watching passersby, waving at those they knew, their heads in public space, their bodies in private. Split in two. Not having waffles with boys.

Earlier that summer, when her father had suggested that they go on the pilgrimage to Mecca, Sharmeena was eager. The pilgrimage to the holiest site in Islam, the city in modern-day Saudi Arabia where the Prophet Muhammad was born and received his first Quranic revelation, was one of the five pillars of the faith, a journey required of all Muslims who could afford to make it. In her community in East London, it was commonplace to go; virtually every travel agent on the high street of any neighborhood advertised hajj travel. She started covering her hair ahead of their trip. While they were there, circling the Kaaba, walking the plains where the Prophet Muhammad, peace be upon him, had walked, Sharmeena wept openly. Her father considered this a most natural reaction. She had recently lost her mother and was on a pilgrimage that deeply stirred almost everyone's emotions. Indeed, that was the very purpose of hajj, a spiritual shake-up, a reminder of the temporality of this *dunya* life, a reminder that growing close to Allah and walking His path would hopefully unite us with our loved ones in the *akhirah,* or the afterlife, which, unlike this one, would last forever.

Apart from the security services, no one quite knows who in East London noticed Sharmeena adrift and lonely that autumn of 2014. Two women, it is said, began sidling up to her at the mosque and making conversation. They were solicitous and friendly, eventually interrupting her sad reverie with their sincere, rapt attention. They began texting and calling her regularly, and invited her to women-only discussions, ostensibly about religion, that she soon found to be hot-talking political grievance sessions laced with some Islamic terminology.

Sharmeena liked sitting and listening. Listening to strangers was actually easier than talking to people she knew, who inevitably asked her how she was coping, which forced her to arrange her face into some semblance of okayness she didn't actually feel. The strangers who had befriended her talked about the world in stark, finite terms: Muslims pitted against the *kuffar,* the unbelievers; an epic global struggle of Muslim suffering in places like Palestine and Syria; the urgency of building a real Islamic state.

They asked Sharmeena if she was sincere in her *iman,* her faith, and if so, whether she was willing to act upon it. They told her there was an Islamic state emerging in Syria, where she could practice Islam freely without harassment and live a life infused with deep spiritual meaning. They encouraged her to contact other women who had traveled to Syria from the West.

Much of what Sharmeena saw being circulated online, among the *muhajirat,* the female migrants who had already made the journey, made it clear that—if you were serious in your faith, in your commitment to other Muslims—traveling to the emerging state was not exactly a choice. As Umm Abayda, a prominent *muhajira* Twitter personality, noted: "To all those in the west chilling in their homes.

Know that just like there is a fardh [duty] upon you for salah [prayer], there is one on you for hijra."

Sharmeena's mosque-going was a great relief to her father, who imagined that his anguished teenage daughter was coping and finding solace in Islam. Piety was an expected coping mechanism—to wake up before first light and read the dawn prayer as a means of solace, rather than taking up yoga or going to drug-soaked music festivals, as the white people around them might do. Sharmeena had stopped obsessively scrolling through outfit lookbooks on her phone and saying she wanted to be a fashion designer; another relief, which spared her father from having to say, "No, baba, we need you to be a doctor!" She did appear changed to him, more pensive and withdrawn, but he felt changed too, by the death of the person who had anchored them both. He thought they were experiencing the same thing on the inside.

The only things that struck him as amiss were the extra time she was spending on her phone, and her hectoring new injunctions. There were certain television programs he liked to watch that she had started saying were forbidden. "Baba, smoking is *haram*," she would say, shaking her head at him. He started resolving to quit each time they saw each other, so he could say, "Sharmeena, I've just quit!" and have it be true. Though she used the term *haram*, "forbidden," her concerns for him seemed more worldly than ideological: his health was poor—he had diabetes and high cholesterol, both of which were aggravated by long hours on his feet at the restaurant, running plates in and out of a hot kitchen.

At a time when her own world in East London was constricting, Sharmeena stumbled across, or was pushed into, a whole new world online. By that December 2014, the Syrian civil war had been burning for nearly three years, ever since Syrians first rose up against Bashar al-Assad in 2011, in the heady early days of the Arab Spring. Her new women friends spoke to her regularly about the horrific deaths of Muslims in Syria and the urgency of building a caliphate, as a means of self-defense against the violence and depredations inflicted upon Muslims everywhere. These views were echoed loudly online. She began following the Tumblr blog of a Pakistani British girl from Glasgow, Aqsa Mahmood, who had traveled to Syria earlier in 2014 to join ISIS. Aqsa blogged under the *kunya,* or nickname, Umm Layth. In regular posts, she described why she had left her family in Scotland to join the Islamic State struggle, urging other young women to do the same.

> First of all wallahi wallahi I know my position, I am not a scholar, a daiee or even a student of knowledge—not even close to it. So please do not assume that of me. These diary posts I write are only and only written with the intention of being a way of encouragement and advice for my sisters and brothers who are still stuck behind the walls of Darul Kufr.
>
> So in this post I am not just talking about myself but in general of all the muhajirat here (all my words are my own). The media at first used to claim that the ones running away to join the jihad as being unsuccessful, didn't have a future and from broken down families etc. But that is far from the truth. Most sisters I have come across have been in university studying courses with many promising paths, with big, happy families, and friends and everything in the Dunyah to persuade one to stay behind and enjoy the luxury. If we had stayed behind, we could have been blessed with it all from a relaxed and comfortable life and lots of money.

Much of what Umm Layth wrote held true for Sharmeena as well, except perhaps the big happy family. Bright and academically successful, socially charismatic, with a path to university and then a decent career within reach—all of this was true of her. And so it meant something to Sharmeena, hearing someone else articulate this longing for something more meaningful, something higher, a testament of devotion to Allah that surpassed any of these worldly accomplishments.

Umm Layth was mostly upbeat and determined on Tumblr and Twitter. She made clear that she believed terrorist acts—like the 2009 attack in Fort Hood, in which U.S. Army psychiatrist Nidal Hasan shot at fellow soldiers preparing to deploy to Iraq and Afghanistan—were legitimate acts of armed opposition to American military atrocities. Umm Layth's tone veered between the reductive stridency of a teenager who has just discovered injustice, and the plaintive voice of a vulnerable child far from home. Sometimes she admitted how hard it had been to leave everything behind. In the spring of 2014, she wrote:

> I'm not writing this because it's mother's day or whatever they call it. I am writing this because I miss my mother, and I want this to be a reminder to all of you, to recognize the worth and value of your mother, because once you lose her, nothing will be the same again. While most of you can still see your mother's smile, I cannot anymore. While most of you can still put your head on your mom's shoulder, I cannot anymore. While most of you can still call out to your mother when you feel pain in your body, I cannot anymore. While most of you can still go and have that heart to heart talk with your mother, I cannot anymore.

Sharmeena read that one repeatedly; it was like an arrow straight into her own heart.

She loved Umm Layth's humility and eagerly followed her postings. It was through her blog that Sharmeena learned about Mike Prysner, a U.S. soldier who spoke publicly about the abuses he and his battalion had committed in Iraq. Umm Layth posted clips from a speech where Prysner described dragging women and children by the arms and confiscating their homes for use by the American military, without providing any compensation; he described violent interrogations, putting bags over detainees' heads. He spoke of his shame at the casually racist terms his battalion commanders used when they incinerated civilian convoys. This former American soldier said, "We were told we were fighting terrorists, but the real terrorist was me and the real terrorism is this occupation." It was essentially what the American Yemeni imam Anwar al-Awlaki argued: that state military violence against civilians was terrorism too.

Sharmeena began following other women to whom Umm Layth was connected across various social media platforms, their feeds converging into one loud crescendo of outrage against Muslim deaths: Palestinians killed in Israel, U.S. drone strikes on weddings in Afghanistan, U.S. drone strikes killing civilians in Somalia, the children killed by Assad's barrel bombs, Rohingya in Burma. No matter what part of the world, it was unsafe to be a Muslim. The women favored online ideologues who argued that armed insurgency, or jihad, was the only way to defend Muslims against these onslaughts. They posted quotes from Anwar al-Awlaki. They were religious too—concerned with being good Muslims, avoiding behavior that was impure—but their faith was more emotionally charged with political fury against the West than desire for spiritual awakening.

It was a whole world of youthful, febrile, intellectual contestation, one in which young Western Muslims who had already traveled to Syria shrugged off the media's depiction of their motivations, hoping to reach those who were sympathetic but wavering, like Sharmeena. It was possible, they argued, to have multiple and sophisticated motivations. A woman using the name Bird of Jannah, who was probably the most popular English-speaking feminine face of ISIS, posted a stylish, filtered image. It showed a couple in the desert, a handsome bearded young man and his wife in full face veil, with a pink heart and the caption "The love of Jihad: Till martyrdom do us part." At the same time a person called Umm Irhab, on Twitter, cautioned women against being made to feel like their commitment was somehow driven by sexual frustration or base desire: "I have never personally met a sister [in] sham who came here because of a 'romantic thought abt war or bcos of a man' We all came bcos of Allah."

For many, the anonymous question-asking website ask.fm became a welcome platform to share views directly. Umm Ubaydah, for instance, received this question:

> Anonymous: I just wanted you to know that the vast majority of Americans don't hate Muslims, & I want to apologize to you & all your people for the terrible things we've done, & all the families & husbands we've killed. It's shameful. I'm American, but my best friend is Palestinian. I love her like a sister. Many of us understand you resort to violence because we've done you so wrong & that is the only way you have to fight us. Inshallah—we would embrace you if you sought peace. We are all one people.

But Umm Ubaydah responded on her Tumblr blog:

We don't resort to violence because of the wrong America has done. We are trying to build an Islamic state that lives and abides by the law of Allah.

It seemed like there was a collective drive by followers, relatives, observers, the media, the government, to find one angle of understanding the *muhajirat*. But online, there were countless young *muhajirat* pushing back against this tendency, saying openly, *Our motivations are diverse. Muhajirat* literally translates as female migrants, but could arguably be rendered as female jihadists. Within the ideological worldview that advanced the notion of *hijra* to the Islamic State caliphate, migration was not such an innocent or neutral transfer of location, for those who were old enough to be held accountable. It meant signing up to the caliphate's disruptive everyone-punishing project of extreme violence, as a female citizen-member and adherent.

Umm Layth, the young woman from Glasgow, remained Sharmeena's favorite. She seemed always candid and reliable, calling out rumors and false information wherever she saw them, even from ISIS supporters. She said that those who claimed that female *muhajirat* could go to the front and fight alongside men were spreading propaganda.

Apparently, head military of Sham said women are not allowed [to fight]. They can do lots of other works. Today I spoke to one of Dawlahs main men in sham. He said even if u wanna start a business here COME. Like if u wanna be a dr here or anything just come, u can do it all inshallah. Lolll

But Umm Layth, like so many other European women, was unable to read the campaigns and manifestos of the most prominent female ideologues of the group who explored these matters—women's fighting roles or suicide operations—in Arabic. Whether she and others would have felt differently if they were able to access and understand these texts is impossible to say. Most likely not. But the shallowness of what the European *muhajirat* wrote about themselves, essentially diary entries about youthful Muslim political grievance and identity agony, stood in sharp contrast to the deeply theorized political and ideological writings of ISIS female leaders in Arabic, anchored in the discord of their societies. For the Arabic-illiterate Western women, going on the hybrid aesthetics and lofty resistance narratives of ISIS videos, and their own scattered, naïve longings for community, joining ISIS was not unlike joining a rebellion. For the *muhajirat* from Arab lands, many of whom had long adhered to strands of extreme Salafi thought and who politically supported the jihadist solution to their societies' ills and their governments' subservience to the Western state order, it was a less random choice, a hardening of existing positions within a political landscape where very little about what the group represented was unknown, in the face of circumstances that themselves grew more extreme.

In Umm Layth's writing, Sharmeena also saw a reflection of her own confused, pain-flecked, teenage Londoner naïveté: it was true that Muslims in all these places were dying, being killed by Israeli snipers or Syrian bombs; it was true that it was excruciating to watch that from the comfort of their British lives, feeling hopeless, useless; it was true that when they read Sheikh Awlaki online saying that change "depends on the youth," that might very well mean her—an ordinary teenage girl, a girl who loved browsing ASOS and chewing wine gummies, sitting in her home in East London.

As she read the comments under Facebook posts and the exchanges on Twitter, occasionally someone would ask one of the women who had already made *hijra* whether the violence that ISIS was meting out—the beheading of the journalist James Foley, the calls for attacks in the West—was theologically ethical or justified. The argument in response often went like this: Such brutality was certainly not desirable, but the West had left the militants no choice, there was no other way left to resist; nonviolent protest would not sway the dictator Assad, whose military was torturing and killing scores in detention centers, nor would it sway the United States, which had invaded and occupied Iraq, killed countless civilians, and sustained and protected Arab tyrants. Western societies were slumbering, had lost all empathy for the plight of Muslims, and needed to be awakened: only when their own citizens were forced to suffer would they be roused to notice the violence Muslims suffered daily.

Sharmeena was only fifteen—what did she know of anything—but the logic made sense to her: extreme violence begat extreme violence. She tried this argument out at school, defending ISIS to a teacher, who disagreed sharply with her. They argued, but the teacher reported to neither the school nor Sharmeena's father that this vulnerable, testy girl, whose mother had just died, was openly advocating on behalf of a group that sliced people's heads off on camera. The teacher didn't suggest that, perhaps, someone might have a talk with her about these radical, violent political views. Perhaps, as might well have happened if she existed in a more educated family and world, someone might have told her there were other avenues for dissent and other ways to help vulnerable Muslims across the world: that she could devote herself to human rights law and political activism, or postcolonial studies or conflict reporting or humanitarian work. There were many things a young woman could do with rage. But it took an attentive, intact family, living rooms with books, a sensitive school, layers of protection that often didn't exist around working-class girls from East London, to introduce those ideas. Even when the government got around to employing British Muslim women who had been through precisely this journey, dispatching them to counsel girls who were "vulnerable to radicalisation," they conceded, as one did in an interview, that there was little to no space for these discussions in British society, no avenue for these angry young women to channel their political discontent to the government.

Bethnal Green Academy, the state high school that Sharmeena and her three best friends attended, had an overwhelmingly Muslim student body. Its teenagers mostly kept to the daily five prayers even while at school, and girls wore long skirts or threw abayas over their school uniforms. Even if their families were conservative about mixing with the opposite sex, boys and girls interacted freely at school; they swarmed into the nearby Nando's or chip shop together after class or congregated in the local park. If anything, they separated along racial lines, Asians and blacks, rather than by gender. Student life at Bethnal Green Academy was, by most reports, relaxed and warm. What was missing was a way for especially unhappy and especially intelligent girls to learn that the world offers many ways to dissent against injustice, beyond violent radicalism.

One day that autumn of 2014, Sharmeena tweeted at @Umm Layth and asked if they could direct message.

THE OTHER THREE GIRLS WATCHED as Sharmeena took these first, searching steps into trying to understand why the world, for Muslims, was steeped in so much blood and loss. She told her friends everything and they followed her, loyally, curiously, tentatively.

After Sharmeena, Amira Abase was the most confident. "Bubbly. Sweet," recalled a friend. "I don't think there was one person who didn't like her. Everyone liked her." She was the only non-Asian girl of the group. Her parents were Ethiopian Muslims who came to Britain when Amira was a small girl. Her father's path was particularly jagged: he left Ethiopia when he was sixteen, smuggled out after protesting the government's war against neighboring Eritrea; he spent six years in a German refugee camp before making his way to London.

Amira was edgy, funny, with a face rather imposingly beautiful for her age, bow eyebrows over sloping cheekbones, and nostrils that flared when she grinned. She was kind too; kinder than a popular, pretty girl needed to be. London was expensive and her father struggled to find work. But money wasn't everything, and he made clear it was a blessing to live in a country that took liberty seriously and welcomed expressions of dissent. Ethiopia, where he had grown up, was highly repressive, especially if you were Muslim; it was the kind of country where the government bought spyware from China, listened to people's phone calls, and detained them for weeks, calling their religious ringtones "illegal." In the evenings, her father sat bent over the table, writing letters to protest the treatment of Ethiopian Muslims. Some accounts hinted that the Abases' home life was troubled; that Amira's parents didn't get along and that Hussen, her father, was physically harsh with his children. But others who knew him well said he was a sensitive man, devoted to his family, if cynical about the realities of global politics.

What is clear is that he was open about his views and didn't think his daughter was too young to learn to protest and demonstrate. The conditions in Ethiopia for Muslims were and remain so dire that many fled to Saudi Arabia to work as migrants, encountering circumstances that were much like modern slavery: long working hours with no time off, beatings, passport confiscations, and other abuse. In 2013, Saudi authorities expelled more than 160,000 Ethiopian migrants, setting upon them with machetes and sticks. They dispatched the migrants back to Ethiopia, where many were tortured in detention, kept in underground holes for months. Amira's father took her to a rally outside the Saudi embassy in London to protest the expulsions; people chanted, *"Stop violence against Ethiopians in Saudi Arabia!"* and *"We want justice!"*

When protests erupted in 2012 over an American film mocking the Prophet Muhammad, Amira's father followed a crowd from the mosque in East London to the U.S. embassy. It was a Friday when Muslims across the world turned out to protest what they felt was a deliberate, racially motivated insulting of Islam, originating in a country, the United States, that appeared intent, in the guise of its war on extremism, to kill so many civilians it had given up even counting them. Like so many second-generation Muslim kids, Amira grew up in a home where global politics were intimately lodged in daily life. She had inherited her father's sense of justice. Growing up in Britain taught her she had the right to speak up. At school, she was a strong debater, making the case for why Muslim women had the right to wear veils, or how rape should be prosecuted.

Not everyone in their group grew up with such exposure to politics. Kadiza Sultana, a girl with a shy smile and dark glasses, lived with her older sister and ailing mother in a household that was less preoccupied with politics. Her sister, who was living back at home after an arranged marriage at seventeen, was the authority at home. Sometimes the sisters clashed, but at school, where Kadiza excelled, she was well liked and admired. She was friendly to girls in younger years, and sometimes helped them with schoolwork. The school told her mother that Kadiza was one of the most promising students of her year; a teacher gave her a novel as a gift, praising her accomplishments in English. She watched *The Princess Diaries* and went to Zumba.

The fourth friend, a girl called Shamima Begum, was by all accounts the most quiet, a fan of the Kardashians. Her sister later told a journalist that Shamima was unadventurous and skittish, the type who "doesn't like to go by herself to buy a pint of milk." She was a typical teenage homebody who liked reading and watching television. "She was a brilliant student," her sister said. As in most families, she measured Shamima's well-being by how she was faring at school: "You don't question a child who's done her homework and has got straight As." Shamima's mother had asked her to start wearing a headscarf in Year 10, when she was around fourteen; Shamima hadn't minded because her friends were all covering their hair, and she didn't like feeling that she stood out.

By autumn, all four girls were dressing differently, favoring long skirts over trousers and looser tops. Kadiza, who had never worn the hijab and loved playing around with hairstyles, started wearing a headscarf. Like Sharmeena before them, the girls all began hassling family members for watching television that was *haram,* but in traditional Muslim families this was easy to mark as a dynamic of teenage power struggle. Like Sharmeena, Kadiza grew preoccupied with the Syrian war, and asked her older brother what he thought about it.

Sharmeena's father remarried that same autumn of 2014. "He seemed completely in his own world," said someone who knew the family. Everyone whispered that the rushed second marriage was unseemly; couldn't he have at least waited a year after his wife's death? But Sharmeena ironed a smile onto her face and invited Kadiza to be with her at the ceremony. She felt small, sad, and alone, forced to contend with a stepmother who spoke halting English, who was young herself and territorial about her new husband.

Sharmeena had her own bedroom at their flat, on a high floor in a Shoreditch council tower block. The apartment was one of those London council flats that made you know your place in the city, and showed you everyone else's: soiled stairwells, poorly lit entryways with signs that warned, in Bengali, "Don't Spit," but with expansive views, London spread out below in all directions, the gleaming skyscrapers of Canary Wharf and the City. In their apartment, there was a textile with a Quranic verse hanging on one wall. Her father's new wife had added some feminine touches, a few candles and a decorative pot of honey. The girls gathered often there, but they went straight into Sharmeena's room. She would occasionally emerge and fetch snacks from the kitchen, but her father rarely spoke with the girls.

He was a traditional, aloof Bengali father. He wasn't that old himself, not even forty, and was working hard to meet the needs of a new young wife. He didn't watch the news or follow the Syrian civil war. He didn't know that a transnational armed group called ISIS even existed, let alone operated fluidly across Instagram, Tumblr, Twitter, and Facebook, spooling its indoctrinating half-truths and seductive promises right into his living room, spinning a web around his grieving daughter. He didn't know there was a millennial honey-tongued blogger out in Syria, Umm Layth, prepping young women for the caliphate as though it were boarding school: "Regardless of how annoying and emotionally draining your parents can get—you have to keep ties of kinship and keep in touch with them. . . . tags: enjoy Raqqah teamManbij bring me my perfume he hehe."

On that December night in the Westfield mall, where Sharmeena was doing her shopping on the eve of departure, the girls finished quickly. Sharmeena's aim was to be done by 6 p.m. and back to her grandmother's an hour later, so she would have time to finish packing before dinner. She wasn't going to return to her father's place that night; his new wife was very young and very alert. It was not worth the risk of her noticing something.

Everything was in place to leave. Sharmeena had asked her grandmother for money, from the funds the family had been given around her mother's death. It was enough to cover the tickets. The rest of the girls, if they decided they were brave enough to follow their friend to Syria, would have to figure something out.

PART III:
Over and Out

ASMA

2012–2013, Raqqa, Syria

THE WAR FORMALLY ENTERED ASMA'S LIFE WHEN AL-HASAKAH UNIVER-sity, where both she and her boyfriend had been studying, suspended classes. The boy's well-off parents dispatched their son to Jordan to finish university. The day that Asma said goodbye to him, in 2013, was the last time she saw him. Asma's family had decided to stay. They didn't stay to fight or support the Assad government per se, or to do anything per se. They were among the many Syrians who were simply weary. Fleeing to Turkey or Europe was full of risks and unknowns: drowning, poverty, squalid refugee camps. They were trying to decide what outcome might damage them the least.

Every war has its stayers and leavers, and sometimes the stagger-ing volume of the latter—the exodus from Syria formed one of the greatest mass movements of people in contemporary history—makes us think that everyone could have chosen that path. That somehow the only moral Syrian story, or the chief story of Syrian suffering, is that of those who left. But there were hundreds of thousands of fami-lies who were already barely surviving, or who were making it within the strictest of margins, who felt they had little choice but to stay. Taken together there would be 6.2 million Syrians displaced within their own country—the largest displaced population anywhere in the world.

By late 2012, what had started as a peaceful revolt against the Assad government had turned into a violent armed confrontation. The way it happened was simple: in the earliest days after the uprising, after the Syrian military finished terrorizing a town, storming houses in the middle of the night and assaulting men before their families, they left stockpiles of weapons behind. To "militarize" a conflict is to humiliate and stoke the rage of protesters with disproportionate brutality, to detain and torture innocent bystanders or peaceful activists, and then handily provide them the means for a violent response. There is no agreed timeline around precisely when this happened, but over the course of 2012 and 2013, the Syrian uprising transformed and splintered into a civil war, and then a proxy war.

Countries like Saudi Arabia, Qatar, and Turkey, seeing an opening to extend their competition and project their influence in this chaotic sphere, began funding and supporting more militant Islamist factions. It created a strange incentive among the opposition: long beards and religious optics secured more funding. Iran, the Syrian regime's only regional ally, began dispatching military advisers to bolster Assad. (Syria had been the only country to support Iran during its eight-year-long war with Iraq, a conflict that ended in 1988, in which Saddam Hussein liberally used chemical weapons and Iran lost a million young men.) These intrusions transformed the Syrian revolution into a proxy war, where regional powers fought for influence.

As though this proxy overlay were not complex enough, a further dimension developed. The U.S. invasion and occupation of Iraq in 2003 had broken the country. When Saddam Hussein's regime toppled, the new orders that arose in its place, first the U.S. occupation authority and then an Iraqi government dominated by Shias, essentially cast Sunnis out of public life; this marginalization provided a social opening for Sunni militants, many of them Saddam-era Baathist loyalists, to exploit ordinary Iraqi Sunni grievances and harness them to their fight against both U.S. occupiers and the new Shia-led government writ large. The radical, violent groups that emerged from post-invasion Iraq were distilled, by 2013, to the predecessor of the Islamic State in Iraq and Syria, what we know today as ISIS. Its aim was territorial: to secede from Iraq and occupy as much land as it could, pushing up through the collapsed border with Syria, to form what it envisioned as an Islamic state.

The Syrian uprising transformed into an even more intricate contemporary approximation of Afghanistan in the 1980s: a theater for the enactment of conflict between the West and Russia; regional proxy battles between Iran and the Gulf Arab states; a leadership competition among the Sunni countries of the region; intra-jihadist battles over competing views of tactics and the ultimate enemy; battles between Shia militias and Sunni jihadists. It was made even more intricate by the weaponization of information and social media on all sides, such that even basic questions—Was a group like the White Helmets really composed of brave medical first-responders, or were they actually al-Qaeda in ambulances? Did Assad use chemical weapons against his own people, or were these attacks false-flag operations?—ended up unnecessarily but wildly contested.

Throughout much of early 2013, the CIA-backed Free Syrian Army and the al-Nusra Front, composed of Syrian Islamists with al-Qaeda leanings, controlled Raqqa. By summer, Raqqa was alight with bombings and clashes, and al-Nusra rebels who saw ISIS gaining strength switched sides. Up went the black flags. The militants, some so young they barely had facial hair, stormed churches and took over municipal buildings.

During the early stretch of the Syrian civil war, Raqqa had been relatively safe compared to smaller cities and towns across the country. But now Syrians who had fled to Raqqa from other cities began streaming out. Well-off Raqqans cleared out their valuables, withdrew what savings they could, and joined the flow of Syrians into neighboring Lebanon, and, if they could afford it, Europe. Those who couldn't, who didn't have the contacts, the cash, or the conviction that one's country could be left behind, decamped to relatives' houses in nearby suburbs or surrounding towns, planning to wait out the worst of the fighting.

By the time the temperatures dropped to freezing in the winter of 2013, ISIS had wrested total control of the city from other rebels. Raqqa was now its bureaucratic command center. Like the Baathist regimes of Saddam Hussein and Hafez al-Assad, under whom many of the fighters had come of age, ISIS began systematically breaking down the local social order. As the group's leadership moved in, it consolidated its hold brutally. Those community leaders who resisted, or whose family and friends had the wrong connections, faced arbitrary detention, torture, execution.

It had been possible to be apolitical in Raqqa under Assad, because politics was essentially forbidden, as risky as quicksand. But under ISIS, from the earliest days, it became clear to Asma's father and his relatives that every spot in the new hierarchy, and any chance to survive, was utterly dependent on the group's whim. It also became clear to Asma that their status in Raqqa—as middle-class citizens in a prosperous Syrian town—had fallen precipitously. Now when she went to the market, she heard chattering around her in Arabic or even French and German. Foreign fighters, known as *muhajireen,* or migrants, began streaming into town—answering the call to fight Assad, to build a state in God's name, to find some dignity and purpose in the plains of Syria that had been absent in their lives in Europe or Tunisia or Morocco or Jordan. These foreigners became the leading lights of the transformed city.

At the beginning, the militants brought security, by then a relative novelty. For a short period of time in Raqqa, some residents said, there was little robbery or theft, no more shootouts in the street. Asma could walk to the market or visit friends without fearing for her safety. It was in the year that followed that ISIS began to use theatrical violence as a tool: to draw more recruits from abroad, to instill public terror in areas under its control, to hasten submission in areas newly taken. The strategy was highly manipulative and effective, cheap kindling for reporting that took the militants' religious claims at face value. Slowly ISIS became, in the Western imagination, a satanic force unlike anything civilization had encountered since it began recording histories of combat with the Trojan Wars. Even *The New York Review of Books,* not known for its analytical inadequacy, ran a piece about ISIS that declared it was "not clear whether our culture can ever develop sufficient knowledge, rigor, imagination, and humility to grasp the phenomenon of ISIS."

The whiff of exorcism and devilry made ISIS a popular intellectual fetish in American journalistic circles, one that overlooked the contributions of American policies and wars to the group's origins in favor of tracing just how much Quranic scripture infused the militants' aims and depravity. Much less attention went to the cold calculation the West had made: that the Assad government was preferable to whatever more religious, militant order that would surely rise in its place. The ISIS chroniclers remained obsessed with religion, vividly portraying every atrocity the group committed as some facet of Islam; rape, that longtime tactic of war used to humiliate the enemy, became a "theology of rape," an Islamic sickness rather than a war crime. From the vantage point of the young Muslim women of Raqqa, women like Asma who heard frequent tales of regime massacres and sexual violations, there was no such hand-wringing about whether ISIS was the evilest of them all, whether it was *really very Islamic*. To them, at that moment, everyone was equally predatory, equally complicit in the rending apart of Syria. Everyone had blood on their hands. Everyone claimed an ideology to justify their violence. Did putting it on YouTube make it that much worse?

NOUR

ONE EVENING THAT FALL, NOUR LEARNED FROM KARIM THAT WALID had gone to Syria. She was stunned. Why hadn't he told her? She quashed that thought quickly; there was no reason why he would have shared his plans with her, even if they were friends.

Following the sermon in central Tunis that led to the violent protest at the U.S. embassy earlier that year, the police cracked down on Salafi activists. The women in Nour's group at the mosque were growing twitchy, worried about attracting police attention. But it was only when Nour heard about Walid's departure that she realized how developments in the wider region were pulling some young activists' attention away from Tunis.

In that fall of 2012, the Syrian civil war was still a just war, to many, a just jihad. It was a clear case of a tyrant, a *taghout,* brutally murdering his people. Young men like Walid did not feel they could watch Assad's slaughter while casually proceeding with their lives.

Islam carries the concept of *ummah,* or a global community of Muslims, all of whom share a spiritual bond and a stake in each other's welfare. This is an unshakable sentiment that rests in the heart of many Muslims across geographic and social contexts; it has a secular variant that may not rest on the idea of *ummah* so much as simple political solidarity. At Tunisian soccer matches to this day, fans drape banners in support of Palestine across the stadium. Was Palestine an Islamist cause, an Islamist value? Not especially—but an individual's political worldview could be shaped by many values, anything from a belief that religious tenets should drive politics, to a belief in self-determination and democratic will. The secular youth of the revolution in Egypt, for instance, also focused on Palestinian rights, demanding that Egyptian foreign policy reflect these concerns.

These new forces in the Arab Spring—the rise of popular Islamists; the emergence of radical young people who believed that religious parties should have a role in politics, young people who felt as viscerally about the sixty-year-old Israeli occupation of Palestine as though it had happened last week—were profoundly disquieting to the Sunni tyrants who had presided over the region for decades, as well as the Western countries whose interests had also upheld that order. The collapse of the Arab Spring revolts led to an even more extreme regime of repression in countries like Egypt and Bahrain; for the autocrats whose power rested on their choking suppression of politics and civil society, their strict control of the media, it became imperative to ensure other countries did not provoke their populations by example.

Even though Tunisia was a pint-sized country of little consequence in the wider world, its internal politics suddenly took on urgent and wide-ranging implications for the region. The emerging axis of Arab authoritarian regimes allying with Israel—particularly Saudi Arabia and the United Arab Emirates—could not tolerate the rise of a popular religious political movement in Tunisia; it would provide too dangerous a model for their local oppositions. Islamists were disruptors. They couldn't be bought off with yachts. They felt the whole game— the Western political and economic ordering of the Middle East, enacted through wars, cultivation of potentates, and arms sales—was stacked against the people of the region, and they rejected this game entirely.

The term itself, "Islamists," was a popular but opaque term that didn't capture the breadth and intention of what such actors were up to: they were often simply socially conservative political oppositions, challenging modern Arab nation-states' failures—to oversee social and economic development, to endow the concept of citizenship with any meaning. These failures, the Islamists maintained, were the real driver of the region's extremism. They had popular support; many had illiberal (in their eyes, orthodox) religious views. And their views on Israel, on America's military footprint in the region, were disquieting. Everything about them was disquieting. But from the bottom up, they were exceedingly strong.

In February 2013, a Tunisian MP who had been critical of Ennahda was shot dead outside his home. Within several weeks of his arrival, another politician was assassinated.

The suspicion immediately turned to Ennahda, fanned by the press, still dominated by Ben Ali–era figures. But the Tunisian police were too ill-equipped to make an arrest and produce forensic evidence showing who was responsible. Hundreds of protesters gathered outside the Kasbah, demanding the Ennahda-led government step down from power. The situation was ostensibly a domestic political crisis, but there were forceful voices coming from outside. Western intelligence agencies sent urgent messages to the government in Tunis, pressuring it to get tougher on terrorism. Ennahda understood clearly that it had to save itself.

By the summer of 2013, when Walid returned to Tunis, stretches of Avenue Bourguiba were lined with concrete barriers and whorls of barbed wire. The first evening of his return to Tunis, Walid met a friend downtown for a shawarma. He was stopped at two checkpoints, each stop necessitating a twenty-minute wait. The cars were mostly full of young men driving into the center of town for an evening of strolling past the avenue's cafés. But the police saw this as an opportunity to resume their old ways: harassing young men for the sake of it, imposing spurious fines that were just demands for bribes.

That night, Walid walked past the Café du Théâtre, past the alleyways that led to darkened cellar restaurants where union and leftist party leaders had wine with lunch. Tanks and barbed-wire whorls formed a cordon between the building and the street. On bad days, it felt to Walid like very little had changed: the police still terrorized you, they confiscated your car, demanded bribes for basic paperwork, turned your girlfriend's family against you. Instead of raping you with a bottle, they savaged your life more bureaucratically, but it felt the same. On good days, he still thanked God that Ben Ali was gone, that there was a transitional justice process underway, where the former regime figures would be held to account in hearings broadcast on national television.

In August, the government declared Ansar al-Sharia a terrorist organization. Whether the majority of the group's members supported violence was unclear; certainly, the majority were not involved in acts of violence. But Ennahda needed to appear tough on terrorism, and the Tunisian security services lacked the capacity to monitor and police the Salafist movement with a fine-tooth comb. The police were used to operating as Islamist hunters, and asking them to do any different would have been like suggesting Joseph McCarthy make investigative distinctions between Stalinists and Trotskyists. Politically and practically, the only course was to ban the organization wholesale.

Walid was livid with this political reality. He had a tendency to spit out Abu Iyadh's name like the shell of a sunflower seed, blaming him for the attacks that triggered the state crackdown. "Abu Iyadh did the greatest damage of any single individual to the cause of Islamism in Tunisia," he said. Walid believed that Abu Iyadh was compromised, that he possessed some other agenda. Security services routinely penetrated Islamist networks and egged on everyone, from sympathizers to militants, to plan and carry out attacks. Islamists whispered this about Abu Iyadh everywhere, from London to Tunis; he was the Keyser Söze of the Salafi movement, a figure whose motivations and allegiances remained a permanent mystery. Walid reasoned aloud, "Why would you do that? Why would you take up arms against the government? Why go on the offensive so quickly? Couldn't he have calculated how the state and the police would've reacted?"

Or perhaps Abu Iyadh had been doing global jihad for so long that it had become a part of him. This was the view of Abu Abdullah, a fellow Tunisian traveler in the world of Salafi jihadism. His history, like Abu Iyadh's, stretched all the way back to the jihad against the Soviets in Afghanistan in the 1980s. When the United States invaded Iraq in 2003, the resulting Sunni insurgency drew old veterans like Abu Abdullah back into the field. He spent two years in Anbar province over 2004 and 2005, fighting U.S. Marines in intense urban combat.

In late November 2005, after an IUD exploded under a Humvee

and killed an American soldier, Marines rampaged through the town of Haditha, in Anbar province. Marines ordered five Iraqi men out of a taxi—a driver and four students—and shot them in the street. Then they stormed into a nearby neighborhood and kicked in the doors of two houses. Inside were families, including a blind old man in a wheelchair and children as young as three, some still asleep in their beds. The Marines gunned them all down, nineteen in all.

This was the fighting Abu Abdullah saw in Anbar. In his eyes, militant groups had no choice, in the asymmetric war in which they found themselves, but to target Western civilians. How was that any different from what the Marines had done that day in Haditha? They were up against a powerful country that had launched an ideological war in Iraq and often deliberately killed civilians and feigned apology afterward. Was that not simply state terrorism?

It was in Anbar that he met and grew close to the Jordanian militant Abu Musab al-Zarqawi, known later as "Sheikh of the Slaughterers," and cemented his belief that the West was inexorably against the development of Arabs and Muslims. He came to believe that the developed living standards in the United States and Europe were dependent on an economy of Arab client-state management, of massive arms sales to dictators, military invasions, and the lucrative Western-contractor-led rebuilding that followed. "They steal our wealth, they oppose our movements, they want to keep us Third World," Abu Abdullah said. To his mind, colonialism had never really ended, it just changed guise. In this new order of things, jihadism was revolutionary self-defense.

There is no consensus perspective on Salafi jihadism, either as an idea or as a transnational militant phenomenon. How much is Salafism itself to blame, and how much the armed, oppositional tendencies of the groups in question? Ideology or context? How genuine and significant are the links between Salafi jihadist groups from one theater of conflict to the next? Just because one group signals ties to a powerful centrist jihadist group to burnish its muscular image and enhance its brand, does that mean we face the same enemy across multiple fronts? Or must different national and regional conflicts be largely understood on their own terms? Ideology or context?

Some view Salafism as inherently toxic, liable to disrupt and fuel tensions in whatever society it takes root because at its core, Salafism is so rigid and inherently intolerant of difference, a sect that cannot help but preach apartness. Salafi jihadism is then a natural outgrowth of such a reactionary and unstable ideology. Others advance the idea that Salafi jihadism flourishes in the cracks of state disorder, that many insurgencies around the world may inflect their campaigns and agendas with its language and aesthetics, but that they are fundamentally local conflicts that must be read and assessed within their own spheres. Those tasked with responding to and assessing violent acts—intelligence agencies, police, scholars, journalists—tend to hew to one view over the other. The distinction matters because the story we agree to tell about extremism, the mapping of who is hurting whom and what should be done about it, as well as the scale and nature of the threat, determines the policies that states put into place.

The ideological reading tends to advance militarized policies—more drone strikes, battlefield onslaughts, and more punitive security policies. The contextual reading promotes engagement with the politics of these insurgencies, perhaps at times even engagement with the militants themselves, with the aim of transforming the conditions that gave rise to them in the first place. The truth is that there is no singular answer to the problem of Salafi jihadism, and scarcely anyone is capable of theorizing it properly.

For his part, Abu Abdullah's views, like most hardened rebels, were sweeping and mechanical.

The old jihadi argued that the Americans and the Europeans would never allow an Islamist government to take hold in Tunisia. He pointed to Ennahda's retreat from mentioning Sharia or even Sharia principles in the new constitution. "Their project is not to create a state where Muslims can be religiously free. Look at them now, even though they're in power. If you go to their headquarters and ask for help, if you say you're a niqabi girl harassed by the police, they'll say, 'There's nothing we can do for you.'"

Apart from finding Ennahda especially useless, Abu Abdullah didn't believe in working within the state's political framework in the first place. He considered democracy to be *shirk,* or idolatry; God had provided all the laws necessary, and overriding them was sinful. This belief was at the core of many Islamist movements, which originated after the fall of the Ottoman caliphate at the end of World War I. The idea of *an* Islamic state—not the organization called the same in Syria, but a modern entity that brought Muslims together under one political banner—remained the ultimate aim of Islamists across the spectrum, from the veteran jihadis to the new generation of Salafi rebels.

Abu Abdullah said the appeal of jihadism signaled a desperation, the failure of the prospect of gradualism. "The system is so corrupt and so oppressive that it seems futile to do anything. That's why you see the rapper, the praying man, the drinking man, the Rasta man . . . all turning to ISIS." But if there was a repaired Tunisian system, would young people still be drawn to jihad or the pursuit of an Islamic state? He considered this carefully. "Young Muslims have this instinct inside them. Something in them will always awaken to fight the enemy. To change things in the world, to make the religion proud and glorious."

BY THE AUTUMN OF 2013, Karim had given up looking for work and was back on the sofa. Most evenings he sat with Nour's father, watching the news. They flipped between the Qatari-owned Al Jazeera, which covered the Islamists of the region as though they were statesmen, and the Saudi-owned Al Arabiya, which dourly warned of Islamism as a creeping terrorist fungus. One night, on the latter channel, he watched the presenter's glossy fuchsia mouth pucker into an O every time she called the interviewee "Doktor." Her high-cheekboned, lacquered face was so beautiful it was almost calming.

Karim had a shift later that night driving a taxi. Two such nights' work would make him about one-sixteenth of a month's rent. His original plan—to get a job at the Ministry of Transportation and then earn enough to rent a taxi on the weekends, rather than picking up just an occasional pity shift—had fallen apart. There weren't any objective criteria for getting hired by the ministry, or making it through the various stages of almost-hiring that might or might not result in an actual salaried job.

Karim was not alone in his mounting disillusionment. Young men gathered almost weekly to protest in front of the ministry; it happened so regularly it didn't even count as news anymore. Sometimes Karim went along, halfheartedly throwing a stone. He was thirty-seven that year, but he felt as though he were living out his third lifetime: the first in corruption-choked Tunis under Ben Ali; the second his escape to France, a nomadic existence where he tried to avoid the easy lure of petty crime; and now the third, here in the new Tunisia, which made his heart tighten up, because if nothing opened up for him here, nothing ever would. Falling asleep at night, he would whisper to Nour to be patient, but she was two months pregnant by now.

It was the season of Mediterranean dust storms that would sweep in from the north and make the sky a glowing saffron haze. It was the season that the men of Kram started to disappear. They were going to Syria, where, it was said, you could make a living by joining the jihad. It wasn't just petty drug pushers who were drawn by these promises, but skilled guys with degrees. Professional soccer players. IT guys. Lawyers, doctors, fine arts graduates. There were tales of large salaries and subsidized apartments.

The story that was making the rounds fastest was that of Hamza Ben Rejeb, a disabled university student who had spent his whole life confined to a wheelchair in a third-floor flat in Tunis, and somehow managed to wheel himself to Syria to join the fight against the tyrant Bashar. Once there, he put his IT training to use and, reportedly, felt respected and productive for the first and only time in his young life. Back in Tunis, his older brother Mohamed went on television, complaining bitterly that the jihadists had so little shame they were even willing to seduce a cripple. Mohamed went to Syria and demanded that Hamza come home. The militants held up their hands, saying they were not in the business of keeping cripples against their will, and Mohamed wheeled Hamza back to Tunis, back to the third-floor flat with the view of no future.

Before 2013, no one talked much about "radicalization" in Tunisia. They talked about fucking off to Syria to find a job, to build a polity for Islam, to fight Bashar al-Assad, to join a militant group, to rescue a dying child, to ensure a place in heaven, or some combination of all those things. Those choices and motivations were taken at face value; no one imagined that the young people going to Syria didn't actually feel these things, that there was instead some fuzzy ideological process called radicalization happening to all of them. Mohamed, brother of wheelchair-bound Hamza, was someone who had seized upon the idea of radicalization that had recently been exported to Tunisia. Each decade tended to have a notion that reliably elicited Western donor funding to local civil society organizations. The 2010s was the decade of "countering violent extremism." Mohamed started an organization euphemistically called Tunisians Stranded Abroad. He held court in local cafés, explaining how online Salafi sermons and targeted grooming had convinced Hamza he was a genius ("Hamza is not a genius," he assured journalists who asked). In all of this, no one was ever permitted to speak to Hamza himself. He had grown depressed and wanted to return to Syria.

Karim hadn't known Hamza, but he did know Saber, the son of a local seamstress. Saber had a scar on his right arm from where a bullet had grazed him during the revolution. Saber applied for work from the Ministry of Transportation and protested outside every day until finally he was accepted into the recruitment process. He made it all the way to his medical exam, the very last phase. He was meant to start work two days after that, but when the final hire lists were published, he wasn't on them. No one from Kram was listed; the only guys hired were those who had connections to the influential labor unions, just as it had been before the revolution. Saber left for Syria, and after about three months, news reached home that he had died.

The same thing happened to a local rapper kid, whose hip-hop name was Kouba. Kouba also spent a month protesting in front of the Ministry of Transportation. He finally sat the national exam, and also, like Saber, passed his medical exam. When it came to the hiring list, though, his name wasn't on it. Again, the jobs went to the union guys and others with connections. Emad, the activist from Kram, knew Kouba. He said that in the end, Kouba gave up on Tunisia. "He didn't have an extremist thought in his head. But he found a way to Syria and died in Syria."

Leaving to do jihad in Syria became a dignified exit from a life that offered nothing else, Emad said, which made vulnerable young men easy prey for militant recruiters. "Imagine yourself a young kid, thinks he's a hero because he carried out the revolution. Imagine after that revolution you find yourself respected by the state, hired, doing well. What would you be thinking about? You'd be thinking about getting married. Buying a car. Living your life. Then you have the opposite taking place. You find your life ticking by. It's now six years after the revolution; if you were twenty-two then, now you're twenty-eight. If you were twenty-four, now you're thirty. You want to build a life, but the doors keep getting slammed in your face. When a man gets to that point, he doesn't think for himself anymore. They think for him."

In the years following the Arab Spring uprising, many young people in Kram reported stepped-up harassment by the police. The old regime's methods of policing—trumped-up charges, no evidence, no due process, physical violence—had never really gone away; now they returned quickly, and with impunity. Mohammad Ali was one of what was called "the wounded of the revolution," protesters who had suffered bodily injury in 2011 and received a small monthly payment from the state. This extra help had allowed Mohammad Ali to take a short holiday in Turkey. Upon his return to Tunis, the police put him under house arrest. "Mohammad Ali was religious, he prayed. And he had gone to Turkey. To the police, this could mean only one thing," Emad said. "Terrorism."

They had no evidence at all, nothing to go on. But they interred Mohammad Ali in his house for long enough that he eventually lost his coveted job at the Ministry of Health. "The police think religious-minded people are the enemy, that they're a danger to Tunisia," Emad said. "It's not easy to get rid of that attitude in just three or four years. It will take ten years, fifteen even, for the police to become republicans and not interrogate people's beliefs."

In the afternoons, during the years after the revolution, Emad often sat at an outdoor café on a crowded street in Kram. Around him men drank coffee and smoked water pipes. The wall across the road bore the giant graffito WE FEAR NOTHING, ALWAYS FORWARD. Emad bristled when people asked about his country's jihadist exodus. In fact, such questions irritated a whole range of people in Tunisia—

sociologists, young graduate students, human rights activists—who preferred to make clear that the nation, even after the revolution, faced a whole morass of problems beyond jihadism. A quarter of Tunisia's population lived in poverty while a sliver grew more affluent; opportunity remained firmly out of reach to those not born to wealth or connections; the government could not begin to shape better economic policies, because the delicate political consensus that was keeping the country together, where the old elites had a stake in the new order, was too paralyzed to agree on and enact necessary reforms. Many young people saw militancy as just one symptom of what was still wrong with Tunisia, rather than a whole pathology or framework of inquiry on its own.

The exception to this were many secularists who specialized in jihadism or extremism. These scholars and analysts tended to hold discussions from about ten thousand feet in the air; they laced their conversations with words like "brainwashing" and "concubine," and believed that religion itself, rather than state brutality or corruption, or some intermingling of all these things, led men and women to militancy. Their scholarship was highly partisan and politicized, and their views quickly garnered them attention in domestic media, similarly partisan, and quickly received recognition, support, and funding from Western organizations who held them up as representative local civil society voices. Often, they reached for English terms like "radicalization" or "violent extremism," policy terms of a counterterrorism discourse minted by the West as part of a foreign and security policy agenda, now spreading out across the world, imposing generic, context-collapsing terms and solutions on disparate societies with widely varying problems.

One such academic had designed a "rehabilitation program" for jihadist returnees that involved sequestration and a deprogramming process that would alter their views on religion. He admitted that it would be challenging to reengineer an individual's belief system. "We would need to fundamentally review Islamic thinking, and that has not been done in the Arab world," he said. "The problem is that political Islam believes in Caliphate."

The secularists sometimes acknowledged that they knew these

outlandish plans wouldn't work. Sometimes they freely admitted that they, the minority, were content to rule by force. Over dinner one evening, a refined professor at the University of Tunis declared that democracy was unsuitable for Tunisia, because until a population had absorbed the values of Rousseau, it could not be entrusted with the freedom to vote. The professor drove a gleaming SUV and in his free time enjoyed limericks and walking holidays in Britain's Lake District. Western liberals who suggested that lasting stability for Tunisia could only be achieved through real public participation in politics—he thought they were delusional Islamo-gauchistes, deluded leftists who were enamored with Islamists and overlooked the sectarian and violent dangers they posed. His life was civilized, protected, and secure, and he didn't seem interested in letting his country experiment with any real freedom.

For the activist Emad, it rankled that Westerners turned their attention to Tunisia only when the country became involved in militancy that impacted the West, and then used the lens of that violence to understand the whole country. He kept pushing his beret back and shaking his head in exasperation. "We have so many kinds of extremism after the revolution, why does the media only look at the religious kind? Why does no one ask why the media outlets and prominent spokespeople, all affiliated with the old regime, were making huge public issues out of the niqab or even just fleeting references to Islamic law, when the revolution had been about employment and development and dignity at the hands of the police? Is it not extremism to make a national cause out of nothing, to sow false divisions about such side issues?"

The new Tunisia was a place where the old grievances held strong. The inequalities remained firmly in place: between poor suburbs and seaside enclaves in Tunis; between the relatively prosperous north of the country and the impoverished interior and south. The country's economy was sluggish. Real economic reform required an aggressive campaign against corruption, but the old-regime elites blocked these efforts, which would undo their ties of patronage. Stoking fears of terrorism was a rapid, effective way to ward off the anti-corruption purges that reform required. For Emad and others, if leaving to wage jihad in

Syria had come to define the new Tunisia, that was a symptom that things had gone terribly wrong. Understanding those things—the many other extremisms that had produced this singular one—should be the focus.

MOST MORNINGS WHEN KARIM LISTENED to the news on the radio or passed a newspaper stand, he felt as though nothing had changed. He was finding it difficult to control his reactions to ordinary things, or to react proportionally to anything. The sounds in the house of Nour's parents, the scratch of her mother pulling the chairs closer to the table, the squawking of the pink rat creature in the cartoon her younger brother always watched, and the excitable boy's mimicked response—all of it made him want to smash something.

He decided it was time to go. He told Walid first, on a warm autumn night at a café in Kram. They smoked in silence for a time, and then Walid said, "You're a total fucking idiot."

He interrogated Karim about his reasons. Did he want to be a martyr? Did he want to save the Muslims whom Assad was murdering? Did he want to serve the jihad? Walid was prepared to counter any of these notions. To die a martyr, no one could deny, was an exquisite fate. But what would become of Tunisia if all its youth abandoned it to help another cause? Who would fight for their country? And by that fall of 2013, the Syrian war had changed; it was no longer a just jihad, and Walid tried to impress this upon Karim. It was drawing mercenaries and delinquents, men without politics, with impure hearts. Abu Bakr al-Baghdadi, the leader of ISIS, was a scorpion, responsible for turning the Syrian opposition into a pageant of extreme sectarian violence that alienated most Syrians and only served Bashar al-Assad. Syria was now a death trap, a war whose combatants and instigators twirled around in a space of funhouse mirrors.

Karim stared at him impassively. It was all well and good for Walid to say these things. He had dropped into the war during its righteous stage and returned with the burnish of a warrior. Karim saw this in the way Nour looked at his friend, that sheen of admiration in her eyes. Who had more dignity in the eyes of a woman: an unemployed man on the couch in athletic wear, or the returned *mujahid* who had fought alongside his brothers and carried injured babies to the hospital?

Karim told Nour late that night. They sat in the kitchen after everyone had gone to bed, with a plate of leftovers between them on the table. Nour didn't know what to say. She still wore her niqab and wanted to lead a fully committed religious life, despite its hardship; she still believed that the people of Tunisia should be governed by Islamic laws. Now that Ansar al-Sharia was banned, some of the women in her prayer circle were talking about joining ISIS in Libya. The women said the space in Tunisia for religious and political activity had closed, and no one, not even Nour, felt like they could go back to how things were before, as though the revolution had never happened.

It took two nights for Karim to convince Nour. On the second evening, they went for a walk, passing through the park where it had all started years ago, the day she told the girls she would be the school's first student to wear a niqab. Ever since the government had banned Ansar al-Sharia, the neighborhood committees that collected rubbish had disbanded. The park was once again strewn with garbage, dirty diapers, and crushed water bottles.

Nour thought about the relief it would bring to her parents, who felt the burden of supporting the young married couple. In three months, their baby would add a third mouth to feed. By now Karim should have had a job, they should have moved out. "Have I not tried here? Have I set my sights too high, for work I could not get?" Karim asked. They sat on rusted swings that punctuated the air with squeaks. Nour frowned and said, "No, you have been sensible."

She could not countenance staying behind. He was her husband, father of her soon-to-arrive child, her lifeline out of her parents' home. Her aspirations were modest ones, ones that could very possibly be met by moving to Syria, if it was true that Karim would have a salary there. She wanted only to have a small space of their own, so they could sleep without her siblings in the room. She wanted to be able to work in a shop and earn some money without having to take her hijab off and show her body. She wanted to live in the caliphate under the protection of Islamic laws, practicing her religion without anxiety, social judgment, and public shaming. She wanted to hang curtains that she had chosen and watch them flutter in the breeze as she cooked dinner in her own kitchen. She wanted to be free of having to hold her tongue when her parents told her what to do, because they were living off their generosity and she could not.

RAHMA AND GHOUFRAN

Summer 2014, Sousse, Tunisia

THE FIRST TIME OLFA HEARD THE NAME ABU BAKR AL-BAGHDADI IN 2014, it meant nothing to her, and she paid little attention. But over time, her daughters Rahma and Ghoufran, enmeshed in their new teenage lives as Salafi activists, mentioned him more and more. They read passages from his sermons aloud to each other and called him by the honorific "Emir." Increasingly they talked about what was happening in Syria and how it was shameful to do nothing when Muslims were being slaughtered across the Mediterranean. "Muslims are suffering right here in Sousse, and five and ten towns away as well," Olfa said tartly, but the girls shook their heads, as though they had become privy to some existential truth that eluded their poor ignorant mother.

If the early months of Rahma and Ghoufran's interaction with the Salafi movement had been social and active, a lively sequence of prayer circles and mosque visits, the girls now seemed to live in their mobile phones. They listened to jihadi *nasheed*s and fielded a stream of Telegram notifications. One night late that summer, like mothers of teenagers the world over, Olfa told Rahma to give her phone a rest. Rahma reached for it again in less than fifteen minutes, and Olfa lost it. She grabbed the phone and smashed it against the sharp corner of the coffee table.

Rahma's face crumpled. For a minute Olfa loathed herself; it was probably her fault her daughters behaved so strangely. They had no father, only a mother half-dead from exhaustion, bitter and volatile. Olfa fell asleep that night regretting the harshness she never seemed able to conquer. But the next afternoon, Rahma came home smiling, with a new, superior phone.

Her daughter Ghoufran worried her less. Her old, cheery personality coexisted with her new religious identity; unlike Rahma, she hadn't lost all sense of perspective or tolerance, which reassured Olfa. One of them was staying sensible.

By June, Olfa had to decide whether to travel for her biannual work trip to neighboring Libya, a chance to earn some extra money during the high season. Usually she found someone to stay with the children, or at least stop in frequently to make sure they were okay. Between them, Ghoufran and Rahma had always been capable of running the household on their own, for the month or six weeks that she was away. Olfa did not like the fact that she had to leave her four children for the sake of making extra money for the family, but she stocked the house with biscuits and tins of tuna, and trusted they would be fine. In Libya, working as a cleaner at a beach hotel or household, she could make in one month what she earned in Sousse in three. They needed this money; not going was not an option.

The girls too had been thinking about Libya. A cadre of jihadists was coalescing there, and would declare allegiance to ISIS under the leadership of al-Baghdadi later that fall. Some of the women the girls knew in Sousse and Tunis worked with an online and recruitment unit run entirely by women. Many had already gone to Libya.

They whispered about it in the mornings, while the younger children watched cartoons and played with their shared doll. When Olfa mentioned that it was about that time of year, Ghoufran made the suggestion: "Why don't we all go?" The course she described seemed so reasonable, so obviously to everyone's benefit—they could all be together, Rahma and Ghoufran could work as well and combine their incomes, they would look after the smallest children.

Olfa was easily persuaded. Going to Libya together, why had she not thought of it herself?

EMMA/DUNYA

February 2014, Istanbul, Turkey

PERHAPS NOT ENOUGH IS SAID OF ISTANBUL'S GRANDEUR AND SWEEP, the role of its extraordinary beauty as the launching ground for impressionable young people journeying to the caliphate, many of whom had never traveled abroad before. It is a city capable of stirring something deep, a quality Orhan Pamuk describes as its ineffable *huzun,* or melancholy. It is a word whose root appears in the Quran five times, and denotes a feeling of anguish at separation from God. *Huzun,* though painful, is spiritually necessary. It is the darkness that impels one to seek oneness, or union, or a state of getting close enough to God. Without *huzun,* how would one even know to seek?

It is this quality that permeated Istanbul, the City of Islam, the capital of the Ottoman Empire—the last caliphate—which ruled from the thirteenth century through the end of World War I. Stretching between Europe and Asia over the Bosporus, teeming with mosques cast in golden light, the city is one of the most physically arresting, historically saturated, cosmopolitan urban theaters, vaster and more majestic than any city that might seek to compare. If Isfahan, Venice, Damascus, and Cairo were all courtly little jewel boxes, Istanbul was the whole world itself.

Dunya and Selim went walking alongside the Bosporus at sunset, watching the ships dock at Karaköy. The light was sinking into a smudge of gray-violet and rose; flocks of birds fluttered black against the dimming light, with the towers of Topkapi Palace in the distance. Despite the drama and beauty of her surroundings, Dunya was anxious. Not only about going to Syria, but also of the prospect of running into her mother-in-law, who traveled to Istanbul every summer to visit her relatives. Dunya had wanted to stay near Taksim Square, but Selim said this area was too visible, so they spent three nights at a motel near the airport, a low-slung, dank place with smoked-glass windows near a club called Big Boss Lounge and dumpy restaurants that all seemed to evoke Dubai in their names, as though this was a code word for sin. When they went outside, she would scan the street ahead, half expecting her mother-in-law to jump out of a shop and snatch Selim away from her. She was almost relieved when Selim said it was time to go.

She slept badly the whole night, watching the shadows migrate across the ceiling, before Selim's phone alarm went off. It was still dark when they left the hotel, the sea glinting in the darkness and the bridge in the distance draped in lights.

The drive to the south took about ten hours. It was past midnight when their car approached the stretch of border where they were meant to cross. The driver turned the headlights off and crept forward, telling them to keep quiet. Beams of light swept through the darkness ahead: border guards, but apparently not the ones they had bribed to let them through.

The driver put the car into reverse. Selim said they would stay for a couple of hours at the nearby home of a local Turkish couple who helped ISIS people trying to cross the border. The house smelled of recent cooking and was spare except for a few chairs and a large metal shoe rack near the door. Dunya wondered how many people had transited through this living room, wondered where they were now.

The second time, they fared better at the border. By then she was so tired that the adrenaline didn't hit until they were actually outside in the darkness, Selim calling her name, hissing "Run!" With her heart pounding, she jogged behind him until they reached another waiting car.

LINA

LINA'S ASCETIC LIFE IN FRANKFURT AT THE WOMEN'S SHELTER WAS RE-markably easy to pack up; she rarely bought anything new, received no gifts, had no travel or lifestyle magazines. And her journey from Frankfurt to Raqqa was easier than it should have been: she flew to Istanbul, ate a cheese sandwich, and took a short connecting flight to Gaziantep.

There was a lanky man in flip-flops waiting for her outside the security gate, holding a sign with an agreed-upon name. He was Turkish and spoke no Arabic, so they communicated with hand gestures. He mimed putting a head down on a pillow: he would take her to a house to spend the night.

The next day, he drove Lina and several other women just a mile away, where a minivan was waiting. After about half an hour in the minivan, the driver asked Lina and the other women to get out and walk briskly. The sun was intense, but Lina's duffel bag was light, and there was a car waiting about two hundred yards in the distance. Up to that point in 2014, thousands of foreign fighters and recruits had crossed the border into Syria with ease; the border was long, porous, and Turkish border guards were amenable to bribes. Car to car, a quick dash across a dark field, it was all routine. It was only much later that year, and into the next two, that the Turkish authorities began to tighten passage, eventually building an imposing concrete wall along the border.

By evening, Lina was in Raqqa. She spent a night in a women's hostel, a bewildering place vibrating with strange energy. She met Jafer for the first time when he came for her the next day. He seemed to her a fine man, true to the personality and voice she had grown fond of over the phone. Had she not been in such strange and alarming new circumstances, she would have liked to have more time to spend with him first. But in her fright at staying alone in this new place, she immediately said yes, she was prepared to marry him. They were husband and wife by that evening.

SHARMEENA, KADIZA, AMIRA, AND SHAMIMA

December 2014, East London

SHARMEENA'S FATHER WAS SURPRISED SHE HAD NOT YET RETURNED home. The rain spattered against the windows and he imagined her without an umbrella, perhaps slipping into the mosque on the way. Finally, as he was preparing to leave for work at the restaurant, he rang her mobile. It went straight to a message in a foreign language. He called the police. A few hours later, they told him the language was Turkish and that it was likely Sharmeena had traveled to Syria to join the Islamic State.

Later, scanning her mobile phone bill, he could see that she had spent several days in Turkey before crossing into Syria—days during which the police were aware of her intention. He would wonder why the British police had not coordinated with Turkish authorities to stop his teenage daughter from crossing the border.

Two days later, the girls came to visit him. Kadiza, Amira, and Shamima sat in a row on the sofa, their innocent eyes staring at the fleur-de-lis pattern on the brown carpet, seemingly bereft at the peculiar vanishing of their best friend. Sharmeena's father quizzed them: "Come on, you guys were so close." But they swore up and down they knew nothing. "Really, Uncle, we had no idea. She was always on her phone. We kept asking her what was going on, but she said she'd tell us later."

Two weeks later, Sharmeena called her father. "I'm happy here. I went by my own decision. Don't worry about me, I'll be okay," she said.

He asked where she was, insisted that he would come and get her, no matter what. "No, you can't come here, Baba," she said, tearful. Her broken voice made him cry too.

At Bethnal Green Academy, administrators called the girls—Kadiza, Amira, and Shamima, along with four others—into the office to meet with counterterrorism police. They were asked to answer questions about their best friend's disappearance, and to give evidence, without their parents present. Were they criminals? Would they be put in prison? The girls, threatened and nervous, focused on speeding up their own departure and ensuring that no one got scared and ducked out of the plan. The police handed them letters to give to their parents. The girls, of course, pocketed them.

Less than two weeks after Sharmeena left, Amira, the popular Ethiopian girl, tweeted, "If you are three [in number], then let not two engage in private conversation excluding the third." The girls grew sloppy with their homework—until then always reliably completed—but their teachers didn't notice. Because the school had only called the girls' parents to say that Sharmeena had "gone missing," leaving out the crucial "to join ISIS" bit, their families had no reason to suddenly grow watchful—to check whether their daughters were doing their homework, or to start monitoring their social media. Kadiza's sister would often ask her if she'd had news of Sharmeena, but each time she repeated, oddly, "Well, I don't know, I don't know."

Amira's persona on social media, posted under UmmUthmanBritaniya and until then mostly concerned with fashion, soccer, and school, pivoted to talk of politics and religion. She and Kadiza, her bookish friend who excelled at school, shared images of injured Muslim children in Syria, and also Myanmar, where the plight of Rohingya Muslims—which the world would finally notice in 2017—was already a focus of online Muslim activism. Amira was transfixed by the extreme violence that accompanied Syria's civil war, a conflict that had raged without any outside intervention to protect civilians. She posted a quotation of a young Syrian boy's last words before death, with the caption "This always gets to me. ♥" and an image of a Syrian toddler with a bowl haircut and eyes full of tears, eating dried bread. Throughout the Syrian war, both the regime and armed groups used and invoked violence against women and honor codes as a way of galvanizing support. Amira, listening to the rhetoric of one side, believed the jihadists were fighting valiantly to defend and protect the honor of women: "Hearing these stories of sisters being raped makes me so close to being allergic to men, Wallah," she wrote that winter of 2014.

Amira also grew more attuned to the vulnerability of Muslims living in the West and the Islamophobic hate crimes they endured. She tweeted and shared posts about a spate of events that occurred in one four-month period, stretching from November 2014 to February 2015: three Muslim students were murdered in Chapel Hill, North Carolina; shots were fired at a Montreal Muslim school; a Houston mosque was set ablaze by arson; a hijabi woman was thrown in the path of an underground train; online anti-Muslim vitriol was stoked by the film *American Sniper*, which celebrated a soldier who killed many civilians in the Iraq War. Amira's tweets reflected genuine distress and bewilderment at popular culture, which seemed to construct a world in which Muslims were the perpetual aggressors, never the victims of violence.

The women who had already traveled to the caliphate echoed this in their online discussions. "The killings of innocent muslims is not just collateral damage tolerated by leaders of the west, but also directed by them," tweeted a woman called UmmYaqiin. These messages sometimes segued into droll encouragement: "Hijra ✔ Just do it," and contemporary images that embraced extreme modesty and yet also craved the public performance of social media, like a photo of two *muhajirat* posing before a Syrian field, with face veils that didn't even include eye slits: "My sister and I ❤."

Amira's nascent understanding of how local Islamophobia as a form of anti-Muslim racism connected with global politics was intertwined with a new, assertive embrace of Muslim identity. Anyone seeking to understand whether the politics drove her religion or whether religion drove her politics would immediately discover how unanswerable that was, because it was all of one piece; the language Amira used to express her political dismay was inflected with religious indignation. She tweeted, for instance, about the case of Omar Khadr, a Canadian child who was taken to Afghanistan by his al-Qaeda father and thrown into battle alongside the Taliban. The U.S. military detained him in 2002, but rather than treating him as a child soldier, they interned him in Guantánamo for a decade under alleged torture. "Sub Han Allah, the ummah is supposed to be one body. . . ."

Amira shared Quranic sayings that betrayed a pricked conscience; whoever had switched the light on in her head about injustice was also telling her that Islam required her to do something about it. "Knowledge without action is arrogance," she quoted the Imam al-Shafi'i as saying; "the truth requires change," she wrote herself, later quoting the Quran: "What is the matter with you? Why do you not help one another?" She began talking frequently about the *kuffar,* or unbelievers, as a way of assigning blame. Sometimes the violence and war and conflict all seemed to stress her out, and this she processed, or was taught to process, spiritually: "Those who are sincere are always in a state of worry."

Threaded through all this nervous, intense religious-political banter was a *Thousand and One Nights* fantasy of what the East might hold in store for a good, pious Muslim girl whose heart beat against injustice. There were memes of an AK-47 twinned with a crimson rose, a bullet-riddled building in the background, with ornate script like a wedding invitation: *In the land of Jihad, I met you O my dear Mujahid.*

The fate of these marriages, though, was apparent from the tweets of British teenagers who had migrated earlier in the year: these young women were already widows. One girl from Manchester tweeted proudly about the death of her fighter-husband: "He was a blessing from Allah swt ♥ please make dua Allah accepts him and I will join him very sooooooon." But life in the caliphate didn't simply clang to an end once one's husband became a green bird, the symbol of the martyr in Islamic eschatology. The Islamic State cared for its widows, and there was always the sisterhood to fall back on, in the absence of family. "My dear sisters come and join the caravan Bi'ithnillah, . . . see the blessing that I see in bilaad ash sham!!! 😍♥."

Amira posted images of camels trudging through a glowing vermilion sandstorm and Moorish palaces set against the moonlight. She became a chronicler of brooding sunsets ("Can't stop taking pictures of the sky 🌙") and assumed the breathless tone of a Victorian woman trying to express her desires chastely; she tweeted a picture of baby clothes, an abaya-clad woman clutching a bouquet of roses ("These are so nice I want some 😊💐"), handsome lion after handsome lion, and her disappointed realization that "honeymoons are haram, what 😞."

She started peppering her English with Arabic expressions and posted photos that showed her friends in London wearing black flowing robes. "Our abaya game is strong 😊🌀," she wrote. Amira wondered whether "nose piercings are Haram," said she was "Connnnfuuuusseeedddd," and finally crossed the aesthetic line after which, for any brown girl with dark hair, there was no turning back: "The Prophet (PBUH) cursed those who pluck their eyebrows." Amira, Kadiza, and Shamima were regularly spending time at the East London Mosque; the turquoise carpet of the women's prayer room often figured in the backdrop of their photos.

Any counterterrorism investigator reading Amira's Twitter account in December 2014 would have immediately realized what was going on: a series of interests, inferences, and views that, taken in combination, reflected a teenager being cultivated by savvy recruiters with one foot out the door to Syria. Each post and tweet and image was a snapshot of her state of mind: *I am getting political and pious and confused between the two; I am suddenly preoccupied with death and the afterlife; my interpretation of my religion is disturbingly narrow; I am looking to learn Arabic; I am admiring jihadi scholars whose work I cannot hope to understand; I am in love with the idea of a handsome jihadi husband; I am in love with the idea of being in love.* Anyone reading her Twitter account would have also been reminded that she was still a British child: "Vans: yes or no?" "Chelsea forever Chocolate waffles, revision is killing me, this is Westfield [mall] right now," "Picking your A levels is the hardest thing ever 😊," "my new socks are so nice I want to cry," a photo of a tower of highlighter pens that she and Kadiza built together while studying. Anyone reading her Twitter account would have seen her announce, in late January 2015, her imminent departure: a selfie of her feet in black Converses, wearing flowing black robes, with the caption "Waiting . . ."

In a page torn from a calendar, the girls scrawled a list of items to buy before leaving: bras, a cellphone, an epilator, makeup, warm clothes. They listed the prices of these items. In the week before they left, their social media chatter reflected glaring signs of growing unease. "I feel like I don't belong in this era," Amira wrote on Twitter. Three days later, she posted a photo of the three girls, swathed in black abayas, their backs to the camera, with the caption "Sisters," and in all caps, "PRAY ALLAH GRANTS ME THE HIGHEST RANKS IN JANNAH, MAKES ME SINCERE IN MY WORSHIP AND KEEPS ME STEADFAST." Two days before departure, Shamima messaged Umm Layth on Twitter. The final night, Kadiza insisted her niece, just a few years younger than she, come over for a sleepover. They danced around in their pajamas and cuddled on the couch. On the eve of their departure, Kadiza, Amira, and Shamima were still very much teenage girls.

The next day, February 17, 2015, they told their respective families they were going to the library. Instead they traveled to Gatwick Airport and boarded a Turkish Airlines flight bound for Istanbul.

IN THE PUBLIC IMAGINATION, THE girls died for the first time in the blurry CCTV images captured at Gatwick Airport. The photo that later blazed across the media was actually a montage of three images, making it appear as though the girls had stepped through the airport's security detectors at once, a synchronized gliding into the twilight world that awaited them. Their appearance was haunting: Kadiza in skinny jeans and a preppy white-collared shirt paired with a gray sweater; Shamima in the middle with a jaunty leopard-print scarf; Amira, at the right, in a canary-yellow top, black pants, and white trainers. They looked like young students off on a cosmopolitan adventure, perhaps their first Eurostar to Paris. For the next four years, no images of them were seen in public. They were as good as dead, even if they were not.

● ● ●

ISTANBUL'S BAYRAMPASA BUS STATION, THE girls learned that evening as they struggled to direct their taxi driver, was called *Otogar* in Turkish. It was a teeming plaza of departing buses, each gate with its own small waiting room, not numbered or ordered in any manner, organized by men bellowing out cities ("Ankara, fifteen minutes!"), overrun by families transporting banana boxes of produce and bags of crinkly brick-red peppers.

It was early evening on February 17 when they arrived, but their bus down to the Syrian border would not leave until the following afternoon, so the girls settled in for what would be their final stretch of time in the Land of Disbelief, as they had come to think of it. They were exhausted, buzzing from adrenaline, and sat for a time in the central arcade, lined with doner kebab stands and clothing shops. They took turns watching each other's bags—they each had a backpack and a duffel—while they walked around, peering into cafés where travelers drank slim-waisted cups of dark tea.

It was chilly outside, with a stinging wind coming off the Bosporus; the pavement was lined with heaps of dirty snow. A yellow dog slept in the corner of the station. Tired children with red cheeks leaned against giant sacks of rice. Everything looked old and faded: the blue mirrored glass that plated the terminal, the peeling paint on the stairwells leading down into the metro, the rickety white plastic chairs. Traveling by bus was cheap in Turkey. Groups of thin young men strolled past, hair slicked back, arm in arm, and occasionally students carrying guitar cases. The buses traveling to the south left from the far southeast corner of the terminal, near the mosque. Destinations like Gaziantep, Urfa, and Dohuk were starting to acquire meaning to Kadiza, Amira, and Shamima. It was a place where people transported all kinds of goods, where you would see many different methods of carrying a rolled-up carpet: hoisted over a shoulder, carried by two people like a log, propped on a wheelbarrow. The girls slumped against a mural of the Anatolian coast and waited to board their bus, eager to be enclosed for hours and sleep.

Eight hours later, after the bus ride, they filed out into another snowy landscape, looking for the man who was supposed to greet them. "John" spoke good English and hurried them into a waiting car. They didn't notice he was filming them on his phone. Turkish authorities later arrested "John" and said he was a Syrian asset working for Canadian intelligence, documenting the names and passport photos of the hundreds of Westerners he shepherded across the border.

As soon as he got behind the wheel, he began speeding into the darkness toward the border. The girls looked at each other with excited eyes. Finally, they were close.

SABIRA

IT TOOK SOHEIL A YEAR AND A HALF TO GET MARRIED IN SYRIA. HE WAS not one of those men who had hooked up with a woman online before leaving, nor had he arrived and swiftly asked for a wife. Soheil had gone to fight in defense of the Muslims who were being killed.

Layla, a young American Pakistani girl who had traveled to Syria on her own, had heard about Soheil. She knew that he was English-speaking, of a similar background to her, that he was a brave fighter and an appealing personality. Soheil had fielded similar overtures from women in Syria in the past and ignored them. But earlier in the spring of 2015, he had been shot in the leg during a firefight, and he was taking time to recover. He figured there would be no harm in meeting Layla. They had both come to a place where there was extreme pressure to marry, and had held out. Perhaps they might have something in common.

After communicating for several weeks, he agreed to marry her. All of this unfolded, for his sister Sabira, as intimately as though it were happening on the next block. She and Soheil's wife started speaking on the phone and exchanging messages. "It's completely fine here. Don't believe what you hear in the media," Layla would tell her new sister-in-law.

THE POLICE RAIDS HAPPENED EVERY couple of months. They would bang at the door and come rushing about, taking away anything digital: Sabira's phone, her laptop, her tablet. They would return them a few months later and she would need to get rid of them, because of course they were bugged.

THAT SUMMER, FOR THE FIRST time in her life since the sixth grade, sixteen-year-old Sabira took off the hijab. Soheil had always made her wear it; she'd had no choice in the matter. Now that he was gone, she just didn't feel like wearing it anymore.

And what a difference it made, walking through the Spitalfields Market with her hair out, the long, light brown wave of it down her back. It was like a different life, the way men responded to her, making comments, sometimes harassing her. The attention was distracting and seductive in its own way. Sabira encouraged it, dyeing her hair red, turning the mass of it into fairy-tale locks. What a sense of power it gave her, being able to provoke men's reactions! And how satisfying to realize she could draw as much attention as the pretty white girls and Indian girls at school.

The family was displeased with her unveiled appearance. "We're all going to pray for you," her aunt said gravely one Saturday at lunch, shaking her head. Sabira didn't care. By this point, she was angry with them all: with her mother, for not having stopped Soheil; with her father, who had finally turned up, too late, in an attempt to persuade Soheil to return. It wasn't that Sabira had no hope. As long as he was out there, alive, willing to speak to them, there was hope. But she doubted that Soheil would ever return. She was the one who saw his pictures, heard his voice all pumped up. He was a twenty-three-year-old man who had gotten used to war: the close scrapes and the intensity, the adrenaline and revulsion. Even if he didn't agree with everything the war entailed, he seemed content to just get on with it, aware that all the doors that led back were closed forever. Sabira was closer to him than anyone else, and she knew, knew, that he was only being kind when he humored their dad by saying he would consider coming back. This awareness produced a misery so deep it felt settled into her very tissue; it made her nauseated, unable most of the time to eat anything but toast or half an apple. Her parents, now consumed with getting Soheil back, hardly seemed to notice that their daughter was getting thinner and thinner.

It was around this time that Imran showed up, with his easy jokes and deep voice and broad shoulders, announcing to Sabira that he was Soheil's friend and ready to "be there for her." His eyes were a beautiful rich brown streaked with green. In the span of a few weeks, Imran and Sabira went from being strangers to being incredibly close. He texted her first thing in the morning and last thing at night. He picked her up in the afternoons and took her out. When they were together, he made her laugh. He would take her to the hospital for her blood tests, holding her hand as she was poked with needles, as the doctors struggled to figure out what was wrong with her, why her flesh was melting away. He was careful and tender with her. At cafés, he would buy three types of cake and arrange them across the table. "Which one do you like? Just have one bite of whichever one you like. Just one bite."

The not eating made her light-headed most of the time, and Sabira had some distant awareness that his attention was peculiar and perhaps not quite right (he was married!), but when you were used to love being swirled through with pain, it felt familiar and warm.

And then, one afternoon, Imran announced it was time for them to go. They both knew exactly where he meant, though he always referred to Malta as their destination. Imran said she was lucky he had picked her, because his wife would have quite liked to go. It was one of tens of discrepancies Sabira noted but didn't think too carefully about—because she felt reckless, because she felt like hurting everyone as much as possible.

And Imran had *deen*, she thought, giving him the benefit of the doubt. A brother who had *deen* like that, who was even willing to pray in a public park or on the pavement if he didn't have time to get to the mosque or back home, a brother like that simply wouldn't mess with you, would he? Leaving this country didn't seem like such a bad idea. Everyone in England had hurt her; it was a place that deserved to be left.

IT RAINED INCESSANTLY THE NIGHT before their departure. She couldn't sleep and lay flat on her back, her hand resting on her concave stomach, listening to splattering against the windows and her parents' voices carrying from below. They were shouting at each other, something to do with a relative, a spurious story that had driven some wedge between them. Sabira couldn't bring herself to pay attention.

A police siren wailed in the distance, the second one that night, a sound that in their neighborhood was previously like white noise, but tonight was suddenly startling. In the morning, a ghostly mist hung over the streets. Imran picked her up after her parents had both left the house. "Let's have a final lunch," he suggested, and stopped at a curry shop on the corner. In their relationship she left all decisions to him, both small and monumental.

Imran ate heartily, while she sipped a diet soda daintily through a straw. She thought of her mother and father finding out later, imagined the conversation and the scene in the house, and the angry words her frantic mother would lash her father with. "Both of them gone! You *kuttha*!" These musings gave her a small relief. Perhaps they should have noticed when an older man was showing their teenage daughter suspicious attention; perhaps they should have asked exactly what was going on. If they were so concerned about her uncovered hair, what about her going around with a man who wasn't her immediate relative?

At the airport, she and Imran sailed through the passport gates and the security check. They walked past sushi stands and a Pret, where Imran bought them popcorn. Sabira wandered into a Boots to get an extra lip balm. At the gate, they found seats together and she looked out at the clouds splayed against the moody sky, the airport trucks moving across the tarmac like little toys in a play set. Sabira and Imran were about to get on the plane when they were stopped. Two officers pulled them out of the queue and asked them to come away for questioning.

Her mouth went dry. The flight was departing in under twenty minutes; there was no way they would make it. The police didn't know exactly what to ask; they didn't seem to have much to go on, apart from the fact that they were young British Muslims about to board a plane. For much of 2015 and 2016, security services closely monitored the airport movements of most British Muslims under the age of forty. They stopped thousands of travelers under Schedule 7 of the UK Terrorism Act, which allows police officers broad powers to stop anyone traveling through a port, airport, or international railway station, to question them for up to six hours and detain them for up to nine hours, to confiscate and download their private data from their phone or laptop, without any suspicion of involvement in terrorism.

In some years, authorities stopped as many as eighty thousand people under Schedule 7, the majority of Asian or ethnic minority background, and prosecuted only a tiny fraction. It seemed both a bewilderingly crude and a very fine net. Critics called it a harassment and surveillance tool, one that allowed authorities to intimidate journalists or activists. It caught activists, honeymooners reading books about Syrian art, and young Cambridge University students traveling on genuine holidays, holding them up for hours with questions and calls to parents. And yet, at the same time, the net failed to catch those of high intelligence value, young people known to the police as targets of ISIS recruiting, or young people in regular contact with known ISIS members already in Syria, like the Bethnal Green schoolgirls.

That night, the net had caught Sabira and Imran. The room was spare and smelled vaguely of disinfectant. "Who is this?" one of the officers kept asking Sabira, demanding to know her relationship to Imran, and where they were going together. She invented a story about going to visit a cousin and was relieved when they stopped asking. Imran was being questioned separately and she had no idea whether their stories even aligned. Eventually they were allowed to leave.

"I just want to go home," she said, as they walked through the passageway to the train station at the airport.

Imran's eyes were jumpy. It was like the adrenaline in his body needed them to just keep moving, moving. "Tomorrow afternoon," he said, "be ready for me."

What could she say? She closed her eyes as he pulled out a laptop and started booking new tickets.

Back at home, she told her mother she'd decided not to stay over at a cousin's after all, and slipped upstairs to take a shower. She stepped in before the water had a chance to warm up, forcing herself to be still as the cold spray pricked her skin, unclenching slowly as the temperature shifted. Sabira was unable to sleep. She spent the short hours till dawn thinking about parents, how they had brought children into this world and forced them to endure all manner of hardship, in the name of obedience and duty.

THE FOLLOWING WEEK, THIS TIME at Stansted Airport, they again sailed through passport control and security. They were sitting anonymously at the gate, amid the mostly Lebanese and Turkish passengers waiting to fly to Istanbul, when two officers approached them. This time, the police were more serious. One of the officers was kindly, but the other made Sabira feel humiliated. She thought they might charge her with something, although she had no idea what. They separated her from Imran and asked the same questions over and over again, tripping her up on small inconsistencies. Hours passed. She felt numb with exhaustion. Her story wasn't adding up, and they came at her relentlessly.

Finally, she just wanted it to stop. "I'm not going to lie to you anymore," she said. "I know I have landed myself in so much crap." She told them everything: about her health issues, about how difficult life had become at home, how one of her relatives was behaving abusively toward her and she could barely bring herself to speak about it, about how she had no idea where she was really going, that she just had to get away.

"You silly girl, what were you thinking?" one of the officers barked at her.

No adult had ever spoken to her like that. Her eyes filled with tears. But she asked herself a similar question: *Sabira, what are you doing?*

It was near dawn when the officers drove her home. The M25, the motorway that ringed London to the north, was eerily empty. During the car ride, she felt the confusion and numbness that had webbed her mind for weeks finally clearing away. In its place, she felt just a hot fury. At Imran, whom she had allowed to have some trancelike hold on her. At the police, for taking away her fourth phone in a year. At the world, for having handed down the cruelty and circumstances that led her brother away.

At her family's home in Walthamstow, she unlocked the front door, crept upstairs, and crawled into bed.

PART IV:
Citizens of the Abode of Islam

ASMA, AWS, AND DUA

January 2014, Raqqa, Syria

WITH ISIS NOW FULLY IN COMMAND OF RAQQA, ASMA'S LIVING ROOM was perpetually dark and stifling, the curtains drawn so that no one outside could see the television, and the windows closed to keep the sound in. Television, music, the radio—everything was kept at the lowest volume that was still audible.

By that time, electricity in Raqqa had dwindled down to two, sometimes four, hours a day. Asma had never realized before that winter how virtually everything in life required electricity: drying her hair, watching movies, listening to Lebanese and Iraqi pop music, reading in the evening. Now her life was filled with hours that could not be filled. There was no more going to the salon for a haircut or eyebrow threading. Traversing the city to visit a girlfriend required a chaperone. ISIS decreed that the internet should only be used for work—like the online wooing of new recruits—and not for entertainment. Asma found herself disconnected from the world.

Her thoughts on a typical day before the war came to Raqqa: *Should I do a master's after finishing my degree, or get a job in Damascus working with foreigners so I can improve my English? . . . Is a keratin treatment going to damage my hair? . . . Is Amman so fun that my boyfriend will not want to ever come back? . . . Should I learn Excel or take a second economics course? . . . Will I ever fly business class like in the movies?* Now that the war had come to Raqqa, the tenor of her thoughts had changed: *How can I avoid the attention of ISIS fighters on the street? . . . How few of these black sackcloths can I get away with own-*

*ing? . . . How can I read a book on my phone when I need my phone for
everything else and the generator isn't reliable? . . . How quickly life can
swing to some previously unimaginable extreme!*

As a female civilian in Raqqa, Asma felt as though her life had
been taken off the circuit of the world. Simply powered off. She could
not attend her university, which was closed; she could not earn money,
because public work for women, save a few specialized jobs, was forbidden; she couldn't even go on a walk through the neighborhood and
watch the finches dart from tree to tree. Her mother unhelpfully said
things like "Try to keep yourself busy." Doing what? The days advanced on her, one after the other. The worst time was just before
midday, when the fact of it not even being lunchtime yet made time
itself feel aggressive. All of it was stifling: the faint smell of vinegar
that clung to their kitchen, the mottled skin of her mother's hands as
she wiped the counters too many times, the solitude a strange contrast to the rattling inside her.

A number of relatives in Asma's family had already started working for ISIS in various capacities, and she deliberated carefully before
joining in January 2014. With her family so enmeshed with the militants, the step seemed shorter, less fraught, almost sensible. She belonged to a generation of Syrian women, born in the 1980s and 1990s,
who were leading more independent lives than their mothers and indeed any women before them. They were a generation who studied at
university before getting married, who got married later, who were
more in control of their destinies. Asma had grown up thinking that
as a woman she should be able to get an education, earn money, and
have authority. The collapse of her country's revolution now meant
that she was putting that belief into practice by working for ISIS.

Asma was unique in her new job for also being single. Most of the
other women who formally went to work for the group had already
married.

There were girls like Dua, the girl with the rose tattoo, who lived
with her sister, mother, and father in a spare, two-room house. Her
father was a day laborer and cultivated the land around the house, but
none of it was enough to support the family. Both Dua and her two
brothers knew their future would be to work hard, from as early an

age as possible. Her brothers moved to Lebanon to work in construction when she was in her early teens, and after Dua finished high
school she stayed home, helping with the farming. It was difficult living like a villager in a fairly prosperous city. In Syria, being poor narrowed the world, especially for women. Dua never could have hoped
to attend university, couldn't even have explained, probably, what a
marketing course would entail or set her up for.

She still wanted the things most twenty-year-olds wanted: to look
pretty, to have fun on Fridays, to please God and hope that He would
find her a good husband. She would have liked to have a collection of
stylish headscarves and shoes. For a year, she saved up to get something that would last, that everyone would always see: a rose tattoo on
her creamy wrist. She had eyebrows shaved into thick, straight arrows,
a round sloping frame, and a voice that was soft and poised. Her family was poor, but there was still enjoyment to be taken from life in
Raqqa, and they were not poor, as her mother liked to say, in their
ethics and in their faith. There was enough to do in the city that cost
nothing. Dua was content to be a good daughter, to be slightly in love
with the Iraqi singer Kazem al-Saher, to spend evenings at home
watching Bollywood films, ideally featuring Shah Rukh Khan.

Dua had a first cousin on her mother's side, Aws, to whom she was
close. Aws's mother had—fortunately or unfortunately, depending on
your calculus—married a liberal-minded engineer who provided her
with a more padded and less religious life. Aws didn't wear the hijab like
Dua. She wore tight clothes and studied English literature at al-Hasakah
University. She was a fizzy, slim girl with a gamine face and a mass of
curly dark brown hair, with no time for the swooning, kohl-eyed hero-
ines of Dua's Bollywood movies, who were always peddling their virtue
for love. Aws was into Hollywood, where women shouted at their husbands and romance came with adventure: Leonardo DiCaprio, Ben Af-
fleck, even Tom Cruise—she watched all of their films. She felt a
kinship with Julia Roberts; they both had big smiles and big hair.

Aws enjoyed her English degree, but mostly she wanted to get
married, hang out with her friends, and have babies. Ideally, to lead a
life that involved spending lots of time at the beach and smoking nargileh, her favorite pastime. She had a photographic memory of all the

nargileh cafés in Raqqa, and could tell you which ones had the rare fruit flavors, like kiwi or lychee.

Aws found Dua a bit severe, but she loved her nonetheless. As cousins, their social lives were intertwined. There was enough to do together that didn't strain Dua's tight finances. There was Qalat Jabr, the eleventh-century fort on Lake Assad, for walking, and al-Rasheed Park for taking coffee. There was al-Raqqa Bridge, where you could see the lights of the city twinkling at night, and gardens and amusement parks in the town center. Aws and Dua were woven into each other's memories of childhood, all those summers of waiting until the cooler evenings to go out and roam the city together. Their lives were a portrait of a single extended family that encompassed both liberal and conservative strands, living aside one another with acceptance.

THE DAY ABU MOHAMMAD, A Turkish fighter for ISIS, walked through Aws's front door to ask for her hand in marriage, her father and grandfather greeted him with warmth and respect. The militants had now controlled the city for almost a year and were sweeping across large swaths of both Syria and Iraq. In June 2014, they captured Mosul, Iraq's second-largest city after Baghdad. Until then they had mostly taken smaller towns and more rural areas, but Mosul was a metropolis of two million, and a coup. The people of the Sunni-majority city, resentful of long years of neglect by the Shia-run central government, were left defenseless against the invaders. The Iraqi army melted away. By October, the militants raged through Anbar province, making spectacular gains, and came within fifteen miles of Baghdad. It was only outside intervention that halted the group from taking most of Iraq. From the vantage of Raqqa, the seat from which ISIS ruled and coordinated this breathtakingly fast spread, the militants' occupation appeared entrenched.

As under any occupation, reality was a muddle, the ethics of not collaborating clanging against the instinct to adapt and survive. During wartime, ideals were a luxury. The Nazi officers who occupied Paris during World War II wanted women, and the women—from brothel sex workers to Coco Chanel herself—eventually complied. So too did the ISIS fighters settling into the homes of abandoned Raqqawis want wives. And so they went calling throughout the community of those who had stayed, making their wartime proposals.

Aws's family had told her she could see her suitor at a second meeting if he offered a suitable *mehr,* or dowry. But Aws was too much of a romantic, and had seen too many Leonardo DiCaprio films, to consider meeting a man whose face she had not seen. When she kneeled down to leave thimbles of coffee behind the living room door, she peered in for a moment and caught a glimpse of him. He had winged eyebrows, light eyes, and a deep voice. As she waited for the discussion to conclude, she flicked through her cellphone photo gallery, the sunset images of couples by the beach and babies swaddled in cabbage leaves, imagining what her life with this man might be like. When her father called her in, she felt a flutter of nervousness, but she was prepared to say yes, ready to begin her new life as a wife and, God willing, a mother.

THEY WERE MARRIED WITHOUT FANFARE because it was wartime. Abu Mohammad often didn't come home at night and was sometimes gone for three- or four-day stretches. Aws minded these absences, but she tried to keep busy socializing with the other fighter wives. Among them, she felt lucky. Some were married to fighters who were abusive; everyone had heard of Nahla, who slit her wrists, and there was the Tunisian girl next door who burst into tears every time someone mentioned her husband's name. But Aws's marriage felt real. Abu Mohammad liked to trace the two moles that made a constellation on her left cheek; he teased her about her accent when she tried to pronounce Turkish words. She disliked his absences and would pout upon his return, and he would have to make silly jokes and cajole her into forgiving him.

At home, her days had become a void. Sociable and lively, a young woman who had grown up studying English literature and reading occult adventure novels, Aws chafed at having nothing to do. She finished her housework quickly, but there was nowhere to go and nothing left to read. ISIS had purged the bookshops and local cultural center of "immoral fiction." The group was even casting its long shadow over the most intimate interiors: marriage. ISIS was determining matters that she thought would be for her and Abu Mohammad to decide.

Aws was desperate to have a baby. It was those baby images on her phone that had nudged her to say yes in the first place—the naked dimpled babies with their plump arms and crinkly smiles, arrayed in flowerpots, curled up in pea pods. But he asked her to start taking birth control pills, still readily available in Raqqa's pharmacies; he said his commanders had instructed their men to avoid impregnating their wives. New fathers would be less inclined to volunteer for and carry out suicide missions. At first, Aws couldn't believe he'd be willing to allow his commanders to make such a decision. She would raise the subject lightly, in passing, as well as seriously, gently—she brought it up in every manner she could think of. But her interventions upset him. She could see how he struggled not to get frustrated with her. His patience with the discussions began disintegrating.

It was one of the early, bitter moments when Aws saw that there would be no normalcy; ISIS was like a third partner in her marriage, there in the bedroom. She asked herself whether she would still want children if her husband were to become a martyr, and knew instinctively that she would. She didn't know how she would cope with a child on her own, but the desire inside her was so strong it overcame these thoughts, as reflexively as oil pulled itself above water.

Without any work to do, without a baby to prepare for, without anything to study or read, Aws started looking forward to her daily trip to the market. One day she saw fighters lashing an old man in a public square. It was late afternoon and passersby crowded around to watch. The old man, about seventy, frail, with white hair, had been overheard cursing God. The ISIS fighters had him kneel in the center of the square. Tears streamed from his eyes the whole time they lashed him. It was lucky that he had cursed God, she thought, because God shows mercy. If he'd cursed the Prophet, they would have killed him.

DUA'S FAMILY, LIKE MOST OF Raqqa's poor, survived by cobbling together scraps of income from disparate work. There was the little plot on their land that they farmed, and her father worked in construction as a day laborer. But now most building work had stopped. They relied on what they earned from farming, but so many people had lost their jobs when ISIS took over that suddenly everyone was selling fruits and vegetables to get by. Some professions, like the practice of secular law, were simply dissolved; other jobs, like that of MRI technicians, became irrelevant in a land where hospitals lacked electricity. The militants had started levying taxes, which cut further into many families' already reduced incomes, and they charged the civilian community for electricity or gas at higher rates. Dua's family was scraping by, just barely.

When a Saudi fighter came to ask for her hand in February 2014, Dua's father pushed her to accept. The Saudi, Abu Soheil Jizrawi, came from a wealthy construction family in Riyadh. Saudi Arabia was one of the leading sources of early ISIS recruits, just as many of the fighters who had traveled to join the insurgency in Iraq in the mid-2000s were also young Saudi men. Saudi citizens also largely financed al-Qaeda in Iraq, one of the insurgent groups that eventually evolved into ISIS. The most prominent and influential female ideologue within ISIS, a woman of Syrian origin called Imam al-Bugha, spent fifteen formative years teaching religion in Saudi Arabia before she migrated to join the Islamic State. The year of her migration, she wrote a booklet for ISIS arguing that the group had simply put into practice the theological ideological worldview she had always had, declaring: "I am a Daeshite before Daesh even existed." Al-Bugha's young daughter Ahlam accompanied her to Syria, and married Abu Osama al-Gharib, the Austrian jihadist who moved in the same circles as Dunya, from Germany. Ahlam wrote poetry and was an influencer to millennial ISIS recruits; her accounts had thousands of followers. Both women's formative intellectual years had been shaped in a Saudi environment where classical Salafism and jihadist doctrine blurred; between them, they shaped and inspired thousands of ISIS women and girls.

For the Saudis, raised in an intolerant Wahhabi Salafi environment that viewed Shia Muslims as enemies and unbelievers, pushing back the influence of Shia Iraqis and the influence of Iran in both Syria and Iraq was an existential and ideological fight. Their contentions were different from the earthly grievances of Sunni Iraqis, who largely opposed the Shia central government in Baghdad because it discriminated against them politically and economically. The U.S. occupation of Iraq provided an opening to the ideologues who were looking to harness these chauvinisms to legitimate and widely held grievances. When a Sunni insurgency eventually developed in response, the Americans incarcerated militants in detention centers like Abu Ghraib, the site of storied horrific abuses. Were the Saudis fighting out of hostility to Iran, out of bigoted hatred for the Shia, or in defense of their genuinely marginalized Sunni brothers, or all of these impulses combined? Either way, the wealth of these Saudi men contributed greatly to the uprising in Iraq. Here in Raqqa, that same wealth promised an auspicious match for Dua.

"If she agrees to marry me, I'll transform her life," he promised her father. Dua was no great beauty; she had no university education like her cousin Aws or other middle-class Raqqa girls. She thought about her life as a farmer's daughter and whatever prospects she might have marrying a village boy or a local laborer. The word that flashed through her mind again and again was *weathered*. Her life was weathered. Her hands often ached from tilling the vegetables; her skin was coarsened; her clothes faded from being washed so many times and dried under the sun. Her purse, her shoes, her spirits—all were weathered. She wanted to lean into someone and know she was taken care of. She deliberated, and eventually agreed.

She met Abu Soheil for the first time the day of the wedding, when he arrived bearing gold for her family. She liked what she saw: he was light-skinned with a soft black beard, tall and lanky, with charisma and an easy way of making her laugh. He never said no to anything she asked for, never raised his voice or looked at the wall when she told him about what she had done during the day.

He set her up in a spacious apartment with new European kitchen appliances and air-conditioning units in each room. No one in Raqqa had air conditioning in each room, and she showed off her new apartment to friends and relatives. Her kitchen became the place where the other fighter wife in the building, a Syrian girl married to a Turkish fighter, stopped in for coffee. Each morning, Abu Soheil's manservant would do the shopping in the market and leave bags of meat and produce outside the door. In the evenings, Dua and Abu Soheil would linger over dinner, and he would compliment her cooking, especially the Syrian *kabsa* he loved, a spiced rice dish with meat and eggplant. Dua, with her round moon face and thick eyebrows filled into an arrow, had ended up marrying well. Abu Soheil didn't even mind the rose tattoo on her hand, though permanent tattoos were forbidden in Islam. He had transformed her life completely, and for that, she loved him.

Abu Soheil didn't want children, but Dua, the pragmatic farmer's daughter, did not mind. She knew how hard life could be. She was enjoying the respite.

IN THE SPRING OF 2014, two months after her marriage, having failed to persuade Abu Mohammad to let her get pregnant, Aws joined the al-Khansaa Brigade. Because ISIS maintained a strict separation of genders in its territory (it upheld the view that women should not have contact with any men but their immediate relatives), it used a special all-women branch of the police to provide security, and enforce dress codes and controls on women's movement. Many residents called it simply the *hisbah,* or morality police. Al-Khansaa reflected, in various institutional forms, the growing and widening place of women in administrative, educational, health, recruitment, and propaganda wings of the Islamic State. The al-Khansaa Media Unit, which merged with another media arm in 2015, produced and disseminated its own bespoke campaigns and messages that catered directly to women. Its major tract, "Women in the Islamic State: A Message and a Report," reviews the degraded status of women under secular feminism and Western culture ("Women did not reap anything from the myth of 'equality with men' except thorns") and then outlines women's rights, potential, and duties under the caliphate. It centers women at the very heart of the jihadist movement—"Know that the Ummah of Muhammad (PBUH) will not rise without your helping hands"—and raises the possibility of women in combat, in cases of extreme military need or even simply a woman's desire for martyrdom.

Dua joined al-Khansaa around the same time, and the two cousins started their compulsory military and religious training together. For both Dua and Aws, already married to fighters, working with the brigade filled time and created a parallel with their husbands' lives in the group, a semblance of normalcy. Instead of thinking about what to cook that evening straight after breakfast, now they could spend much of the day outside, and still return home in time to prepare dinner.

The outside world might have branded them terrorists, or terrorist wives, but Aws and Dua felt themselves to be military wives. They heard justifications each night for the bloodshed: the fighters had to be more brutal when taking a town; this would minimize casualties later. Assad's regime forces were targeting civilians, sweeping into people's homes in the middle of the night, assaulting men before their wives, raping women in detention centers. ISIS had no choice but to respond in kind; it was the regime's violence begetting their own. They heard these things from the mouths of the men they had cooked for, waited up for, would go to bed with. How much of it they believed is something they could hardly say themselves.

Dua, Aws, and Asma all attended the compulsory military and religious training for new recruits. Roughly fifty women took the fifteen-day course that taught them how to load, clean, and fire pistols, and practiced on targets in fields. It was more an introduction to the simple handgun than preparation for the front, even though there were rumors that some of the foreign women who had traveled to join ISIS were getting trained on *russis,* Kalashnikovs.

Dua liked the religion classes best. They were taught mainly by Moroccans, Algerians, and Saudi women, and focused on religious laws and principles of Islam. She'd never had the chance to learn about her religion properly before. And her teachers were extraordinarily learned; many, but especially the Saudi women, had doctorates and years of advanced learning in jurisprudence and religious sciences. Because these veteran ideologues moved between the caliphate's religious and media departments, they deployed their religious learning, digital skills, and capacity for persuasion all at once. Dua was dazzled by them. She appreciated that someone was bothering to teach her, that she was deemed worthy of education. She found her-self attracted to the idea of a real Islamic state.

DUA HAD ONLY BEEN WORKING for the al-Khansaa Brigade for a couple of months on the day her friends were brought to the station to be whipped. When she heard the voices she knew from childhood speaking heatedly near the entrance of the station, she stood up from her desk.

Her colleagues escorted the women in, a mother and her teenage daughter, both distraught and speaking volubly. They had been picked up for wearing overly tight abayas. When the mother saw Dua, she rushed over and asked her to intercede. The room felt stuffy as Dua weighed what to do. Their abayas really were very tight. It upset her that they hadn't been more careful, and were now expecting her to bail them out. "You've come out wearing the wrong thing," she said quietly.

The woman looked stunned. Dua watched as her colleagues took the women into a back room for their lashings, which were usually administered with a whiplike instrument by one of the more senior figures in the brigade. The intensity of the lashing, whether the woman was lashed through clothing or asked to bare her skin, depended on the whim of the person in charge. Some were vicious and foul-mouthed, screaming reproaches about shame and relishing the spectacle; others were milder, since they knew that being lashed, even without great force, was traumatic. When the mother and daughter took off their niqabs, they were found to be also wearing makeup. It was twenty lashings for the abaya offense, an extra five for the makeup, and another five for not being meek enough when detained. Dua tried not to listen when she heard their cries. They weren't very intense lashings, she told herself. It was more humiliation than actual pain.

In the weeks since she had joined al-Khansaa, the brigade had grown more stern in its policing. Mandatory abayas and niqabs were still new for the women of Raqqa, and the brigade, at first, had wanted to give the community a chance to adapt. The patrols would pick up women for wearing abayas that were too short, transparent, or tight, and take them back to headquarters. But the fines were small, less than five Syrian lira. The offending abaya would be burned and a more appropriate one donated in its place. The women of Raqqa found the consequence so light that they openly flouted the rules. Many young women were becoming repeat offenders, calling their fathers to the station to pay and get them released. This state of affairs was making the rules ridiculous. So the brigade decided to increase the fines and started punishing women with lashings, twenty to forty, depending on the severity of the infraction and whether the woman resisted.

That night, the mother and daughter came to Dua's parents' house. The two families had known each other for years, with a shared history of Eid gatherings and children's birthday parties. The woman was furious. She railed against ISIS. "Everyone hates them, we wish they had never come to Raqqa," she said reproachfully.

Dua explained she worked for them, she had to follow orders. "I can't play favorites, can't you understand?"

The woman could not. She left without even looking at her, and their families never saw one another again.

BY MARCH 2014, AWS AND Dua were out every day working the brigade's street patrols, driving around the city in small gray Kia vans with AL-KHANSAA stenciled on the sides. There were women from across the world on their unit—British, Tunisian, Saudi, and French girls—but ISIS had issued a strict rule to its Syrian recruits: no talking to foreigners. Aws would have liked to speak to the foreign women, but tensions were already high between Arab and European fighters; each suspected the other of allocating cars, salaries, and housing by nationality, favoring their own countrymen. Less communication, the thinking went, might bring more harmony to the occupied city, at least among the occupiers.

Status within Raqqa—how it was derived, and how it was enacted—was slowly becoming a grievance among women as well. In the female hierarchy, Dua enjoyed more status than most, to her gentle satisfaction. Her Saudi husband was not only senior in ISIS security, but also independently wealthy. But she, Aws, and other Syrian women began noticing that the foreign women, especially the Europeans, had more privileges. They appeared to have more freedom of movement, more disposable income, and small perks: jumping to the front of the bread line, not having to pay at the hospital. Their manner in the market, in shops, was often brash and high-handed.

"Why do they get to do whatever they want?" Aws complained. They really were completely spoiled. It was appalling to her that a European teenager should have more power than she, an educated and formerly middle-class woman of Raqqa, in her own hometown. But Dua, the good military wife, always reluctant to criticize the militants, offered a justification: "Maybe because they had to leave their countries to come here, it was felt they should be treated more specially."

AS MIDNIGHT DREW NEAR, ASMA dressed for the night's work, pulling on her black abaya and the niqab that covered her eyes. Her role in al-Khansaa involved meeting foreign women at the border and accompanying them into Raqqa. With her smattering of English and cosmopolitan air, she was suited to this task. She would receive a slip of paper with names and, along with the driver and sometimes a translator, would start up the highway toward the border crossing. The road to the border was smooth and clear, and she leaned her forehead against the car window, imagining the olive trees and pines hidden in the darkness. At the border crossing, she drew a shawl around her shoulders and waited, clutching the slip of paper in her hand.

The girls she was meeting that night came from London, a city Asma associated with Agatha Christie and good-looking English soccer players. When the girls emerged from a white car, their bags lugged by a Syrian man who hurried them along, Asma was startled by their youth. Most of the women she met and escorted back to Raqqa were young, but these three looked like children, barely sixteen. "Tiny," she said later, to her mother. "They were just tiny." They were wearing Western clothes and their eyes were twitchy bright with fatigue and fear and excitement. Once inside the car, speeding toward Raqqa in the darkness, the girls talked quietly and laughed.

At this moment, they were still deferential and polite, but Asma suspected that within a month they would behave like the rest of the Western women who arrived in Islamic State territory—brassy and bold, believing themselves superior to local women like Asma. One girl's headscarf slipped back, and the driver snapped at her in coarse Arabic to fix it. The girl perhaps did not understand his words, but his meaning was clear. She pulled her headscarf up obligingly, her smile steady.

How happy she is to obey, Asma thought, *and how naïve. Where does this conviction come from? Where do they think they have come to, these London girls?* She couldn't understand everything they were saying, they spoke so quickly, but she picked up snatches. They were anticipating introductions to husbands and acquiring their own long black abayas. They thought they had arrived at the gates of Dar al-Islam, the land ruled by the Prophet's law, where they would finally belong.

She looked at the girls in the shadows of the backseat, as they drove past grain silos whose towering outlines were visible in the dark. How little they knew what awaited them. They would soon find out that the caliphate ruled by Abu Bakr al-Baghdadi troubled itself little with the Prophet's law. That his men used the ancient punishments meant to instill an otherworldly fear—the chopping off of hands, of heads—as bloody, nihilistic gang rituals. The girls seemed to imagine they were en route to some *Romeo and Juliet* scenario in the desert. How could they not know? Asma wondered what or who had bewitched these girls, that they would travel all the way across Europe and cross this desolate stretch of border in the dead of the night, in order to voluntarily become citizens of the place that, every day, made Asma question the existence of God himself.

She accompanied them to a private home and helped them get settled, providing the loose black abayas and niqabs the command kept in stock for new arrivals. Eventually, once they had been observed, they would go to a guest house for women in Raqqa. As with most of the foreigners she escorted, she did not see them again. It was only later she saw their faces plastered across the internet, identified as Amira, Kadiza, and Shamima—the three schoolgirls from Bethnal Green, in East London.

That night, at home in her bed, she powered up her phone and saw a message from her boyfriend, now in Amman. He teasingly asked her whether she had budged yet on wearing hijab. She didn't even respond. She hadn't told him she was working for the brigade, that she had become a collaborator. The lie, or the absence of truth, made their exchanges feel inauthentic and brittle to her. She felt intense spurts of anger at him that she couldn't even voice. Anger for being safe in Amman, for not being able to protect her, even if just from herself. She fell asleep listening to Evanescence on her phone, mourning how disappointing men were, to judge a woman's faith in inches of skin covered.

ONE MILD SPRING DAY, THE women in Dua's brigade went to one of the city's main squares to watch two local women get stoned for alleged adultery. Dua stayed back, uneasy. The religion classes in her training course had dealt substantially with jurisprudence, and she had learned about the evidence required to apply this punishment: four eye-witnesses to the adulterous encounter, *four* eyewitnesses to the act itself. Evidence that was in the overwhelming majority of cases unattainable, impossible.

Her instructor had explained the intention of these old *hadd* punishments, reflecting the Islamic approach to jurisprudence: the horrific penalty for such acts was meant to underscore their reprehensibility and prevent them from ever being normalized as "just human"; at the same time, the evidence demanded was so outlandish as to make the punishment virtually inapplicable. In this way, she learned, Islamic law regulated the public sphere: if a couple committed adultery, they knew to keep their own betrayal private, so as to avoid gradually tearing away at the sanctity of marriage for others. It was inconceivable to her that a judge would have been able to meet the evidential standards required to correctly implement the punishment for adultery. She hated how the group prized slickness and spectacle over proper justice. It was in this strange way that the Islamic State instilled in Dua the awareness with which to repudiate it.

Within hours, word spread that one of the women had not been involved with a man at all. Instead, she had showed up outside the main police headquarters holding up a sign that read *Yasqot al-Tanzeem* ("Down with the Organization"). Could it be true? It almost didn't matter; everyone believed her to be innocent one way or another. By the time the trees were blossoming that spring of 2014 it had become commonplace to see heads hanging in the square, near the clock tower. Bodies sometimes lay in the street for a whole week. The militants, Dua thought, were growing openly sacrilegious. Islam forbade the mutilation of bodies.

The brigade itself was deteriorating. At first its remit extended only to holding up dress codes, the rules around abayas and niqabs and makeup. The brigade's role was to sow distrust and resentment, minimizing the likelihood that people's dissent would coalesce into defiance. But now, the young women of the al-Khansaa Brigade had started using their authority to settle petty quarrels or enact social revenge. Even girls who weren't employed by the brigade turned up to accuse their social enemies of some infraction. Sometimes women who had done nothing wrong were brought into headquarters.

The social fabric of Raqqa had collapsed. That everyone was probably two-faced was the only reliable assumption. "Many times, I saw women I knew smiling at me when they saw I'd joined. But I knew inside they felt differently," Aws said. "I knew because before I joined myself, when I saw a girl I knew had started working with ISIS, I didn't like it."

ONE ESPECIALLY WARM WEEK IN July 2014, around the time when the terebinth trees could be cut for their sap, Abu Soheil did not return for three nights. Dua grew restless, and on the fourth day, a knock came at the door.

It was a fighter, there to tell her that Abu Soheil was now a martyr; he had blown himself up in an operation in the battle for Tal Abyad, fighting the Syrian army. The fighter didn't even come inside to tell her the news; the car he'd arrived in was idling just outside, with another militant inside it, waiting. Dua was devastated. The tears came fast. "He asked for the mission himself," the fighter said, awkwardly turning away. Abu Soheil had never told her about such a plan, and this made her break down and shut the door.

She was too loyal to feel he had betrayed her, and she considered him a *shaheed,* a martyr. But days later, she learned something that made her honorable widowhood harder to bear. Abu Soheil hadn't killed himself in an operation against the Syrian army, as the fighter had told her, but against opposing rebel forces, the Free Syrian Army. Many armed factions viewed the FSA as traitors and unbelievers for receiving support from the United States, and believed they were permissible targets. But for Dua, this news was the greatest part of her grief. She called her sister-in-law in Riyadh and they cried on the phone together. Abu Soheil had not died fighting the Assad regime, but other Muslims. She struggled to sleep for many nights, in a stupor of shock and sadness.

Ten days later, another man from her husband's unit came to the house. He told Dua she could not stay at home alone and would need to marry again, immediately. Islamic law, under all universal interpretations, holds that a woman must wait four months before remarriage, after widowhood or divorce. This is mainly to establish the paternity of any child that might have been conceived, and the period, called *idaa,* is not only required of every Muslim woman, but is also her right, to allow her to grieve. But even here, in the realm of divine law, ISIS was disregarding the tenets of Islam. Dua was wearing her face veil and her tears made the fabric cling to her cheeks. "Can't you see I can't even stop crying? I'm very sad. I want to wait the whole of the four months."

The commander seemed impatient to get away, and spoke tersely, as though she were a child who couldn't understand simple things. "You're different than a normal widow," he explained. "You shouldn't be mourning and sad. He asked for martyrdom himself. That makes you the wife of a martyr! You should be happy."

She said nothing in the moment. She nodded her head, as though assenting, and rose for him to leave. Dua felt a sliver of loyalty to the Islamic State as an extension of the loyalty she felt to Abu Soheil, who had been an upstanding husband to her, even if only for a few short months. She felt changed by her relationship with him and the world he had brought her into; she had enjoyed the feeling that she was worth educating. But she saw that ISIS was claiming the mantle of Islam as a means to justify its own ends; the same way it was willing to stone a woman without any evidence, it was willing to dispatch her into another marriage before it was time.

She knew at that moment that she was done. She knew it instinctively and also spiritually: she could not remain in Raqqa to become a permanent temporary wife, passed from fighter to fighter. She walked from room to room of the beautifully decorated house that should have been her inheritance, committing the curves and whorls of the wood furniture to memory. It felt like the simplest thing to mourn, this air-conditioned house that had surrounded her in brief, plush comfort. The loss of Abu Soheil, her neighborhood, the city, the whole country to a never-ending war of mercenaries and madmen—that was too much to carry.

THE NEWS CAME FOR AWS not long after it did for Dua. Abu Mohammad had also killed himself in what Aws, like Dua, considered a martyrdom operation.

To be an ISIS widow was to experience loss so anonymously that Aws sometimes dug her nails into her palm to remind herself that she was alive, capable of feeling pain, that Abu Mohammad had been real. There was no funeral to attend, no in-laws to spend long hours grieving with; there was no wardrobe full of clothes to go through or mementos to organize, no dinners to plan for visiting family, no chance to fill those stunned first hours with cooking and mindless chatter. There was just a sudden blaring emptiness. Aws curled up in the same leggings day after day, alone with her thoughts: Had he been brave at the end, or terrified at the impending explosion that would rip all his flesh and organs to shreds? Had he thought of her in the final seconds?

Soon, the commanders came knocking at her door as well. The one who spoke was stocky, with a slight limp; he gestured for her to pass through the doorway into the living room first, a strange gallantry, she thought. "Abu Mohammad is now a *shaheed,* thanks be to God, so he obviously doesn't need a wife anymore," he began.

It was such bizarre phrasing she had to fight back a bark of laughter. Abu Mohammad, due to being a martyr, also didn't need pajamas and a cup of tea anymore. And a wife. The commander continued: "There's another fighter who *does* need a wife. He knew Abu Mohammad well, he was his friend, there with him when he died. He wants to protect you and take care of you, on his friend's behalf."

Aws was one month short of her widow's mourning period. She wasn't sure how she could take on a new partner, sit with him in the evenings, be intimate with him, feign concern for his well-being. But she agreed reluctantly. She thought she would be safer with a man around, and perhaps this other husband would be decent as well; perhaps he might want a family.

He was Egyptian, and unpleasant from the beginning. She hadn't anticipated she would so dislike his chalky smell, his indifferent attitude to her. Unlike Abu Mohammad, he didn't notice or observe anything about her; not her Levantine pronunciation or her cooking or her morning curls. Nothing between them clicked. Thankfully, he turned up at home even less than her first husband had.

When Dua asked her cousin about him, she shrugged off everything about him—his looks, his manners, his personality—with a sour expression and a single word, *aadi,* "regular." He didn't even brush his teeth. She discovered this when it became clear that he simply had no toothbrush. Was it because he anticipated imminent death, and so what was the point? Was he just slovenly? When he fled back to Egypt with his salary two months later, without even a goodbye, at least she could conclude it was the latter.

Back at her parents' house, Aws touched her old photos and books, thinking about the life she had had before, the evenings lingering over nargileh, the days at the beach, and how it all seemed light-years away from where she found herself now.

Late Summer 2014, The Caliphate Ascendant

ISIS releases a video called "Message to America" that shows the beheading of American journalist James Foley. At its end, it warns that the group will kill another captive, the American journalist Steven Sotloff, if Obama doesn't halt American air strikes.

At its height in 2014, ISIS controls a stretch of thirty-four thousand square miles across Syria and Iraq, a territory roughly the size of the United Kingdom, reaching from the areas east of Damascus all the way to the western suburbs of Baghdad.

In September, the militants behead Sotloff and British aid worker David Haines.

In October, they behead aid worker Alan Henning and raise the black flags over parts of the city of Kobanî in Syria, a city that sits directly on the border with Turkey.

EMMA/DUNYA

Spring 2014, Raqqa, Syria

DUNYA KEPT HER EYES CLOSED IN THE EARLY-MORNING HEAT, REFUS-ing to be roused by the child screeching from the neighboring bedroom. She and Selim had parted the night before, when he dropped her off at the guest house where arriving women stayed, awaiting husbands who, like Selim, were off doing their military training. The official ISIS employment/identity form listed his religious knowledge as "rudimentary," so after his weapons training he would do a course of religious instruction. He was not allowed to use a mobile phone during this period, so for nearly two months Dunya neither spoke to nor saw her husband.

The guest house was something between a hostel and a reality TV show, the days bleeding into one another in a tedium of sameness: cooking, eating, repeating the same inconsequential but sometimes tense conversations. There was no television. There were no books to read. There was nowhere to hide from the ever-present children, who shrieked from boredom and shrieked while playing and generally just shrieked. It was, however, international, and this was something Dunya appreciated. There were women from everywhere coming through: Afghanistan, Saudi Arabia, Tunisia, France, the United States. Most were very young.

The people who migrated from Germany she divided into various groups. The do-gooders, who wanted to fight Bashar al-Assad and then were eventually indoctrinated, inured to the violence. The convert freshies, who didn't know a thing about Islam and watched the wrong videos and met the wrong people, and were convinced that the path to heaven led through Syria. The psychopaths, attracted to violence. And the submissive women who followed their husbands, who for whatever reason—codependent personalities, misplaced loyalty, fear of divorce—went along with the plan.

Dunya viewed many of the girls as inexperienced boy-band groupies, having understood ISIS as some kind of trendy rebellion. They watched ISIS videos on their phones and laptops, droning on about the delight of finally living under a caliphate. They huddled together on WhatsApp groups and Facebook groups. Dunya viewed herself as superior to these unsophisticated young women, who seemed only to memorize the words and concepts that had brought them to the Islamic State, without actually understanding what lay behind them. She had actually studied Islam over the months and years since her conversion. She had some *ilm,* or Islamic knowledge, whereas they mostly seemed to have hormones and attitude.

She slept late. The summer heat made everyone in Raqqa nocturnal, staying up later and later to benefit from the evening coolness, and sleeping through as many hours of the searing day as possible. She eventually found some other German women in the city to befriend. Even though the caliphate was intended to erase the ties of nation-state and tribe, most women still preferred the company of those like them. Partly this was a matter of simple communication; exuberant pantomiming and Google Translate could take you only so far. But it was also true that no one shed their prejudices upon arrival in the caliphate. The racist superiority the Saudis felt toward Pakistani or Bangladeshi Britons ("they are not *British* British"), the superiority the British Asians felt toward the British Somalis, the superiority German Turks felt toward the local Syrians, the superiority the Lebanese and Syrians felt toward the Saudis, the superiority the Syrian Arabs felt toward the Syrian Kurds—none of these impulses dissolved. Indeed, they were harnessed into sweeping generalizations about who was most hapless in warfare and thus best assigned to suicide operations (Europeans), who was the most brutal (Tunisians), who was the most zealous (Saudis).

About a month after her arrival, Dunya went shopping in the market in Raqqa and saw the bodies of about a dozen men lying on the street. Not even on the side of the street, or in the middle of one of the central roundabouts, but directly on the sidewalk. The shoppers and pedestrians were forced to step around them. Their limbs were splayed out, and their faces were frozen in some final expression.

FROM RAQQA THEY MOVED CLOSE to Manbij, which in that late autumn of 2014 was the favored destination for Europeans seeking a leisurely, chill-out jihad. The town was quiet, surrounded by ruddy desert plains dotted with pine trees. There was round-the-clock electricity and there was no fighting for miles in any direction. The area was especially popular among British fighters who, depending on who was judging their motivations, were too squeamish to fight or preferred to gauge the caliber of the caliphate before deciding to give it their life.

The Syrians viewed the British fighters as colonizers, and were bewildered by the insertion of these London-accented, brown-skinned Brits into what was, to their mind, their local civil or regional proxy war. The British fighters behaved like conventional overlords. They viewed their mission as legitimate and just. They thought it correct that they should appropriate the homes of Syrians who had fled, and to impose their rule on those who had stayed behind.

Many of the British jihadists were descendants of South Asian Muslims who had lived under British colonial rule in India; their families had been displaced by the violence and instability that followed the 1949 partition. That the British fighters lived in such exalted comfort over the Syrians—their status in 2014 recalled that enjoyed by low-ranking English civil servants dispatched to colonial India in the mid-nineteenth and early twentieth centuries, experiencing for the first time the delight of structural superiority over others—was an unforeseen long-term colonial residue. Perhaps the colonial past endured by their families didn't color their hatred for Britain, didn't spur their escape into this nether region of Syria. But the racism they had contended with, the mocking in school or taunts of "Paki" in the street, fit within the scope of Frantz Fanon's belief that the "indelible wounds" of colonialism—and the racism it engendered for the descendants of the colonized living in Europe—would take years to recover, and often resulted in acts of reactionary violence. The young overseers of Manbij imagined themselves to be there in benevolent solidarity with the local population, but in the eyes of Syrians who had lived there for generations, they were nothing more than colonial interlopers, despite their brown skin and Arabic names.

When ISIS took over the city of Manbij in the spring, they painted the courthouse black and imposed the *jizya* on local Christians. This was a tax that Islamic states had historically imposed on their religious minorities, in exchange for various privileges and protections. Fighters and their families tended to live in apartments and houses on the outskirts of the city. The proximity to the Turkish border, just thirty miles away, meant that foreign goods streamed into local stores. Dunya was pleased that she could buy Raffaello chocolates, Nutella, superior Turkish potato chips, and American cigarettes. The Saudis, nearly always somehow wealthier than everyone else, would often glide up in their gleaming SUVs and clear out these shops. Selim was away for long stretches, sometimes three weeks at a time. At the beginning, he was able to keep a cellphone with him, but as the coalition air strikes began, then became a perpetual buzzing-and-exploding part of the night sky, phones were forbidden.

The very beginning of that first year was special. Everyone agrees on this, even those who later renounced the caliphate for its wanton brutality, its devotion to earthly power and indifference to Islamic procedure and values. At the very beginning, when the men were fresh from military training and the women were freshly arrived, those who migrated to the Land of Islam felt it was the best decision of their lives. The foreign recruits, who were illiterate to local dynamics of the civil war and intoxicated by the compelling, sophisticated videos the ISIS media arm steadily produced, believed that everyone behaved mostly with goodness; the fluttering of the black flags still inspired a heady feeling of righteousness.

In the small village house Selim had secured on the far outskirts of Manbij, Dunya was much happier. Not because the house was physically nicer—some of the spoiled German girls had secured more comfortable flats in the city and said things like "Finally, insulated windows!"—but because it was more peaceful. Each day went the same way: clinging to sleep for as long as possible, cooking, tidying, going to sleep again. The internet connection sustained Dunya, and the indolent lifestyle was not, to her mind, altogether disagreeable. There was a procurement man, a sort of virtual personal assistant, charged with dropping off pillows, duvets, anything that was lacking in the homes that had been occupied. You could send in your request by text message and he would drop off the items that same afternoon, leaving them behind the door. No need to ever speak to or lay eyes on the man. Sometimes checking WhatsApp, to monitor the status of quarrels being waged among the local German ISIS women, seemed the most taxing part of her day.

It was a Kurdish village; the surrounding land was dotted with waterfalls and brick-colored ridges. Its inhabitants had no wish to be ruled by the Islamic State, which had banned the simple pleasures that enlivened their rural existence: smoking water pipes outdoors, playing cards in cafés, listening to music. Dunya felt the locals' animosity every time she bought milk or a kilo of tomatoes. She saw it in how the women turned their heads when she walked past, how the produce seller left it to her to put all her small bags into one big bag, a task he performed for the other women.

In larger cities where ISIS had established a municipal presence, local residents had learned to be fearful and deferential. But in small villages like this one, where the group's administrative presence was light and there were fewer or no public displays of violence, locals were more openly hostile. One day, Dunya visited a doctor in the village to get some migraine pills. The woman examined her brusquely, her face tense with anger. "Where are you from, anyway?" the doctor finally asked her. "Why don't you go back to your own country? You're a young woman from Europe, what are you doing here in Syria? What have you to do with us?"

Dunya's face felt hot. She gathered her things and hurried out, and later considered saying something to Selim. Such talk was very dangerous—didn't the woman know she could get into trouble? The idea that Dunya could mess with the woman's life gave her a satisfying sense of power; deciding not to gave her a satisfying sense of benevolence. Selim was worried about her staying alone for long stretches, surrounded by villagers hostile to ISIS. But Dunya didn't want to move. She enjoyed the solitude and fresh air of the countryside, the farm animals and the groves of olive trees and the scent of the night-blooming jasmine in the garden. It was true that the utter stillness of the evenings, punctuated only by cricket song or a rustle in the fruit trees, made the roar of the warplanes more terrifying. In the city, their sounds were muffled by the cars and city noise. But even this she got used to. She agreed to stop going out on her own and limited herself to a twenty-meter radius around the house.

The cat arrived late one morning, ambling down the dirt lane that ended at their house. Her fur was matted in places, but she moved her head from side to side energetically and licked everything in her path with much curiosity. Dunya leaned down to tickle behind the cat's ears, pleased to be interacting with a creature that didn't shrink from her. The cat followed Dunya toward the house and wandered around the back garden as she searched for scraps in the kitchen.

Dunya and Selim wanted a baby. They had talked about it many times, but agreed that it was not the time and place. They were too new, and the conflict was too uncertain. Many of the wives were pregnant or had small children already, and this filled their time with care-taking. But Dunya did not mind her days requiring little of her. She liked the cat's company and named it Simsim, Arabic for "sesame seed."

There were evenings so romantic that she tried to etch them into her memory: the great expanse of the sky and the smell of the trees and the dirt after the rain. Because the safest place was often in a car, and because both she and Selim had watched enough road trip movies to appreciate the appeal of driving simply for the sake of it, they started going for long evening drives. Dunya loved the little she had seen of Syria and wanted to explore more of it.

"Can't we do something?" she asked plaintively one evening. "Can't we drive into the city and get a burger?" And so that's what they did, stopping to buy fried chicken at a fast-food place in the city. They did this many evenings, alternating the chicken with burgers, all of it excellent, and in those moments, with her handsome husband at her side and the desert stretched out before them, it felt like a glorious adventure. It almost felt like a life.

LINA

FOR ABOUT SIX MONTHS, LINA AND JAFER'S EARLY MARRIED LIFE IN TAL Afar was tolerably safe. The small Iraqi town sat on a dry desert plain near the border with Syria, and before falling to ISIS, it had been mostly populated by Iraqi Turkomen, who spoke a language close to Turkish; it made the area a good match for the couple, as Jafer spoke Turkish. Jafer had left Germany for Syria in 2013, before the emergence of ISIS, and his reasons were the typical ones: indignation at the atrocities being committed, a desire to live among brothers in a more religious milieu, and an eagerness to commit himself to a project that helped his fellow Muslims.

Lina and Jafer were content enough with their new marriage, but the war around them grew more intense by the day, and Tal Afar was witnessing increasingly heavy bombardment from the U.S.-led coalition. The jet planes streaking across the sky each night terrified her. She was pregnant by then, and wanted to cross the border back into Turkey, but Jafer said leaving was far too dangerous. If ISIS were to catch them, it would be certain execution for him. "Don't you want our child to have both parents?" he asked her. And she did. That's what she wanted more than anything.

Jafer did not fight on the front lines, but worked in the ISIS communications center on the outskirts of the city. These sites, which usually gathered intelligence, ran radio broadcasts, and oversaw command and control of the local front, were frequently targeted by air strikes. About eight months after they arrived in Tal Afar, one such air strike ripped through the building where he was stationed. Jafer was pinned under the rubble from the collapsed walls and ceilings, one leg so badly crushed that it had to be amputated at the mid-thigh.

The injury kept him at home for months. Lina found herself once again a caregiver, as if this were the role God had ordained for her: changing bedpans, administering medication. Two months after Jafer was injured, their son Yusef was born. Lina's days revolved around cooking and cleaning, and looking after baby and husband, both dependent on her for everything. Sometimes Jafer's friends from Germany came to the house with their wives, and then Lina would have women to chat with. She had her mobile phone and very occasionally there was internet, but she had been a lonely woman in Germany before she was a lonely woman in Syria; she didn't really have anyone in the outside world to contact, apart from Jafer's parents. Most of the time it was just the three of them, husband and wife and baby, keeping each other company, pretending that within the walls of their house their lives were normal.

When Yusef was just a couple months old, Lina fell pregnant again. Time passed more quickly here, she thought each night as she fell asleep, her hand grazing Jafer's forehead. His leg was not healing properly and he was in constant pain, the lines in his face making deep furrows. The only thing that eased it was Tramadol, a heavy-strength opioid painkiller that was highly addictive and intended only for immediate postsurgical pain. But Jafer needed it all the time.

He couldn't sleep without it, and on the few occasions when there was none to be had from the local pharmacy, he writhed till dawn. Sometimes Lina felt that the opioid took him into some distant land of fog and forgetfulness. His eyes were open, but he wasn't there. Sometimes he became aggressive and said terrible things to her, but when she asked him about it the next day, he wouldn't even remember having said the words.

She pressed them to leave and return to Germany. "I'm scared they will put me in prison," he would say. To be imprisoned with his body in that state of pain and addiction was unthinkable to him.

EMMA/DUNYA

Fall 2015, Manbij, Syria

FOR A TIME, THE TUNISIAN GYNECOLOGIST'S OFFICE WAS THE PLACE TO go in Manbij. There weren't many outings for women permissible under the Islamic State, save going to the doctor. For Dunya, who spent long days waiting for Selim to return from fighting, superfluous doctor's visits became a mode of socializing and clinics became de facto social spaces where women gathered, lingered, chatted, gossiped, and took the measure of other women in their city, distilling all the casual human interaction they were meant to have in the course of a week into a couple of voracious hours at a medical office, pretending to have a mole examined.

Dunya heard about the Tunisian doctor through the local expat-wife network, a German friend who had heard about her through a French friend. Being in this network carried some appeal, the frisson of having interesting friends and acquaintances from across the whole world. For young people who lived so predominantly online, social media cultivated an aspiration to be cosmopolitan. This desire was savvily exploited by ISIS, which realized it had that in abundance. And because moving to the Islamic State required no actual capital for initiation—unlike cosmopolitanism in Western societies, which was predicated on being able to afford travel and lifestyle goods—in its own unlikely manner, the caliphate dream was the very height of *accessible* cosmopolitanism.

In the West, the Islamic vision of a state centered around social justice—the idea that society should be ordered such that every citizen has access to a decent quality of life—shared some commonalities with other political currents. In America and Britain, young voters were flocking to politicians who described themselves as socialists, who called for an end to austerity and promised to place education and home ownership within everyone's reach. The financial crises in Western societies, and the democratic erosion that came with the revelation of the extent of financial misdeeds and the inability of states to regulate or penalize such behavior, encouraged young people to look for alternatives to the systems that were failing them. Just as some millennials were realizing that socialism wasn't necessarily an ideological evil, some young Muslims were drawn to the idea of an Islamic caliphate out of similar motivations. Social media helped crystallize and connect young people across both these impulses. It is said that everyone wants freedom most of all, but if the Arab Spring and the bewildering appeal of the Islamic State suggested anything, it was that freedom meant quite little if unaccompanied by dignity and meaning. In the months and short years before it became clear that the Islamic State was a morass of atrocities and gratuitous violence, there were elements of its overture that resonated with young Muslims around the world.

The women who had come to Syria were told that they would receive advanced medical care. And for long stretches, before the assault on major ISIS strongholds began in earnest in 2016, many women in many areas could access a doctor. The Tunisian gynecologist's office occupied a large sitting room of a substantial villa in Manbij. The doctor was a den mother, a polyglot true believer with genuine faith in the idea of caliphate; she viewed it as her duty to provide medical care to women, to make them feel comfortable and welcome. She spoke French, Arabic, and English fluently, along with a smattering of German, and chatted with each patient, inquiring after their sleep and whether they had everything they needed. When she laughed, her teeth flashed white in her square olive face.

The British girls in Manbij flocked to her office, and the waiting room chatter, each time Dunya visited, was dominated by English. At a certain time each day, the doctor finished her clinic and prepared for Arabic lessons, which she offered in the late afternoons. Initially the doctor worked closely with ISIS and didn't charge for her services. Women just had to show their (pictureless) Islamic State ID cards, which also secured them free medicine from the pharmacy and free baby formula. But after about a year, the gynecologist fell out with the ISIS authorities. She carried on running clinics, but started charging women for visits and made clear she was operating independently. She never talked about what happened.

THOUGH SHE WAS CARRYING AN AK-47 herself—she was scared to go outside without one—Dunya was startled to enter the new doctor's office and see a desk piled high with weapons. There were long rifles, like her own, and small handguns, enough to make the room seem like a small arms depot. At the sound of the door, the local doctor, a long-nosed Syrian woman, stuck her head out of the examination room. "Leave that gun on the table, please," she ordered Dunya. "I work with the Red Crescent, not ISIS, so next time you come here leave your weapons at home."

Dunya refused to put her gun down. Sometimes you had to re-solve things mafia-style, she thought. The doctor walked up to her and said that if she wasn't willing to disarm, she would have to leave. Dunya squared her chest. She paced back and forth in the small space. The waiting room went silent, anticipating a fight. Finally, Dunya pulled the rifle off her shoulder and flung it onto the desk.

There was a certain romance to guns in the thug-life culture she had grown up around. In her rough neighborhood in Frankfurt, every-one had internalized the codes of *The Godfather*, used names like Corleone in their Facebook profiles, and shared memes of passionate moments in Italian crime dramas. For young people like Dunya, grow-ing up on the margins of German society in fractured families, build-ing up some bravado through street culture was second nature. The German jihadi scene back home was rife with people like her, tasked with raising and nurturing themselves. They converted to Islam in part to secure some meaning in life, in part for a measure of commu-nity and support.

This was the story, also, of her friend from back home in Germany, Denis Cuspert, the German rapper known as Deso Dogg. Cuspert was raised by a German mother and an African American stepfather who served with the U.S. Army. Their home life was troubled. Cuspert and his soldier stepfather did not get on, sparring over everything from America's role in the world to the rules of the household. When he was young, his mother and stepfather sent Cuspert to a home for juvenile delinquents. A grudge against authority and American heavy-handedness emerged as themes in his life and music. He wrote songs like "Gangsta Inferno" before converting to Islam in 2010. Then he assumed the name Abu Maleeq, and joined a street gang in Berlin, composed mostly of Turkish and Arab young men who tussled with neo-Nazis.

In Germany it was mainly second-generation Arab, Turkish, and Kurdish boys who produced rap music, searching for identity between two cultures and coping with racism and discrimination. Later, Cuspert's German record producer would say that for these kids, hip-hop was an artistic family, a place to vent their grievances peacefully. The hip-hop community took in Cuspert with open arms, hoping he would get out of crime.

IN POLICY CIRCLES, THERE IS something called the "al-Qaeda narrative" of contemporary history—the idea that the West invades Muslim countries, cultivates and backs corrupt dictators who subvert the will of their people, and overthrows popular leaders it deems hostile to its interests. In response to this, political violence in places like Palestine and Iraq is an acceptable form of self-defense against occupation.

To many Muslims the world over, this doesn't just sound like the "al-Qaeda narrative." It sounds like a recognition of their lived reality. This perception is chiefly political rather than religious, held by even secular or liberal Muslims (or indeed Middle Easterners of other religious backgrounds) who have lived in the West for decades. It is discomfiting, because it runs at such crosscurrents to acceptable opinion in the West, where political violence of many varieties had long been referred to as "terrorism." Terrorism, as the word is presently used, is a condition of ideological wickedness, stripped of any rational or legitimate context or motivation, and associated culturally with Islam and racially with Muslims.

At the U.S. State Department's terrorism conference in 1974, the American scholar Lisa Stampnitzky notes, terrorism was recognized as "the production of frustrations induced by unresolved grievances" and a tactic that could be used by "established regimes." But by the late 1970s, terrorism had become a tool confined to nonstate actors, driven by motivations whose political or socioeconomic basis was "doubtful." Stampnitzky argues that we stopped trying to understand and diagnose political violence when the political violence began to spread.

The 1970s saw a rise in international hijackings, bombings, and kidnappings. They were the work of the very same armed groups who had been operating militantly the previous decade, who in that period had been called by the word *insurgents,* and whose goals and aims had been dissected along with the political strategies that might quell them. But when the violence spilled out into the wider world, when it went transnational and hit European capitals, forces began to shift, in Stampnitzky's words, to invent the problem of terrorism. This new terrorism was an amorphous thing, an evil that required demonologists to decipher it, supplied by the fast-growing industry of terrorism experts.

These experts sought to promote the idea, which culminated after 9/11 in the War on Terror, that the West was up against enemies of such unfathomable evil that engaging with their causes or motivations was pointless, and that virtually anything the national security state did to combat them, including a dramatic rise in civilian deaths, was justified. To the millions of people whom it impacted—Arabs, Iranians, Afghans, Pakistanis, and Africans of secular background or various faiths—the terrorism paradigm created a painful double existence. Those who believed that, in many instances, violence committed in their countries of origin stemmed from legitimate grievances—that the violence was not legitimate, but the underlying pathologies and grievances were—felt themselves unable to acknowledge this in public life.

This was not an inheritance that anyone wished for, having to equivocate about what constituted legitimate violence. Better for a child to grow up not having to consider the intricate ethical, legal, even theological dimensions of when violence is justifiable. But this deliberation was the fruit of contemporary history.

The British psychoanalyst D. W. Winnicott's concept of the "good enough" mother is one who is initially emotionally all-giving, but steadily allows a child to experience enough frustration to develop in harmony with external reality: a world in which all of his or her needs won't be met. Growing up in a "good enough" Muslim household in the West required this same introduction of frustration. It enabled second-generation Muslim kids to inherit this narrative of grievance while also internalizing that none of it excused killing civilians in the West. In functional or "good enough" Muslim families, children are instilled with an intense, deeply felt concern and responsibility for the plight of Muslims everywhere, but made to understand that they must also bear this reality without resorting to indiscriminate violence. Frustration is inevitable; emotional needs won't be met. It was the struggle of all such families to explain to their children that they could simultaneously feel revulsion for the violence of September 11 and also a glimmer of schadenfreude; that Osama bin Laden could be valorized for his intentions, but that his means were grotesque, deviant, and impermissible; that Islam did not allow and would never allow the killing of civilians. In a good enough Muslim family, one learned to live with these contradictions.

It was not so much, then, that people like the rapper Denis Cuspert and Dunya were "brainwashed" into an "ideology" of radicalism; they simply lacked the intellectual and psychological coping skills to channel their newly found beliefs into more productive and legal means: activism, charity work, human rights law, citizen journalism. They didn't have the living room culture, the ethical conditioning passed down through good enough families. They were not raised to understand that the correct response to terrible injustice was *not* wanton violence. Arguably, they didn't even have good enough parents to teach them not to hurt themselves, let alone teach them not to hurt others.

European converts to Islam were more vulnerable to extremist groups because many lacked this lifelong socialization. Many came from deprived social backgrounds and were primed to be drawn to aggressive, militant strains of anything, from local gangs to local extremist ideologues. They were quick to subsume their personal grudges against family and society into transnational political grudges against the West. Cuspert fell readily into the arms of shadowy German jihadist figures who promised that extreme stance.

In fact, Cuspert didn't convert to Islam so much as initiate himself straight into a radical Islamist group called the True Religion. It was as though he had pressed a button and changed the aesthetic theme of the WordPress site of his life from gangsta to *mujahid*; the chaotic structure and violent impulses were all the same, but were now overlaid with Islamist imagery and themes. Suddenly causes like Iraq, Chechnya, and Afghanistan mattered to him deeply, and Germans, Westerners, and a broad swath of humanity became "unbelievers" who were complicit in Muslim suffering.

His old friends on the Berlin rap scene were devastated, and furious. They were from "good enough" Muslim families and were adept at living and rapping about the painful contradictions. They didn't turn to violence. They all knew where the lines were. His record producer later complained bitterly about Cuspert's betrayal: "He disgraced everyone, all of the Muslim MCs. He ruined the community. May Allah forgive him. But we don't."

Cuspert was at home on YouTube, on the stage, on the screen, and rapidly became as high profile on the German jihadist scene as he had previously been in the hip-hop world. In 2012 he traveled to Egypt and Libya for military training, and in 2014 he moved to Syria to join a jihadist rebel group, eventually jumping to ISIS and assuming the Kunya Abu Talha al-Almani. Abu Talha imported his insouciant humor and rapper sensibility to Syria, posing in Raqqa as he nibbled a sprig of grapes aloft in the air, standing before an SUV in a long white *thobe*, with electric-blue sneakers.

There was something of the air of Tupac about him—his handsome, soulful face, his songs about a life of pain, his air of embracing violence reluctantly, as though heaven itself had ordained it for him. He even titled one album *Alle Augen auf Mich,* a German rendering of Tupac's *All Eyez on Me.* From Raqqa he started putting out *nasheeds* and video messages with titles like "Against the Infidel Hypocrites and the Saudi Palace," with cinematic graphics of him clutching a rifle with desert scenes and Saudi figures in the background, a mash-up of *Lawrence of Arabia,* Spike Lee's *Malcolm X,* and *Scarface.* In one propaganda video, he held the severed head of a man who had received the "death penalty" for fighting against ISIS.

Dunya knew Cuspert from Germany. She was reticent about the nature of their relationship, but said he had helped her out when she was going through a rough time back home: he had arranged a place for her to stay and dropped off food. She thought that he was, at core, a good person. Or at least he had been, once. "The world is not black and white," she said. "He had a good heart before he came to Syria. He met the wrong people, and they changed his life."

ON THE DAY THE TALL, willowy blonde arrived to marry Cuspert, the heat was so oppressive that the women were waiting to see how long it took a raw egg to cook through on the pavement (eight minutes). The midsummer heat, that June 2014, sometimes approached 130 degrees, an intensity that pushed it beyond weather into a searing physical dimension unto itself.

The blonde was dropped off by the unit that ferried women into Syria from the border, the al-Khansaa unit that Asma worked for. She arrived exhausted, wearing a black dress. Dunya and the other German woman rose to take her inside the house, offering her grapes and cold water. She said she had converted to Islam three years ago, but later, when it was time for evening prayer, she fumbled and said she wasn't "one hundred percent comfortable" praying yet. Would they forgive her? She was so tired. Once alone, Dunya and the other women rolled their eyes and talked in low voices, agreeing it was just like Abu Talha to get some barely practicing Muslimah who was pretty and slim enough to be a model to come out to a war zone for him. "Abu Talha's funny. And women like funny men," Dunya said dryly.

When they walked back into the living room, where they'd left her dozing on the sofa, the blonde was rather more alertly examining a bookshelf and seemed startled to see them. She didn't say much over the next few hours. She was friendly and, oddly, said she didn't mind sharing Abu Talha with another wife.

"It might be *two* others," Dunya warned. "Are you sure you don't mind?"

The blonde shook her head, but looked paler.

"I converted years ago, but if my husband came home with another wife, I would *kill* him," Dunya said.

"But if it's allowed . . . ," the blonde said.

"Allowed! Lots of things are allowed, doesn't mean you're supposed to like them. Doesn't mean it's good for everybody."

Dunya tried to impart some basic Islamic thinking about jealousy to their new arrival, but the blonde half listened with a weary expression and asked if she could go lie down. She stayed in the bedroom till after dinner, when Abu Talha arrived to pick her up in a beat-up old Peugeot, and they drove away into the night.

Dunya never saw the blonde after that, though she did hear from one of the ex-wives of another fighter that the blonde had been caught eating before *iftar* during Ramadan. Abu Osama's wife had said there was something strange about the girl. Dunya defended her. "Don't you remember when you started fasting, in the early years? When you were so hungry you thought you couldn't take it anymore and felt like killing anyone who took the wrong tone?" Abu Osama's wife was unconvinced. More likely, Dunya thought, she was envious of the blonde's slender figure. Life under the caliphate, sedentary and confined, had made all the women fat, but it did not seem to thicken the blonde at all.

THE SUMMER IT TRANSPIRED, A German newspaper reported that an American spy had managed to seduce Cuspert and escape with intelligence about him and his associates. "We are already a long time in the bedrooms of the terrorists," a German security official boasted. The story did not identify the woman by name.

Two years later, American news reports revealed her identity and cast the operation very differently, presenting it not as a premeditated infiltration but as a real love story—an agent who fell for her target.

The blonde was FBI agent Daniela Greene, who had been assigned to investigate Abu Talha but instead left her husband in Detroit to travel to Syria and marry him. Greene was born to Czech parents in Germany. When she was young, she married a U.S. soldier and moved to the United States. There, she became an agent for the FBI.

Was it a coup for Cuspert, seducing an American FBI agent into abandoning her country and her soldier husband and joining him in the caliphate? Was it a coup for the FBI, sneaking an agent into the heartland of ISIS and then pulling her out without physical harm? Was she a double agent? A triple agent? And why did her story garner scant attention in the media, when it was far more sensational and dangerous to U.S. security than the breathlessly recounted tales of American and European country bumpkins who were lured or even just *thought* about being lured to ISIS?

They reported that Greene was prosecuted upon her return to the United States and served two years in prison on a reduced sentence, in exchange for cooperation with government officials. Partially unsealed documents from her case include a memo from a prosecutor in the U.S. attorney's office writing that she had put national security at risk by "exposing herself and her knowledge of sensitive matters to those terrorist organizations," but that she managed to "escape from the area unscathed, and with apparently much of that knowledge undisclosed," a "stroke of luck or a measure of the lack of savvy on the part of the terrorists with whom she interacted."

If this was truly the case, Greene would be the first and only American who experienced anything approaching "a stroke of luck" at the hands of ISIS, and it would certainly be one of the rare instances when the finely tuned, twenty-first-century militia-cum-state showed a "lack of savvy," especially given that Greene disclosed to Abu Talha that she worked for the FBI.

As Dunya said, "I cannot understand this woman."

SHARMEENA, KADIZA, AMIRA, AND SHAMIMA

February 2015, East London

THE FAMILIES IN LONDON DISCOVERED, ONE BY ONE, THAT THEIR school-age daughters had gone missing. Kadiza had said she was going to the library. Amira and Shamima had said they were going to Kadiza's cousin's wedding. It was winter and the sky darkened early, but by around 8 p.m. the girls still weren't back and their phones were either switched off or not answering. Shamima's sister finally decided to ring the police.

The next morning, police officers visited each family and said the girls had flown to Turkey. In the days that followed, the full circumstances leading up to the disappearance of their daughters emerged to the families: that their best friend Sharmeena hadn't just "disappeared" but had traveled to Syria to join ISIS; that the school and the police had neglected to share this with them, and had tasked *the girls themselves* with bringing letters home.

The families were stunned and enraged in equal measure. The officers would show up at their houses with detailed, endless questions, and little information about the girls' movements. Often the news media seemed better informed. The families began to feel like the police were vacuuming their lives and minds for intelligence, but were uninterested in actually getting the girls back—girls who were schoolchildren, who were British citizens.

Shamima's sister called the mosque, weeping. Shamima had constantly said she was going there—had anyone seen her? Could anyone not help? As Kadiza's sister was going through her room, she found the letter from the police tucked inside a schoolbook. Through conversations with the liaison officers assigned to them by the police, it became clear that when Sharmeena disappeared in December, what had begun as a missing-person investigation quickly turned into a counterterrorism investigation. Their daughters had been questioned twice at school by counterterrorism police without their parents' knowledge. When Kadiza's sister confronted one of the police officers, he told her the girls had been "giving him the run-around." She was incensed. Since when did teenage girls "run around" the most highly trained, competent police force in Europe?

Finally the families stopped speaking to the police altogether. They went to the East London Mosque for help instead. One went to CAGE, a human rights group that offered advice to Muslims impacted by terrorism laws. The mosque introduced them to a lawyer, Tasnime Akunjee, who specialized in counterterrorism cases. Details piled up, and accusations flew. The UK authorities said they had sent an email to the Turkish authorities with the girls' names. The Turks said the email had arrived blank. The families were beside themselves. Amira's mother felt like her life had ended. Her mind did a continual sweep across the past several weeks; she castigated herself for missing clues. On February 22, Amira's father, the man who had fled Ethiopia so his daughter could lead a more secure life in the West, went on television, clutching her teddy bear, imploring his fifteen-year-old daughter to reconsider. "We miss you. We cannot stop crying. Please think twice. Don't go to Syria." His English was halting and his voice soft.

For many in Britain, the fact of the girls' youth—that they were schoolchildren and minors, that they had been preyed upon by recruiters—was irrelevant. A right-wing commentator for *The Sun* newspaper blamed the parents of "The Syrian Three" for not preventing the girls from "[scurrying] off to be brides of jihad, sporting nothing more than a burka and industrial lubricant." He demanded that the government drop its efforts to bring them back: "Given we know where The Syrian Three are, maybe we should leave them to get on with epilating their leg hair and pleasuring spawn of Satan, and focus on *our own* missing kids?" And so it was: voices in the media made the case that Kadiza, Amira, and Shamima were no longer *our own* kids; their Britishness evaporated, as though it had never existed in the first place.

It was not only the right-wing press that blamed the girls and their parents; one columnist writing in the liberal newspaper *The Independent* mocked Amira's father's appearance on television:

> I wanted to ask Abase Hussen, as he clutched his daughter Amira's stuffed toy, what exactly he thought was the tipping point that made his delicate, innocent baby-girl leave the country in such a rush that she left teddy behind? Was it the video of Alan Henning—a man who stood for nothing but kindness—having his head removed? Was it photos of crucifixions in central Raqqa? The reports from Kobani of raped, mutilated six-year-old female corpses lying in the streets? Which image of a future life excited her the most? Submissive jihadi bride with a big strong executioner boyfriend? Machine-gun-toting trained killer? And all this without her teddy bear?

The writer concluded by addressing the girls directly:

> I'd go as far as to say you shouldn't be allowed back into the country ever, when surely there are dozens of other bloodier, more depressing places that suit your lifestyle choice better. However, I've asked my liberal friends what we should do and they all wring their hands and say after some mumbling, "Nothing." So give me a call when you're bored with all the stoning, crucifying and beheading. I'll meet you at Heathrow Arrivals with your teddy.

Once the newspapers discovered that Amira's father had attended political rallies in London—protesting the mass Saudi expulsion of Ethiopians, protesting against the American film mocking the Prophet Muhammad—they annulled his right to blame the police for any negligence. They said it was his fault that his daughter Amira had gone to "take up an exciting and challenging position as an in-house whore" for ISIS.

AMONG THE MUSLIM COMMUNITY, IN living rooms and dining rooms across London, the conviction grew that a failure of such massive proportions was simply inconceivable. The families were so distraught and furious with the police that Salman Farsi, the spokesman of the East London Mosque, started acting as intermediary, though he too was stunned by the lapses. "The conversations that were coming out, that were being repeated, was that they were allowed to go," he said. "People thought, they said, they let them go because they wanted to make a point." Or they let them go, perhaps, for the purpose of watching them and collecting intelligence, so they could better understand the chain of handling and command that scooped up girls from East London and deposited them into Raqqa. Or even, the family's lawyer suggested, to boost the status of whatever mole the UK security services already had inside ISIS.

If anything, Prevent, the government's counterterrorism policy charged with identifying young people at risk of extremism, was primed to overreact. So how had it failed to mark the girls as being at risk? How had officers failed to act when Shamima contacted Umm Layth, a known ISIS recruiter? "This was all done under the watch of Prevent and it was a complete failure of Prevent," said Farsi. "If the police were aware of this situation, if the school was aware, how were these schoolgirls then subsequently allowed to stroll out of Britain and travel to Turkey? How on earth did that happen?" The families began planning a trip to Turkey. Like many families in the same situation across Europe, they did not feel the police were interested in helping them get their girls back.

The police confiscated the mobile phones of other girls at the school, girls who they knew were in contact with Kadiza, Shamima, and Amira after they left; they returned the phones, presumably bugged, to monitor their contact even more closely.

Though much of serious academia rejects the notion of "radicalization"—there is no empirical basis for predicting when an individual will commit acts of violence—the approach generally followed by law enforcement, whatever its flaws, follows the "bunch of guys" theory: the idea that young people join radical groups through peer pressure and in clusters. The police started applying this thinking after the Bethnal Green girls had left. But, apparently, none of this had been applied to these girls before it was too late.

When a parliamentary committee held a hearing to examine the failures—misstep after misstep, each lapse more implausible than the last—the commissioner of the Metropolitan Police said he was "sorry" the letters had never made it home, and the head of the committee said it was "a big blow to the credibility of what is supposed to be . . . the best police service in the world." The girls had funded their journey with a sizable amount of cash and with considerable logistical support. "This was not a package holiday," the families' lawyer said. Who had helped them? Why was no one telling them anything? Jewelry, the police finally said. Everyone knew Asians kept gold jewelry in the house. The girls must have taken gold and sold it. The families were incensed by this suggestion. With the exception of one girl, who'd taken two gold bangles, the girls had left behind even their jewelry.

Bethnal Green Academy hired expensive lawyers. The tabloid press sent reporters to loiter outside the school, bribing teenage girls for any tidbits about the three runaways. One newspaper sequestered one of the girls' parents in a hotel, extracting an exclusivity agreement in exchange for a sizable sum of money. Suddenly the extended family around the girls, many of them on pinched incomes and living on council estates, realized that newspapers were willing to write hefty checks for anything they said. They obliged: It was the police's fault! The school's fault! The teachers' fault! The mosque's fault! Mr. Abase's fault! Tabloid reporters assumed multiple identities, ran stories under fake bylines, pitted families and institutions against each other. The bribery and the payments corrupted the story, clouding a clear picture of which institution should be most accountable. And the girls remained lost.

It took a fellow millennial, the mosque spokesman Farsi, to figure out how to reach them. He came up with a social media campaign, #callhomegirls, and launched it across Twitter in late March, just over a month after the girls disappeared. The next morning, Kadiza, the studious girl with the glasses and winsome smile, accepted her sister's request to follow her on Instagram, and they began to private message. Kadiza asked after her mother. "She is on her prayer mat asking Allah to help her find you," her sister wrote. Kadiza said she would call soon. She seemed suspicious of her sister's efforts to find her. Her sister decided to test her, to make sure it was really Kadiza messaging. "Who is Big Toe?" Kadiza responded: "lol, our cousin."

When Kadiza got in touch again the next day, she said she was staying in a comfortable house, "with chandeliers." When her sister asked if she was getting married, Kadiza chafed at the question. "You know me too well. I'm not here just to get married to someone." But when pressed, she said she was "considering." Her sister told her the police had promised the family that if the girls came home, they would not be prosecuted. She begged her to consider returning. Kadiza said flatly, "They're lying."

ACROSS BRITAIN, SCHOOLS WITH LARGE Muslim student bodies reeled. In East London alone, police confiscated the passports of around thirty schoolgirls believed to be at risk of traveling to Syria. Skittish teachers and administrators awaited instruction on how to respond. "We're all bloody terrified it'll be our school in the papers next," one principal whispered to a journalist. Teachers in London received an open letter from a women's-rights campaigner to read to their students.

> Dear Sister, You won't know me but like you I too am British and Muslim. Some of your friends may have gone out to join ISIS and you are also considering going out too. . . . I have no other intention of writing this letter but to tell you that you are being lied to in the wickedest of ways. . . . Dear sister, do not destroy your life and your families lives by buying into a lie. . . . You will find many of your fellow Muslim sisters have also rejected the

call of ISIS as they have seen through the poisonous ideology it peddles.

The letter detailed ISIS's violence and rapaciousness, its corruption of core Islamic tenets. It was a moving and persuasive critique of ISIS and its messaging. The author was a British Muslim woman in her late thirties called Sara Khan, an activist who ran Inspire, an organization that worked on countering extremism from a women's-rights perspective.

By the mid-2010s, Khan had become one of the most vocal and visible Muslim women working on issues of extremism and women's rights. She enjoyed easy access to prominent television and radio platforms, appeared in the pages of *Vogue,* and toured schools to share her lessons for keeping girls safe from the lure of extremism. She was unflinching in her criticism of patriarchal practices in Muslim communities and argued that religious ideology was the root cause of the appeal of ISIS and violent extremism. "I feel like Wahhabism and Salafism have stolen my faith away from me," she said publicly, talking about her drive to "reclaim my faith from these fascists." What young Muslims needed, she insisted, was to receive the right kind of messages, what Khan called "online counter-narrative products." She proceeded to launch a #makingastand campaign against ISIS in *The Sun,* a tabloid newspaper that relished publishing lies about Muslims.

This position made her an ideal voice and advocate for the British government, which by that time had moved to classifying extremism as an ideological condition, divorced from politics. Khan's slow rise into the limelight coincided with the steady intensification of the state's Prevent counterterrorism strategy. By the mid-2010s, British Muslims found themselves disproportionately incarcerated and targeted at airports and borders; they saw their strongly performing faith-based schools scrutinized and shut down for often minor or exaggerated lapses; and, most frighteningly, they found the state increasingly willing to take their children away, on grounds of safeguarding them against radicalization. These very real anxieties underpinned much of the concern about Prevent, but Khan accused what she called an "anti-Prevent lobby" pushed by "Islamists" of creating a "toxic" climate and narrative about the state's strategy, a strategy she insisted was largely working and needed.

Khan presented her group, Inspire, as a grassroots women's group, but it emerged in 2016 that her #makingastand campaign had not only received government funding, but had also been crafted by a branch in the British government's Home Office, the Research, Information and Communications Unit (RICU). RICU produced what it called "strategic communications," or, in Cold War parlance, propaganda, aiming "to effect behavioral and attitudinal change," according to its own documents. When Khan released a book in 2016 called *The Battle for British Islam,* her coauthor was a consultant who worked for this same government unit.

The term "the Muslim community" was problematic, Khan regularly pointed out, as it glossed over all the diversity, rifts, and contradictions among Britain's almost three and a half million Muslims. But if this monolith called "the community" had one thing in common, it was resentment at being manipulated, increasingly treated by the state as a security threat and second-class citizens. It had become routine for the government to surveil Muslim Britons and interact with them through layers of subterfuge. Social workers later turned out to be counterterrorism officers. Teachers handed out surveys to kids in primary schools with large Muslim intakes, asking them questions about God and identity, in what later emerged to be a state effort to "identify the initial seeds of radicalization with children."

It was precisely such an atmosphere that made Muslims resent the rise of Khan. As the government steadily cut ties with a broad array of Muslim community groups, on grounds of their social or political views, it appeared to be willing to interact only with a specific current of civil society that it had largely funded and cultivated. What the state presented as engagement with Muslims was largely just a conversation with itself.

Khan reacted defensively to the criticism about the lack of transparency about her ties to the government, portraying it as an attack on her gender-equity message by Islamist radicals. As early as 2014, a female Muslim blogger wrote that Khan had "really lost the plot, from a reasonably Islamically grounded Muslim to, well, a frankly confused

stooge who has completely lost her way." By late 2015, a popular La-
bour MP called Khan's group "the most loathed organization among
Muslim communities," and in 2018, the former chairwoman of the
Conservative Party called Khan a "Home Office mouthpiece." The
government nonetheless appointed her Commissioner for Countering
Extremism, charged with, ironically, community engagement.

In public discussions around ISIS and the girls' disappearance,
there was suddenly very little diversity or real exchange of views, and
instead a desperate push to identify a single cause, a single story of
culpability. The government blamed ideology. Think tanks refined
that, and blamed Saudi-exported Salafism. The tabloids and right-
wing figures blamed ordinary Muslims. It was like a Rorschach test:
much of what people identified as important reflected more about
their own tendencies, whom they wished to exculpate or blame. A
British Muslim journalist on the terrorism beat spoke of "toxic activity" among Deobandis in Walthamstow. The former member of an
extremist group, now working for the government, had a psychosexual
take, that girls were trying to "break away from the daily grind of their
traditional roles in families that see them as objects." Pro-Israel activists warned there was anti-Semitism at play. Muslim activists pointed
to the War on Terror and harassment by the security services. White
feminists blamed toxic masculinity and "intimate terrorism." The
mother of a young woman who left for Syria said small-town racism
and her ex-husband were to blame: "He is a villain. Everyone in this
town has heard of him, and no one has anything good to say."

AT BETHNAL GREEN ACADEMY, IT soon became clear that the school's
official response to the girls' disappearance would be a severely English silence. It would not be discussed that the authorities had confiscated the passports of several other girls from the school and made
them wards of court, a designation that made the family court system
their ultimate legal guardians, without whose permission they could
not leave the country. Shortly after the girls' disappearance in February, the head teacher called an assembly. Students and teachers were
openly distraught, but he spoke about the girls' departure in clipped

terms that ended the discussion. Teachers were instructed not to talk about it, even off the record, long into the future.

Was it upsetting, bewildering, and possibly traumatic to have four girls from your school—the smart, popular ones at that—disappear to ISIS? No longer sitting next to you in English class poring over *Animal Farm,* discussing why the pigs (the girls sometime spelled out P-I-G when speaking aloud, to minimize its *haram* grossness) embodied tyranny and propaganda. No longer kneeling next to you on Fridays in the prayer room, pressing their foreheads to the ground. Someone could have helped the students of Bethnal Green Academy to make some sense of it all, but making sense of it, as some students would discover later, was dangerously too close, in the eyes of the police and other community authorities, to sympathizing.

SHARMEENA, KADIZA, AMIRA, AND SHAMIMA

July 2015, London and Raqqa

SHORTLY AFTER THE ISIS BEACH ATTACK ON BRITISH TOURISTS IN TUNI-
sia in June 2015 that gained attention around the world, an under-
cover reporter with the tabloid *Daily Mail* contacted Amira on Twitter,
posing as a young girl interested in going to Syria and asking her if
what the news media reported about ISIS was true. Amira responded:
"Don't believe anything they say about islam because they are the
enemies of islam and they will never speak good about it. Everything
they say is a lie, trust me." The reporter then fished for her views on
the Tunisia attack. Amira responded only with "loool." When asked
whether the tourists were innocent, she advised the reporter to "research, like read about it."

The newspaper splashed Amira's face on its front cover, a hammed-
up photo from her school days where her eyes are rolled back in mock
comic horror. The July 2015 story accused Amira of trying to lure the
reporter to join ISIS and documented how "the joking London teen"
delivered a "sickening verdict on beach atrocity." A couple of months
prior, in the spring after her arrival in Syria, Amira had married an
Australian fighter called Abdullah Elmir, a former butcher from Syd-
ney. In what was possibly one of the most peculiar confrontations in
the history of the British press, Elmir contacted the *Daily Mail* and
threatened it with an attack if the newspaper did not stop harassing
his wife.

All throughout that summer, the families of the British girls who had gone to Syria nervously monitored their phones and the daily newspapers, wondering how their daughters regarded the violence and inhumanity that now surrounded them. The parents of Aqsa Mahmood, the Scottish blogger known as Umm Layth, found out by reading her blog that she praised ISIS attacks that summer. They issued a stern public disavowal, making clear that Aqsa represented neither their religion nor her family:

> The family of Aqsa Mahmood became aware yesterday of her blog Umm Layth posting praise for the attacks in Tunisia, France and Kuwait. They are full of rage at her latest diatribe masquerading as Islam during the holy month of Ramadan. Whilst their daughter may have destroyed any chance of happiness for her own family, they are sickened that she now celebrates the heartbreak of other families. The Mahmood family have a message for any young person attracted to Isis: they say there is no honor, no glory, no god at work in the cowardly massacre of holidaymakers, people at prayer in a Shia mosque or an innocent man at his place of work. As for Aqsa's words, they can only be described as twisted and evil, this is not the daughter that they raised.

Aqsa's parents knew that her blog offered easy material to newspapers that were already determined to portray British Muslims, most of whom hated ISIS's nihilistic brutality, as sympathizers.

Later that year, in November, a little over a week after the terrorist attacks in Paris, *The Sun* ran a front-page photo of Jihadi John, the young man from London who had become an ISIS executioner, wielding a knife. Above him the headline screamed, "1 in 5 Brit Muslims' Sympathy for Jihadis." The headline distorted the findings of a survey about British Muslim political opinion, which had asked people to what extent they had sympathy with "young Muslims who leave the UK to join fighters in Syria." The government press regulator said the paper had conflated many things that were not equal at all: traveling to Syria versus going there to fight; sympathy for those individuals having taken such a path versus support for their actions there; the terms *fighters* and *ISIS*.

One of the young pollsters who conducted the survey later wrote anonymously for Vice News about how uncomfortable he had been with the strangely worded, reductive language of the poll, how it elicited answers at odds with the views of the respondents. "Every single person I spoke to for more than five minutes condemned the terrorist attacks carried out in the name of Islam," the pollster wrote. "These thoughts and feelings were lost in a small set of multiple-choice questions. The idea that that one badly worded poll can speak for complex and emotional topics such as identity and religion would be funny if it wasn't so damaging."

The same week in November as the poll appeared, anti-Muslim racist attacks in the United Kingdom tripled. Women wearing hijab were spat at and had their headscarves ripped off. On social media, hijabi women shared safety tips for train platforms, to minimize chances of getting pushed onto the tracks. The British government press regulator ruled against *The Sun* for its distorting survey. But the regulatory body was ultimately powerless over the press. Its conditions for investigation were so finicky that it regularly passed over complaints; it imposed no fines, and when it told papers to make corrections, it demanded neither apology nor any placement of prominence. The press suffered no lasting consequences, and as a result had no incentive to change their practices.

Hatred of Muslims sold. As the editor of *The Sun* said after facing a ruling on a separate incident, he would do the exact same thing again.

RAHMA AND GHOUFRAN

September 2014, Zawiya, Libya

OLFA HAD SPENT YEARS WORKING SEASONAL SHIFTS AS A CLEANER IN Libya, and if there was one thing she could do, it was pick a suitable household in which to become a maid. The lady of the house had to be sufficiently pretty, otherwise she would resent the presence of an attractive woman around her husband and punish her for it with unpleasant tasks and harsh words. She had to be decently tempered, not the sort to scream if the eggplants ended up costing a dinar more than she believed them to be worth. This was easily gauged by a quick chat with the existing housegirls. Olfa was pleased: that summer, she had found good households for both Rahma and Ghoufran in Zawiya, a small city on the Libyan coast.

Zawiya, with its palm trees and apricot municipal buildings, housed one of Libya's largest oil refineries. The country's oil wealth, though not evenly distributed, enabled many Libyans to live in sprawling villas staffed with help. Olfa liked Zawiya. The streets were cleaner and there were cafés that served pancakes and mille-feuille. Sometimes the bodies of drowned migrants trying to sail to Sicily washed ashore and were lined up on the sand in black body bags, almost like sardines when you squinted from a distance.

Libyans had risen up against their dictator, Muammar al-Qaddafi, in February 2011, and in March NATO led air strikes ostensibly to protect civilians from government killings. The NATO mission quickly shifted to one of deposing Qaddafi, who was killed later that same year. Chaos engulfed the country, which soon became a breeding ground for various extremist groups, attracting militants from abroad. Competing militias financed by various Arab states vied for control of key cities and oil-rich regions in Libya. The city of Zawiya was locked in confrontation with other armed groups, and the girls' households were associated with the local militia that ruled the city.

The woman who hired Rahma was welcoming, but had looked confused when Olfa escorted Rahma to the home for her first day of work. "She wants to wear that?" the woman asked, looking at Rahma's full niqab.

"Yes," sighed Olfa. "But, inshallah, you can persuade her to take it off during the day, at home at least."

The matron made clucking noises, and smiled at Rahma. "Here we are like family to you. Don't feel like you're with strangers."

Rahma smiled back with her eyes. Olfa asked to speak privately to the matron, in the kitchen. In a low voice, she explained that her daughter had fallen in with some unsavory groups back in Sousse, and that if she behaved oddly, could the woman please let her know.

The household Rahma worked in was awash in arms. It might have been a depot for the local militia, or perhaps every militiaman's house was so stocked, Rahma had no idea. While she was cleaning the house, dusting and vacuuming, her gaze moved from a spindle of rifles in the corner to a wooden bureau stacked with teacups on the top shelf and pistols on the others. She couldn't wait to be alone with these weapons, to peer at her reflection in the gilt-rimmed mirror, with a rifle slung over her shoulder.

Olfa viewed Ghoufran as more sensible than Rahma, and allowed her a phone. She was working in an equally comfortable home, the household of an oil engineer whose grown-up children were away, and the workload was light. In the ground floor of the apartment block where Ghoufran worked, the girls started attending Quran classes. Rahma was in her second year of trying to memorize the Quran.

In the late afternoon of each day, when she was done with her own cleaning work at her own household, Olfa alternated paying calls to the girls' households, to help them out with whatever work they had left to do. One hot weekday morning, as Olfa was preparing to mop the floors, Ghoufran showed up at the home her mother worked in.

She flung her arms around Olfa and gripped her tight. "Please forgive me," she whispered in her mother's ear.

"Forgive you for what? You haven't done anything wrong. Why aren't you at work?" Olfa asked suspiciously, disentangling herself from Ghoufran's dramatic grip.

"Rahma needs your help today," Ghoufran said. "They're having guests, so even though it's my day, could you please go to her instead?"

Olfa agreed and shooed Ghoufran off; she wanted to get the mopping done before lunch. After she finished her own work, she went to Rahma's home and stayed with her until sunset, even though she didn't see any preparations under way for a party. "It got canceled," Rahma said, shrugging.

The next morning, Olfa's phone rang. The woman who employed Ghoufran said she hadn't come home the night before. She hadn't left a note. The panic struck Olfa so completely that she ran out of the house without her shoes, flying the three blocks to Ghoufran's house. She stopped every person she passed on the way and asked, panting, "Do you know my daughter Ghoufran? Have you seen her?" She had thought Rahma was the impetuous one, the one in danger of going astray. Never did she think that Ghoufran, her confidante, her wise eldest and most beloved child, would be the one to go! Olfa imagined what might have happened. Perhaps she had met a man, a nice man, and run off with him. Perhaps she would hear from her soon, a phone call to say that his stuffy middle-class parents hadn't approved, so they had eloped, and were living in Tripoli and could Olfa make arrangements to visit soon.

When she arrived at Rahma's household, her daughter looked at her disheveled clothes, her bare feet caked with dust and dirt. "Don't stress yourself, Mummy, there's nothing you can do. Ghoufran has gone to Syria," she said in a mild voice.

"Syria!" Olfa hissed.

The woman who employed Rahma, the wife of the militia leader, overheard the exchange. "Has she really gone to Syria?" she asked, curiously.

Olfa knelt down and began kissing Rahma's feet, weeping and begging her daughter, "Tell me where she's gone, don't take your sister away from me."

"Calm down," Rahma's employer told Olfa. "Let's find out exactly what's happened." She called her husband and asked him to come home. The militias operated a tight security cordon around the city, and if Rahma helped them with a bit of information—told them who Ghoufran had left with, what kind of car they had been driving—her husband could probably track her down.

The husband, a tall man with a clipped beard, soon arrived, followed by two men wearing beige camouflage. One of these camouflaged men sat across from Rahma and tried to reason with her. "Listen, girl, we can dispatch to checkpoints on all roads going out of this city, but we need a scrap from you. A name, a town, a direction, a call. Something." Rahma sat silent. He tried, and the other man tried again, but with no luck. Olfa beat at her chest and shrieked. Her histrionics made the militiamen grow impatient with Rahma. One of them pushed her down to her knees. "How dare you do this to your mother! Tell me right now where your sister has gone."

Rahma slipped a hand into her pocket, waved a scrap of paper with a phone number, and shoved it into her mouth. "I won't say a thing," she said. Olfa grabbed her throat. Rahma grasped at her mother's hands, her eyes watery, and swallowed.

The militiaman turned to Olfa. "Lady, your daughter is really pissing me off. I'm gonna kill her if she doesn't give me something to go on."

Olfa was fed up too. "I don't care, kill her!" she shouted. She was furious with Rahma, this girl who had been trouble from the start.

Rahma straightened her headscarf, pulled back her shoulders, and smilingly began to recite, "There is no God but God . . ."

At this, Olfa smacked her in the face. "Shut up with your *dawla* bullshit!"

By morning, her eyes raw from crying, Olfa accepted that Ghoufran was gone. Overnight she had called friends and acquaintances in Tunisia asking for help, and everyone had advised her to return home; Libya didn't have a government, and you needed a government to get a missing girl back.

Back in Tunis, the weeks that followed were a blur of meetings in police stations and lawyers' offices and television appearances. By this point, Olfa told the police that they could do what they wanted with Rahma. "I don't need her anymore. Just make her tell you where her sister is. All I want is her sister back."

The security services interrogated Rahma on and off for days, sometimes keeping her in detention overnight. Rahma, the fearless and stubborn daughter, actually seemed to thrive on the ordeal. She told her mother that if she was hurt or killed before she made it out to the caliphate in Syria, she would still qualify as a martyr. Often the police permitted Olfa to sit in on the interrogations, as Rahma was still a minor. What came out of her daughter's mouth stunned her. Rahma admitted openly to being with ISIS; she declared she had given her allegiance to Abu Bakr al-Baghdadi. She mentioned sites on the internet she had used to learn about handling weapons.

The policeman looked genuinely tired of taking these notes. "If you're such a true believer, why didn't you just go with your sister?" he asked.

"Because I want my operation to be here in Tunisia," she replied.

"Lady, you really should advise your daughter to keep quiet. She's going to spend her whole life in prison," the officer said to Olfa.

But it seemed to Olfa that the security establishment wanted the exact opposite: they wanted Rahma to run her mouth, to glean intelligence. To show up at the security directorate every morning looking at Facebook Messenger, where she messaged with Ghoufran, so the police could monitor their exchanges. Perhaps they were using her daughter to collect intelligence (likely). Or perhaps it suited those in power to let this fester and blow up (also likely). The political and security machinations that shaped the official handling of her daughter eluded Olfa, who felt like a pawn in a much wider, more intricate game.

By that time, the end of 2015, hundreds of Tunisian women had left the country to join ISIS. Olfa was the rare mother willing to go on television and speak about her experience. The public conversation about young Tunisians joining the jihad in Syria tended to overlook women, and when they were addressed at all, the media cast their motivations as purely sexual. Media reports claimed that Tunisian women were traveling to Syria and Libya to become Islamic concubines under a practice breathlessly termed "sex jihad." It was a fake, mash-up concept of layered misrepresentations: one, that women were traveling to Syria as comfort women to fighters; two, that they justified this behavior theologically.

The "sex jihad" coverage emanated from media outlets associated with either the Tunisian security services or the Syrian state, both of which were keen to portray the fighters and women flowing into Syria as deviants or terrorists, or, in this instance, deviant-slut terrorists. There were headlines everywhere in the Tunisian press about women returning en masse from Syria, pregnant or with HIV. Among the Tunisian media and political establishment, there was no wish for a conversation about why hundreds of women were voting with their feet—voting against the failed promises of the new Tunisia, voting against the present regional order—by going to Syria. It was far easier to cast blame on violent extremists motivated by deformed religion and lust.

Olfa knew her girls weren't motivated by sex. They weren't even motivated by finding a husband. Of course they were, to varying de-grees, romantics, but what teenage girls weren't? But they hadn't been seduced into the cause by a particular young man. In fact, both girls had received numerous proposals from local men after the *dawah* tent, but neither had shown any interest. When a TV presenter confronted Olfa with the sex jihad theory for the first time, as an explanation for her wayward daughters, Olfa was furious. "This idea is just ridiculous. I am not defending these organizations by saying that, but the idea that my daughter went as some sort of sex slave is just not true. She had choices and she made this choice."

NOUR

NOUR FELL ASLEEP EVERY NIGHT WITH HER MOBILE PHONE IN HER palm. It was how she kept in touch with Karim, who had flown to Paris, then driven to Brussels, and from there gone on to Turkey. She had given birth to their daughter in the spring and sent Karim a photo of her on Telegram, although the picture didn't seem like enough. She wished he could smell the milk breath and feel the strangling grip of their daughter's little fist.

She thought they would join him after a few weeks, after the baby passed her forty-day cocooning period, but everything started going wrong. She learned from the passport office that she would need her husband's permission in order to leave the country with the baby, and her father's permission to leave at all. To stem the flow of young Tunisians to Syria, the government had started imposing often arbitrary travel restrictions on citizens under thirty-five. The cost of the journey, the air tickets alone, amounted to more than she had.

In the ten months that had passed since Karim left Tunis, there were moments when she despaired of their plan. She tried to imagine what life would be like in Syria, but her mind could produce no images at all. Would there be ice cream shops and Sunday afternoon strolls? Would there be bombing raids? Karim told her that she should see if there were other women who could be persuaded to come. He said *dawla*, the Islamic State, struggled to recruit among Syrian women. They had been harsh in taking over new towns in Syria, and had alienated local women. For the caliphate to be able to function as a state, it needed more women, and they would need to come from abroad.

She was furious with Karim, who was supposed to be sending money but hadn't managed to yet. Nour didn't have coherent ideas about what to do, only flashes of rage that she then used to justify things she knew she shouldn't be doing. Like texting with a friend of Karim's and meeting up with him. Conducting illicit exchanges at night, before she fell asleep. Laughing at his jokes and allowing his knee to press up against her own, under the table. Some afternoons, Nour asked her mother to watch the baby while she had coffee "with friends." She put on more makeup than just eyebrows and foundation, and felt a bit pretty when she caught her own reflection in the mirror of the bus.

She had always believed that God knew best for her, and that by heeding His dictates, she would win His favor. But the recent months were testing her. She knew it was wrong to interact freely with another man. But it was summer, and she needed distraction. Otherwise, everywhere she looked, she saw couples holding hands, sharing a pastry, taking selfies by the ocean, smiling at some private exchange.

IN JANUARY 2014, ENNAHDA AND its coalition partners voluntarily relinquished power, facing sustained pressure over security. The international community, especially the Europeans, were greatly relieved that Tunisia's experiment with political Islam had evolved so gracefully, without the massacre and military coup that ended Egypt's, or the collapse of neighboring Libya. Leaders across the world celebrated Ennahda's pragmatism and maturity and lauded Tunisia as a democracy capable of peaceful transitions. Later that year, the French celebrity-intellectual Bernard-Henri Lévy, shirt as ever unbuttoned, floated into Tunis and praised Tunisians for their victory in the electoral "battle against the religious obscurantists," referring later to a key Ennahda as "the most objectionable company to be found on the political scene." An indignant crowd of protestors at the airport demanded he leave, and please never return.

In May 2014, the new government banned the annual conference of Ansar al-Sharia, which they considered a terrorist organization. Ben Ali–era controls over the religious sphere continued, with imams harassed and prosecuted on trumped-up charges. Certainly some imams were inciting violence against minorities or political foes, but some were simply challenging the long-time hold anodyne state-oriented imams had held over the religious sphere. The security sweep appeared not to differentiate. No one asked what was to become of the thousands of peaceful Tunisian youth who had gathered under the Salafi banner. As one young Tunisian said, "It's like shutting down a factory. Where are all the workers supposed to go?"

Many activists resigned themselves to a retreat from civic life. For others, going underground again, as though the revolution had never happened, felt unthinkable; they saw only two possible directions: Libya and Syria. By the accounts of security groups and the Tunisian authorities in 2016, around six to seven thousand Tunisian men and at least one thousand women had left their country to travel to Syria. Jamal, the Communist in Kram, said around five hundred men from the district had gone, and that the recruiters received a generous fee, about $3,000, for each young man they sent to a battlefield. Female recruits garnered slightly less.

Jamal knew many of the emigrants personally, and took a psycho-analytical view of their motivations. Many of the women were simply troubled; they had body image issues and were desperate to escape their families. Jamal remembered one neighborhood boy who had been bullied intensely as a child. Jamal later spotted him on an ISIS video, in the background of the shot, transporting prisoners for execution. He had seen friends being courted by the Salafis. "They prey on the most vulnerable, exactly at the moment when they're not educated enough to know better, but religious enough to feel the impulse," he said. "They ply them with YouTube sheikhs and fatwas and *nasheeds*, and six months later the guy finds himself in Syria, smoking weed, convinced it was the right thing to do."

But bullying, body image issues, toxic families, broken families— these were the ordinary challenges of life. Was it enough to drive a young person to join the jihad? Jamal sat smoking under a canopy in the rain at a café with exposed concrete walls, filled with young people on MacBooks. He crushed a cigarette and lit another. "Islam is the main pillar of our society. Sometimes I even sympathize with what they feel. Salvation through violence. Pining for the past."

Some days, Nour felt as though the revolution were a private dream. Despite hijabi women now sitting in parliament, despite the fact that a good half of the women on public transport or walking down Avenue Bourguiba now wore hijab, the public culture of bullying hijabi women had not been shed in the new Tunisia. Nour never looked askance at a girl who wore a short skirt on the tram, or glared at a woman in a tank top. They would answer to God on the Day of Judgment. The point of freedom was that everyone could dress however they wanted, was it not? Was it genuinely such a point of offense to women who dressed more liberally that she, Nour, chose not to? They were accustomed to harassment by the police, because the police harassed everyone. It was the contempt of ordinary women that she found harder to reconcile.

On a spring Friday, Nour had dressed carefully to go give blood at a clinic near Carthage. She wore a loose blouse, one with sleeves she could pull up easily, and waited for Walid to pick her up. Walid looked out for her while Karim was away. The clinic was on a residential road, lined with gated villas that were covered in bougainvillea. The woman behind the reception desk wore a nurse's uniform, and elaborate eye makeup. She looked Nour over and shook her head. "You can't come inside looking like that."

Nour willed her features to stay impassive. *"You can't come inside looking like that"* was meant to have died with the old regime. "We're just here to give blood for a friend; what does it matter what she's wearing?" Walid asked. The nurse started to answer, but Nour was already out the door.

That day, they came from the clinic to a beachside café in La Marsa, a well-heeled northern suburb of Tunis, to have coffee. Across the street from the café was a boutique hotel with an infinity pool, where the air smelled like jasmine and the bartender mixed gimlets. Six months prior, Abu Bakr al-Baghdadi had declared a caliphate in Raqqa. Karim, like many Tunisian fighters, left the Nusra Front, which he had initially joined, and migrated to ISIS. Nour supported this, and she was still eager to join him. Her daughter was now almost two and had never met her father. "She thinks my father is her father," she said.

Walid scanned his eyes around the café, keeping his voice low. He thought Nour was foolish. The Tunisians going now, he said, were nothing like the idealistic first wave that had joined the jihad, when he did, back in 2012. "They're not going to free Syria. It's their last solution. They're either mercenaries or going for martyrdom, and taking the shortest path to get there." Unlike when he was a teenager, listening to jihadi cassette tapes and videos, young people now drew their information about jihad from the internet. This had changed everything. "Now it's about the power of the medium, not the content," he said. "It's all about aesthetics and who produces the most beautiful video."

The seaside café was among the more modest in La Marsa, but even here, Nour's outfit—a dark two-piece cloak and trousers over black Converses—drew attention. La Marsa was the quarter where affluent, foreign-educated Tunisians and expatriates lived. The neighborhood had the requisite nail bars and gluten-free bakeries. Here, liberals enjoyed a comfortable majority, and as such, it was an active theater where emancipated secular women bullied emancipated religious women. When a rising star in the Ennahda party, the Sorbonne-educated Sayida Ounissi, attended a lecture in La Marsa a year prior, a woman accosted her in the bathroom and said, "You're so beautiful and clever, why do you wear this stupid cloth on your head?"

From her seat in the café, Nour stared out at the sea. A camel ambled across the beach with fluorescent tassels around its neck, looking, like most camels, wryly content. LIFE IS IN OUR HANDS, announced a nearby billboard advertisement for the British International School. A group of women in flamenco skirts and matching crimson hijabs posed for a photo shoot along the Corniche. The Corniche was lined with wilting, half-dried-out palm trees that were battling the red palm weevil, a palm-decimating pest that had originated in Tunis and migrated north to attack the palms of Palermo and Cannes. Tunisians whispered that the weevils were a curse brought to Tunisia by the son-in-law of the deposed president, the one with the pet tiger.

Nour said she believed it was acceptable for ISIS to kill civilians in the West, but couldn't articulate what religious rulings allowed that. As ISIS grew more savage, many Salafi clerics condemned its acts of violence. Nour seemed perplexed by not having any theological evidence for what she felt—politically, emotionally, morally—to be right.

Walid interjected here, feeling the need to explain why Nour knew so little about the religion she followed so devotedly. The education system under Ben Ali, he said, deliberately kept religious instruction spare and shallow. He remembered being taught a Quranic passage in school, concerning rightful behavior in the face of injustice. At home, when his father opened the Quran to the relevant verse, Walid discovered that the teacher had bowdlerized it, leaving out the more forceful passages. This poor instruction encouraged curious young people to seek out information online, where they stumbled across sermons, sources, and texts of unvetted authenticity and background. "They're like a blank board ready to be written on," he said.

Flimsy religious knowledge was common among young Tunisian women who had joined Salafi networks or traveled to join militants in Libya or Syria. One woman, who died in an air strike on an ISIS training camp in Libya, had failed the entrance exam for the Sharia law degree at the University of Tunis. This is what Walid meant when he said that an education system in a largely religious country that neglected religious instruction left the doors open for manipulation, by actors who used the language of religion for other aims.

Nour didn't feel especially conflicted by her support for a group that was, by that point, heavily involved in theatrical violence. To her, the crucifixions and sex slave markets were the fanciful propaganda of the group's opponents. She seemed skeptical that ISIS had done all of those things. Many young people like Nour didn't believe what they heard about ISIS. The media in most Arab societies was deeply politicized, enmeshed with authoritarian political regimes and reflecting those regimes' agendas and biases. Many young people had simply disengaged. Asked whether she accepted ISIS's tactic of targeting other Muslims, even at prayer in mosques, on the grounds that they had become unbelievers, she nodded in assent. Walid, lighting a cigarette, snapped, "So it's all right for them to target al-Nusra?" She responded feebly and they sparred for a couple of minutes.

After Karim left for Syria, the police started "inviting" Nour to have conversations with them. This involved her going to a police station about twice a month, to sit in a room with a metal desk, usually responding to the same questions posed by the same unibrowed officer: *Why are you wearing those clothes? Why don't you take them off? Who are you in communication with? Who is your religious mentor?*

For a while, Nour had managed to hide the police surveillance from her friends and family. She would come up with elaborate excuses for needing to change plans, but there was nothing she could do about the unmarked number flashing on her phone. In Kram, rumors flew quickly. Some of her friends started shunning her. No one wanted to be associated with a girl who was being watched by the police.

When the neighbors asked her mother where Karim had gone, she told them he was attending to some business in France. But Nour suspected that many of the neighbors realized the truth. A family friend, a taxi driver, blamed Karim and his Islamist brothers for the fact that the cruise ships had stopped coming to Tunisia. In earlier years, the ships had dropped anchor in La Goulette harbor, pouring thousands of cheerful Europeans into Tunis for a few hours of spending each day. The taxi driver repeated the ships' names lovingly, as if caressing a rosary: "The *Majestic,* the *Fantastic,* the *Adonia* . . ." Nour sometimes caught him looking at her with anger in his eyes.

Ricocheting Out

By the middle of 2015, ISIS establishes itself as a global menace whose reach extends across Europe, North Africa, and beyond, upsetting the political order in states from Germany to Tunisia. So many hundreds of Britons have traveled to join the Islamic State that a former UK counterterrorism official suggests the government should "lay on charter flights to Syria."

A Jordanian fighter jet crashes near Raqqa, and the pilot, Muath al-Kasasbeh, is captured by ISIS. After feigning interest in a prisoner swap with Jordan, they ask for recommendations on Twitter as to how he should be put to death, under the hashtag #SuggestAWayToKill TheJordanianPigPilot. The world, seemingly, fails to notice how social media companies are enabling the war, gaining traffic and therefore profiting off people's interactions with such content.

ISIS releases footage of the pilot being burned to death in a cage. Leading Islamic scholars across the world condemn the killing. Jordan and the United States retaliate with air strikes, and the group claims these strikes have killed American hostage Kayla Mueller.

Throughout the spring, the group's affiliates unleash bombings in Yemen, Afghanistan, and Tunisia. They hold a theatrical mass execution in the ancient amphitheater of Palmyra.

This summer, the population exodus unleashed by the Syrian civil war reaches its peak, destabilizing Europe. German chancellor Angela Merkel calls it a "national duty" to host the largest refugee influx in Europe's history, declaring, "We can do this." On some days, Munich processes thirteen thousand refugees in a day, sometimes forty thousand over a weekend. Thousands of refugees die before arrival, asphyxiated in trucks or drowned in the sea.

The European far right treats the war-fleeing refugees as unwelcome invaders, and exploits their plight to gain electoral ground. There are hundreds of attacks on asylum centers each month. A Hungarian camerawoman becomes the global face of this hatred, recorded on camera tripping a man running with a child in his arms for the border. Hungary erects a barbed-wire fence. The European

Union confronts the fact that many of its members do not share liberal democratic values such as human rights.

In September, a photo appears on the front page of newspapers around the world: the drowned toddler Alan Kurdi, wearing a red T-shirt and navy shorts, facedown on an empty beach, hands turned out against the tide.

Despite the backing of Iran-led militias, the Assad government appears in real danger of falling. On the last day of September, at the behest of Assad, Russia launches its first air strikes in what will be a definitive turning point in the war.

RAHMA AND GHOUFRAN

May 2015, Tunis

WHEN OLFA CAME HOME AND SAW THAT HER PHONE CHARGER WAS gone, along with all her headscarves, she knew. It was a cloudless late spring morning and Rahma was gone.

Rahma called two days later, but wouldn't speak to Olfa. "Put one of the girls on," she texted first. When the phone rang, Olfa obliged, because she knew Rahma would hang up otherwise. It had been the same with Ghoufran, who communicated only with Rahma, not with her mother. To both of them, Olfa was a pariah, an unbeliever.

Olfa could understand. She had sat with the same sheikhs and found their ideas appealing. She had briefly considered wearing the same severe clothes that her daughters had adopted. Amid their lives of deprivation and hardship, Olfa saw the appeal of situating herself in the path of certainty. Whatever problem you had, they had a way of solving it. Anything you felt hurt by, any injustice or slight, they had a balm for it. Who wouldn't want such solace?

Olfa blamed herself for all of it; she blamed her parenting and Tunisia itself. She knew, in her heart, that she had not been a friend to Rahma. That she had been harsh with her, had responded to her moodiness and troubled behavior with anger and slaps, that she had allowed herself to take out her own suffering and resentment on her daughter.

And as for Tunisia, how could any child growing up in this country grow up normal? What was a normal response to religion in a country that seemed hospitable only to the extremes?

June 2015, Sousse, Tunisia

On a cloudless June day, at around noontime, a young engineering student walked out onto the beach of one of the coastal luxury hotels in Sousse. There were tourists everywhere, mostly British, lounging on beach chairs, standing ankle deep in the sea. Seifeddine Rezgui held a beach umbrella awkwardly at his side, concealing the Kalashnikov wrapped in its folds. The young man pulled the rifle out and started spraying bullets in every direction.

People screamed as he stalked up and down the beach. Some dove into the water to escape. Others ran, stumbling in the sand, or crawled under beach loungers for cover. He pivoted toward the hotel compound, reloading round after round, pausing to lob grenades. In all, Rezgui killed thirty-eight people—mostly Britons—in a shooting spree that went on for forty minutes before the police finally arrived and shot him dead.

Rezgui was not from a religious family. He was a break-dancer; he admired leftist politicians; he drank alcohol and had a girlfriend. He lived with his family in a one-bedroom house in Sousse, not far from where Olfa lived with her children, and was finishing a master's degree. His family were stunned. They remain stunned to this day, and believe Seifeddine was brainwashed or set up.

His friends tell a different story. Here was a man who, like them, was young at the time of the revolution in 2011 and expected change to come quickly. With the fall of Ben Ali, he believed that society would move away from its authoritarian secularism and embrace more religious values and social justice in governance and public life; when that didn't happen, when even the narrow openings for Islamist politics closed off, he began spending time with some local young Salafi men, who shared his fierce disappointment. Bashar al-Assad's war in Syria, friends said, tipped him over the edge.

His transformation was slow, and happened on the inside. He became a religious young man with sharp political grievances. He developed the conviction that violence was the only way to express them. The local Salafis put him in touch with militants in Libya, who ran a training camp. His father said these young men infected Seifeddine with "evil thoughts" and that he was a victim of "radicalization." But in the words of Olfa, who struggled with this question every day, "What is the difference between an extremist and a very upset Muslim?"

There was a thin invisible line connecting Olfa with Seifeddine. He had been dispatched to the beach that day by Noureddine Chouchane, an influential senior figure with the Islamic State in Libya. There was a hub of Tunisians in Sabratha, in Libya, where Noureddine sometimes sheltered. It was there that a newly arrived Tunisian sister caught his eye: Rahma.

Two months after her arrival in Sabratha, Rahma finally condescended to speak to her mother, despite her status as unbeliever. Like many mothers who receive phone calls from daughters who have absconded to ISIS and are ringing from conflict zones, Olfa kept in character and elected to vent, screaming at Rahma for a full five minutes. When she finally calmed down, Rahma apologized. She said it had been her duty to come. She hoped one day Olfa would understand.

"What of Ghoufran?" Olfa asked. Apparently one man had proposed to Ghoufran not long after her arrival. "When she met him in person, Mummy, she thought he looked weird, so she said no!" Rahma said. "You know Ghoufran, she always thought she was going to marry some handsome guy. So she waited until she found a prince," Rahma said. Ghoufran married this second man. It was another layer to her heartbreak. Olfa had thought many times about the sweetness of planning or approving her daughters' marriages.

When she put the phone down, Olfa consoled herself with the belief that Ghoufran must be happy. No other mother and daughter could have been as close; they were more like sisters than parent and child. The part of her that ached for Ghoufran knew, on some level, that if her daughter didn't miss her, she must truly be contented. At least this is what Olfa told herself.

LINA

March 2016, Tal Afar, Iraq

THAT SPRING, THEY EACH HAD THEIR TASKS. LINA'S WAS TO GIVE BIRTH and bring their second child into the world. Jafer's was to travel to Mosul and undergo a second operation to remove a further piece of his injured leg. The doctor in Tal Afar had advised this, saying, rather ominously, that it appeared the first surgeon "had been unfamiliar with such cases."

In March, when the labor pains started, Jafer had already gone, so Lina went alone to the hospital. As an ISIS wife, she had priority over civilians; hospitals operated on an ISIS-first basis, regardless of triage, and basic hospital infrastructure was still intact. But over half the city's residents had fled, emptying the ranks of competent doctors; of those who remained, many chose not to practice, or practiced privately, outside the public hospital system that had been commandeered by ISIS.

It was Lina's fifth time giving birth, so she knew what was coming. But when it came time to push, something felt wrong. The baby wasn't moving and the pain was different. There was a lot of shouting, and Lina clung to the sides of the bed. She tried to focus on the cracks in the ceiling above her head. Finally he was out—they said he was a he before they whisked him away—and she kept asking for him and asking for him, lying there drenched in sweat.

After an hour the doctor brought him back, a tight smile plastered on her face. "He's in perfect health, thanks be to God," she said, handing Lina the baby. But she knew instantly that her son was not fine.

There were purple bruises along one side of his head and near one eye. Because they hadn't held him up to her as he came out, she suspected that they had done this to him. She decided they must have injected something into his face with a syringe. "This baby needs oxygen!" she shouted. But the doctor ignored her and kept repeating that he was fine. Lina put him to her breast, but his mouth was listless. The doctor huffed in irritation when Lina pointed out that he wasn't suckling. She told Lina to take the baby home and that when she was more relaxed, he would latch on.

But a woman knows when her baby is very ill. She knows it as surely as if it were her own body, because only moments ago it was. Lina decided to go home; they weren't going to do anything more for her here. They were the ones who had hurt him in the first place.

At home, she wiped the baby's body with a wet cloth. He was hot with fever, and coughed little spittles of blood. She fanned him as he slept. She awoke in the night to find his body burning with a fever that must have been over 105 degrees. She had no medicine at home, certainly no infant medicine, and ran to the next-door neighbor's house. She pounded on their front gate, but it was the middle of the night and they couldn't hear her. When Lina got back, the baby's arm was sticking straight out at a ninety-degree angle. He was slowly stiffening. She tried to massage his arm; she thought if she could just keep him supple he would make it to morning, and then she would find another hospital. *He must not go stiff. He must not go stiff.* She whispered in his ear and massaged his miniature, perfect feet. Eventually he took two deep, shuddering breaths, and then he was still.

She stared at the blue tube of hand cream on the bedside table, the tin of hard candy Jafer sucked on when he couldn't sleep, the striped rug between the two beds. Two impulses tore at her: the first to be perfectly composed and wait for the baby's spirit to return to God, who must have loved him so much that He immediately wanted him back; the second, to be entirely certain that he was dead. She needed someone else's confirmation. She banged again on the neighbor's door, this time screaming and screaming until finally the husband came to the gate. "I need you to come see if my baby is really dead," she said. "Please go get your wife."

In the morning she wrapped the baby in a bedsheet and, together with her neighbor, took him to the morgue.

Lina spent the afternoon at the home of another German woman, but she suddenly had a feeling that Jafer might have come home from his surgery. When she returned, she found him lying on the couch, pallid and weak. He was meant to stay in the hospital at least two days to recover—the surgery had involved cutting into his femur—but he had come back to see his wife and their new baby.

Lina perched next to him and told him what had happened. Jafer wept, and she held her husband's face in her hands. It was a turning point for her. After a lifetime of caring for others—her children, her first husband, her in-laws, the abandoned pensioners of Frankfurt, her invalid second husband—now, finally, she needed someone to take care of her.

PART V:
Love, Mourn, Repeat

ASMA, AWS, AND DUA

January 2015, Raqqa, Syria

TO THE OUTSIDE WORLD, THE TERRITORY CONTROLLED BY THE ISLAMIC State seemed hermetically sealed. But the routes into and out of its capital, al-Raqqa, were porous and regularly crossed by both ISIS fighters and the ordinary people interacting and doing business with them. Its territory was still a market, and Raqqa, perched on the banks of the Euphrates, had been a significant commercial and geographic crossroads since the eighth century. Truck drivers streamed in and out of the ISIS caliphate daily, supplying the militants with everything from gasoline to chocolate wafer cookies and energy drinks.

It was this porous commercial normalcy, especially up to and around the end of 2014, that enabled Dua, Aws, and Asma to escape. Dua, the farmer's daughter with the rose tattoo who married the wealthy Saudi, left first. She discussed leaving with her father and brother, and both agreed that if she could not accept another marriage, as the caliphate wanted her to do, the only choice was to go.

Her brother started making calls to Syrian friends in southern Turkey, people who had experience with the border crossing and could meet Dua on the other side. It was a frosty January night when Dua and her brother boarded a small minibus for the two-hour ride from Raqqa to the Tal Abyad crossing. At that time, refugees were streaming across the border daily into Turkey. Dua and her brother passed through easily.

When Aws, the feisty, romantic English literature student who hated her second husband, decided to leave four months later, it was getting more difficult. Turkey had tightened security at the border. Aws contacted her cousin Dua, already in Sanliurfa, a Turkish city about sixty miles north of the border, and asked for the phone number of the man who'd smuggled her out. He was part of a network that specialized in extricating people from within ISIS, men affiliated with one or several rebel groups, often with the cooperation of someone inside the organization. The man dispatched someone to escort Aws to the border. She emailed him a picture of herself, and when her escort arrived on the appointed night, he had fake identity cards for both of them, bearing the same last names; that night, they were brother and sister. They took a taxi to the same crossing, Tal Abyad, but the checkpoint guards did not ask her to show her face. The identity card, unused, stayed in the front pocket of her black handbag.

By early spring of 2015, when Asma, the marketing student whose boyfriend was still in Jordan and who refused to marry a fighter, was agonizing about what to do, the city had been transformed. Most days she went around Raqqa without seeing a single familiar face. Everyone who could afford to had fled, even many of the families who had initially collaborated. In the market, people spoke Arabic with North African and Gulf dialects. It was common to hear French-accented English, people speaking a third language, trying to conceal their identities, as though spies might be lurking amid the produce.

When Asma and a cousin plotted their escape, they told no one, not even their families, and took nothing but their handbags. A friend inside ISIS agreed to get them out. They drove to the border under the blanket darkness of a new moon, a journey Asma had made so many times to ferry women into the caliphate that she could tell, from the pacing of the bends in the road, how long was left to go. Her body felt itchy with fear, mostly for her friend inside ISIS, the fear of what could happen to him if it was discovered he had helped them. When she handed her ID card to the ISIS border guard at the checkpoint, she was convinced he knew they were trying to escape. She felt short of breath and bit her tongue, trying to control the adrenaline that was coursing through her body. The more frightened she looked, the more suspicious she would seem. She tried to remind herself that her thoughts and terrors were inside her head, not visible outside her like free-floating ticker tape. The Turkish guards on the other side were having a tea break, and waved them through. The car waiting for them, a modern Korean four-door, glinted gray from the light at the checkpoint.

URFA, THE TURKISH CITY FORMALLY called Sanliurfa, sits sixty miles north of the border with Syria. The dry grass plains on its outskirts are dotted with almond and plum groves, pines and olive trees. The housing boom of recent years has seen low-slung apartment blocks rise up on its outskirts, providing the cheap accommodation that made it possible for so many Syrian refugees to slowly rebuild their lives. The Syrian war had permanently changed the face of the city, just as it had done to cities like Istanbul and Beirut; its central boulevards and thoroughfares teemed with impish, rumpled Syrian children begging and selling packets of Kleenex. But there were opportunities for work, and the rent on a two-bedroom apartment in Urfa was not staggeringly out of reach, as it was in those bigger cities.

As cities went, it was provincial and understated. Its mixed Kurdish and Arab-origin populace tended to social conservatism, most women covered their hair, and there was no great political Truth hanging over the place—no giant Assad statue bearing down or black flags whipping in the wind. The local squares contained statues of things like giant red bell peppers. The pool adjacent to the ancient mosque swarmed with fat carp that were considered sacred, swimming in the spot where King Nimrod was believed to have thrown the Prophet Abraham into the fire. The fort of Sanliurfa loomed from above. The gleaming new mall, Piazza, seemed out of place, as though airlifted in by the Turkish state to tutor local residents in buying shoes from air-conditioned shops, rather than the shoe heaps spread out on blankets at the mouth of the bazaar.

By the time Aws, Dua, and Asma arrived in early 2015, there were enough Syrian residents to run and sustain Syrian restaurants and baklava shops in the center of town; there were Syrian men who had cooked *molokhiya,* a green, clingy stew served with rice, for years in their hometowns of Aleppo and Homs, and were now doing the same in Urfa. The merchants in the bazaar were practiced in saying, in Arabic, "This price is just for your sake!"

For the women, what they had done back in Raqqa was a tightly guarded secret. They were exiled, dislocated, hiding pasts they knew could hurt them. They missed their families and felt alienated and out of place in Urfa, which felt about three generations behind Raqqa before the war, and they hoped to move on to a more lively, modern part of Turkey. They attended English- and Turkish-language classes, knowing they would need some proficiency to help them chart a future elsewhere. They lived with Syrian families whom they knew from home, who had arrived earlier and were more established; Asma even stayed with distant relations. The families helped cover much of their living costs, and they used what they brought from Syria to cover their language courses and daily expenses.

Aws woke up each day to the same reviving ritual: coffee and the Lebanese singer Fairuz.

Her two Raqqa marriages had not dented her light spirit; she was resilient and young, she was an educated woman who loved reading novels, and she still wanted those babies wrapped in cabbage leaves. The Urfa album of her cellphone gallery approximated her life in Raqqa before ISIS: handsome friends posing by rivers, endless shisha cafés. She managed to speak to her family about twice a month. The family she lived with treated her like a daughter; they even paid her mobile phone bills. She wanted to find a way to finish her university studies, but most of all, she wanted to be normal again. In Urfa, no one ever let you forget you were a refugee. Once, while walking with a Syrian male friend in town, they had been stopped by an angry Turkish man. "If you were a real man, you wouldn't have left your country," he shouted at her friend.

Asma was more fearful and rarely went out. Urfa was crawling with intelligence agents from various countries. ISIS militants transited in and out, and sometimes hunted Syrian dissidents. She had severed all contact with her family, worried that ISIS would punish them for her escape. Once a week, Asma emailed and called a friend in Raqqa to complain about her heartless family and how they had spurned her. This was untrue, but she hoped that ISIS intelligence would hear it—they monitored the phone communications of many Raqqa residents, especially those who worked with them—and that it would protect her family from blame.

Asma felt reduced to her melancholy. She was not the Asma who had studied marketing and wanted to work in hospitality, who had a Galaxy Note II and wore musky perfume and revered Taha Hussein; she was not the woman who had turned down the love of her life over wearing the hijab and yet had ended up working for ISIS. Here in Sanliurfa, she was only a refugee. When she wore stylish clothing or made an effort with her hair, she felt reproachful eyes on her. It was as though she was not allowed to be happy or laugh, as though the only permissible way to act was sober or, more ideally, distraught. She found pleasure where she could; she had recently had a Brazilian blow-dry that took three consecutive days of treatment at the hair salon. She saved up enough to spend a couple of days in Antalya, on the Turkish coast. Every day after her trip, she watched the clips she had recorded on her phone: the nightclub with its anonymous darkness, flashing lights, moving bodies.

Asma, Aws, and Dua sometimes had lunch together. Occasionally they argued about Syria and the future, even though none of them knew when the war would end or what would come after that. Aws saw no place for the intolerant sectarian armed groups in power. Syria was too mixed, had too many religious minorities—Christian, Druze, Alawite, Shia—to make a Sunni Islamist government an option.

But Dua, more pious and conservative, had learned about Islam only when ISIS took over, and wished to see religious politicians— moderate and genuine ones, certainly not these fanatics who used religion as flourish—in power. Her problem with ISIS was not that it had sought to establish an Islamic state and impose Islamic law, but that it showed disregard for basic Islamic legal tenets. ISIS had instrumentalized Islam, made it a means to its political ends; it had hollowed the faith out of everything it stood for and reduced it to a tactic: *takfir,* designating opponents as enemies whose blood could be spilled.

Dua had come to prefer Jabhat al-Nusra, or the Nusra Front, one of the most prominent rebel groups fighting in the Syrian war. It was Syria's avowed al-Qaeda affiliate, but it was also mostly Syrian in membership, and it was at the forefront of the opposition's armed struggle against the government. Unlike ISIS, Nusra had not imposed a jihadist "state" on local populations. Instead, it cultivated popular support and coexisted with other currents of the Syrian opposition.

"No, no, Nusra is not an option," Aws said, annoyed at what she saw as her cousin's naïveté. This point of view was shared by many Western states, which ultimately calculated that a jihadist rise to power in Syria—either ISIS itself or the most extreme of the rebels— was a greater strategic threat than Assad. Many Syrians agreed. Whether enough agreed to tip the balance in Assad's favor, absent Russia's military intervention, is a question people will argue for years to come. But Assad had cultivated an opposition so radical that the world would be obliged to side with him—that was simply a truth, a tactic that insulated his rule, however unjustly, against real challenge.

The women avoided discussing the future, because when they did, as was the case one sweltering afternoon in the summer of 2016, their conclusions made what felt like a shabby, temporary existence seem permanent. In the apartment of the Free Syrian Army man who had helped them escape, where they gathered, a sour, salty smell wafted up from the sheep-brain restaurant on the ground floor of the building.

So much had changed since they had joined the early demonstrations in Raqqa, when they had chanted alongside their neighbors for the fall of the regime. Now they all three said they would never go back to Syria, because there was nothing to go back to. Their Raqqa existed only as a collection of memories in the photo galleries of their phones, to run a finger across in the dark before falling asleep.

"Who knows when the fighting will stop?" asked Asma. "Syria will become like Palestine; every year, people think next year it will end, we will be free. And decades pass. Syria is a jungle now."

"Even if one day things are all right, I will never return to Raqqa," said Aws. "Too much blood has been spilled on all sides. I'm not talking just about ISIS, but among everyone."

LINA

Spring 2017, Raqqa, Syria

THE CALIPHATE SUFFERED AN ABUNDANCE OF WIDOWS, AND WIDOWS, as everyone knows, are especially prone to envy. If the widows were widows twice or even thrice over, as was the case with many women, the problem of envy took on monstrous dimensions. To be a widow in the Islamic State was to be condemned to a rough, deprived existence in a guest house for widows. In the midst of the turbulent war, these women coveted the protection of a husband who would provide them a home. They shamelessly angled to become the second wives of already married men, indifferent to whether the first wives accepted this. Such was the state of things in Raqqa in 2017 that a woman like Lina could be envied for a one-legged man. As she walked down the street with Jafer limping along, she could feel the eyes of other women on them, actually *feel* them, even through the black flaps of cloth the women were now obliged to wear over their eyes.

They had moved away from Tal Afar in the early spring of 2017 in anticipation of the city coming under attack. Lina was pregnant again, and she and Jafer wanted to start over, to erase the memories of their baby boy's death. In their village on the outskirts of Raqqa, life was preternaturally good at first, as if they had landed in some bucolic German village. The evenings were cool and families went out to the park. The night sky was littered with stars; so many, in fact, that shooting stars were commonplace and soon lost their wonder. Jafer's family sent money from Germany and he bought a new car and a whole new kitchen—a fridge, a stove, a brand-new washing machine.

They bought new clothes for their son. And best of all, it wasn't Daesh money. The distinction mattered to her. She would have felt tainted having such comforts supplied by the organization and would have preferred to go without.

But as the local women witnessed Lina and Jafer's comfort, they began inflicting them with *nazar,* the evil eye. This was not mere superstition. The Quran acknowledges the evil eye, and includes a reference to seeking refuge "from the evil of envying enviers." Many *hadith* narrations of the Prophet describe the evil eye as an arrow that soars straight from the heart of the envious into the body of the envied. Lina and Jafer went to see a local sheikh for a recitation of the Ruqyah al-Sharia, an incantation of the Quran meant to ward off or dispel the evil eye. The portly, wispy-bearded sheikh announced that their condition was quite serious. Someone had cast a spell on them. "I'll take care of it," he promised, and asked them to return the next day.

On that second visit, his waiting room smelled of sweat and unwashed clothes, and overflowed with other families suffering from evil-eye afflictions. The sheikh started what was apparently a group incantation. In her chair, Lina closed her eyes. Partway through, she sat bolt upright. Lina had read the Quran many times. What she was hearing was decidedly not from the Holy Book. Was the sheikh a charlatan? Were they hearing voices? Jafer also shifted uncomfortably in his seat, noticing something was odd. The moment the sheikh was finished, Jafer grabbed her hand and their son's and said, "Let's get out of here."

Whatever had transpired in the sheikh's house that day, it seemed evil and unnatural. At home, Jafer held a bottle of water to the baby's lips and Lina recited the Quran, the proper Quran, over his head.

LINA WAS AN ADEPT COPER, too adept, perhaps, in that she coped so hard and so well that usually when she decided it was time to extract herself from a situation, it was well past the point of deadly. So it had been with her abusive marriage; so it had been with her depressed solitude in Frankfurt; and so it was now with the final months of the caliphate. She had survived since the death of the baby by narrowing her world down to the island of her household.

But now, in the summer of 2017, a clear, unambiguous voice told her it was time to leave. Perhaps the birth of the new baby infused her with some courage, or perhaps the encounter at the sheikh's house made it apparent to her that the Islamic State was collapsing; in times of desperation, people's behavior would only grow more dark and unpredictable. Perhaps amid the crumbling there would be a chance to flee, with fewer chances of being caught.

No matter how annoyed Jafer looked, Lina worked on him about leaving. His mother back in Germany, whom Lina had never met, turned out to be an ally. She begged them over the phone to come back. She told Lina she was like a daughter, that they would all be a family if they came back to Germany. The words were like a soft caress. No female figure had spoken to her in such caring tones since she was a little girl in Germany, before her father had kidnapped her back to Lebanon, after which she never saw her own mother again.

Jafer's position was impossible. If he was caught escaping, he would be executed or imprisoned. And in prison, would they give him Tramadol? Unlikely. But Lina kept insisting. If they tried, at least they would have a chance; if they stayed, they would die in an air strike or be captured by the Iraqi army or the Shia militias, which were now rapidly closing in and reportedly executing ISIS detainees on the spot.

Once Jafer changed his mind, things moved quickly. Lina would go first with the children, and he would follow. Jafer gave her four thousand dollars and told her to give half to the smuggler, a friend, upon reaching the border between Syria and Turkey. The smuggler would take Lina and the children to his house; when the road was safe and open, he would drive them into Turkey.

When she met up with him, the smuggler asked Lina to let him hold on to her cash, for safekeeping—not just his half, but all of it. He was a friend of Jafer's, she reasoned, so she didn't think not to trust him. The next day, as they prepared to leave, everyone in the car had a role to play. Lina was to be the smuggler's wife; her children would be their children; an old man they were taking along was to be his father, her father-in-law; and a fleeing fifteen-year-old was to be a deaf-mute cousin. They were posing as an ordinary civilian family from Raqqa, people who had no ties or sympathies to the Islamic State. If all went well, they would be allowed to pass into Turkey, where they would be free.

But the smuggler wasn't driving north. Instead the car went in the wrong direction, through empty brown plains, past shattered remains of buildings hit in air strikes, collapsed walls and twisted rebar. The smuggler stopped the car a hundred meters from a checkpoint, ordered everyone to get out, and drove away, taking all of Lina's money with him.

This wasn't the Turkish border. This was the border with northern Syria, the area under the control of the Kurdish militia known as the YPG, or the Syrian Democratic Force, SDF. Two female Kurdish soldiers with AK-47s slung over their shoulders approached her. They were part of the Kurdish force that was creating casualties each day in the battle for Raqqa, the fresh graves in nearby cities multiplying. They had no reason to treat fleeing ISIS women kindly. Lina trembled, and the two children clung to her.

EMMA/DUNYA

Spring 2015, Manbij, Syria

EVERY TIME DUNYA WENT TO THE PRODUCE MARKET, LITTLE CHILDREN noticed the rifle slung over her shoulder and shrank from her, reaching for their mothers' hands or hiding in their skirts. At first she averted her gaze, pretending not to see that she had become something that scared children. Many of the foreign women thought that this, this fear they struck into Syrians, was the correct response to their authority as ISIS women. But Dunya could not adjust in this way; all these little things, the frightened stares of the children, the snubbing behavior of the local vendors, hummed inside her, reminding her she was despised and that ISIS might not always have the upper hand.

Going out unarmed was unthinkable. She had a scare, one day, walking just two blocks to the home of another German woman for coffee. It was prayer time and the streets were empty. A car slowed behind her, trailing her with the engine running; she had steeled herself not to run, to stay calm and walk straight ahead until she reached the house.

Selim taught her how to shoot a rifle after that, and told her never to leave the house without it. But the stares of the children distressed her. She wanted a small handgun, but Selim said they couldn't afford it, the little guns were expensive. Eventually she borrowed a handbag-sized gun from a German friend, who had an extra.

Selim too was changing. He was frequently ill and his commander refused to give him time off from fighting, because more and more foreign fighters were feigning sickness to avoid the front line. Many recruits had not expected that the Islamic State would ask them to fight against and kill other Sunni Muslim insurgents. But even the faint suspicion of not wanting to fight—or worse, wanting to leave— could result in severe punishment. One German fighter told his friends he was considering going back home; within a week the organization took him into custody. He was waterboarded and given electric shocks, and then sent back out with the hooded, grave look of one who has been tortured. He would serve as an example to others.

The Islamic State leadership disappointed Selim—he recognized its brutality and unfairness, but he seemed to be internalizing its extremism all the same. When the authorities ordered women to cover their eyes and hands in public—to wear face veils that obscured the eyes and black gloves in the heat—Dunya thought he didn't seem as distressed as he should be. He had started using pejorative terms for the Syrians.

One evening Selim walked into the house and peered over Dunya's shoulder. When he noticed that she was downloading an app onto her cellphone, he exploded. "Don't you realize by agreeing to the terms and conditions, you're consenting to American law? *Kuffar* law?"

She couldn't believe he was serious, and tried to make light of it. "Selim, do you actually read web agreements? The whole thing? Who does that!"

But he was genuinely angry. "I don't need to read them to know that you're contractually agreeing to terms under their laws. *Manmade* laws."

"I need to use this app. It's useful to me. At what point are you going to stop making *takfir* of everything? Are you going to make *takfir* of the spider crawling on that wall?"

It was one of their first major arguments, and it marked the point when she began to realize that—apart from the hardship of living in a war zone, apart from the stretches of time he left her alone, without her knowing whether he was dead or alive—he was turning into a different person. They had supposedly come here because Selim wanted to defend the Muslims Assad was slaughtering. But as time passed, his personality grew more rigid; the austere rules of the Islamic State infiltrated their daily life.

It was like walking across a minefield without a map, her body permanently clenched. Dunya felt as though she had coped with a great deal; she could endure the uncertainty and threat of air strikes, but the emotional toll of enduring Selim, constantly hearing that everything she was doing was wrong, was now the hardest of all.

THE GUEST HOUSE FOR WIDOWS was a place of such deliberate torment and uninhabitability that few women could stay long without going mad. This was precisely the intention. Every town or city controlled by ISIS had one or several of these guest houses, depending on its size, but they all resembled one another in condition and atmosphere. The Guest House for Widows was a state of mind. Across the caliphate, women passing through them were made to understand that a female ISIS member's place was at the side of her husband, *any* husband, and that refusing to marry was recalcitrant behavior that would not be enabled by a comfortable private room with en suite bathroom.

Sleeping arrangements were usually several women to a room. Trips out to the market were tightly controlled by ill-natured house wardens, usually Moroccans, who barked at the residents and withheld toiletries and other necessary items as punishment. One German woman Dunya knew was widowed when her husband blew himself up with a car bomb. When the ISIS commanders came to the house after three or four weeks to ask her to remarry, Mildred refused, and was sent to the local Guest House. After a week there, she changed her mind. Mildred married another man, but after three days concluded that she could tolerate neither the second marriage nor a return to the Guest House. When he was out one day, she arranged to meet up with a smuggler, who helped her get to the Turkish border, where she turned herself over to the border guards.

When Dunya had first arrived in Raqqa, the hostels weren't called anything in particular; they were sometimes referred to generically as *maqqar*, base, or a *modafae'eh*, a guest house. With time, when there were no single women left at all, some women began calling them the Guest House for Widows.

Dunya knew she didn't have much time. Many women she had

met upon arriving in Syria were dead, and many others were leaving. The early days in Manbij, of relative safety and sunset road trips, were a faint memory. Now everyone was terrified; every day, there were tales of someone who had been accused of being a spy and thrown into prison. Behavior that had in the past been acceptable—being in contact with your family, being on the internet when you weren't supposed to—was suddenly grounds for intense suspicion. Not fighting was not an option. Not fighting other Syrian rebel groups, composed of Sunni Muslims, was not an option. Being a private citizen who stayed at home was not an option. The only option left to her looked to be escape.

June 2016, a Small Village Northwest of Raqqa

There was a darkness at the center of their marriage. No matter what happened to the Islamic State, no matter what ultimate fate awaited the Syrians themselves, Selim wanted to live an austere, orthodox Islamic lifestyle forever. Ideally they would settle in Turkey, where he could live among Muslims, hear the call to prayer five times a day, and nurture the hope that one day, a better caliphate would rise from the ruins of the one he was fighting for. Selim seemed to hold out some hope that with time, things might improve; if ISIS fighters managed to get the upper hand and al-Baghdadi didn't feel so besieged, if recruits continued to arrive and swell their ranks, then perhaps the leadership would behave more correctly.

Dunya felt his hope and loyalty were naïve. She no longer entertained these conversations. She let him believe what he wanted and told him simply that she was too scared to stay, that she would try to leave and wait for him in Turkey.

Leaving required connections, and being well connected was something Dunya was good at. She spent hours in the evening bouncing between WhatsApp chats, setting everything up. An acquaintance connected her with a mid-ranking figure in the Free Syrian Army (FSA), the so-called moderate anti-Assad rebel group that received CIA funding and arms. Because ISIS viewed the FSA as traitors for working with the Americans, she could not tell Selim who was helping her. She told him nothing, actually, about her plans, because she feared ISIS intelligence was monitoring his phone communications and would punish him for letting her escape.

The night of her departure, she packed carefully and made sure to tidy up after herself, so that Selim could return to a neat house. She filled the fridge with juice and fruit and put the unwelcome thoughts, of him coming back from the front lines to an empty house, out of her mind. She ran her fingers over the sofa and said a silent goodbye to this last of so many temporary homes.

It was past eleven when there was a rap at the door. She turned the lights off and grabbed her purse. Outside stood a man and behind him, a motorbike. Dunya said, "A motorbike? No one told me anything about a motorbike. There's no way I can bring my stuff along on that thing." The man surveyed the hulking suitcases in the doorway, the duffel bag, a basket that was mewing furiously. "What's that sound?" he asked. She opened the basket to show him the cats, staring up with their glinting eyes.

He was flummoxed. "Fucking hell, lady, are you kidding me?"

"Well, you don't expect me to just leave them behind, do you? I'm their mother!" She had bothered to put on mascara and blinked at him with her long lashes.

This European princess act had carried Dunya far in the world of Middle Eastern men, who found it, initially, disarming. They usually snorted with laughter, recognized her demands as absurd, and then humored her. But the act wasn't working anymore.

"I'm leaving, suit yourself," he said with a shrug, turning toward his bike. He suggested Dunya speak to their mutual friend again. Then he started the engine and disappeared into the night.

"YOU DIDN'T TELL ME YOU had so much stuff," the FSA contact told her, annoyed, when she rang him to complain. Fifteen members of his family had been killed in the past year alone, and the rest were living in displaced-persons camps in Turkey. It was war. What did this woman think he was offering her, some TripAdvisor-reviewed extrication service?

She cried into the phone about how the cats would starve without her, how nobody here cared about animals. It would be better when she got home. Did he know that in Germany, there were state-mandated rules about the size of a hamster cage?

"Fine," he sighed. He would send a car the following night. But she would need to do the crossing without her things. He would arrange for them to follow her later, on a commercial truck.

She was pleased when he followed through on his word. For a week she stayed at a house near the border with Turkey, along with other women waiting to be smuggled out. The border wasn't really a border, though; it was more like a hazy line that demarcated territory controlled by ISIS from that controlled by the FSA. The smuggler said nearing the line was safer by night, so it was past midnight when they finally set out walking.

The moon was round and bright and they could see clearly. But this meant they could also be seen. About five miles into the walk, shots rang out. The only cover was a few trees ahead. They were four in all, Dunya and two other women and the smuggler, and they sprinted to the trees. "Just rest," the smuggler instructed them. He lay down with his head on a root and closed his eyes. "We'll walk at first light."

The ground was cool at first, but soon a chill seeped into Dunya's bones. Her stomach was collapsing against itself from fear. She listened to the breathing of the woman next to her and tried to match her inhalations, to calm herself. She slept only a fitful few minutes and was awake to watch the night sky gently lighten to a rose pink. The smuggler soon woke as well, roused the others, and led them all the final mile to the waiting car.

November 2016, a Village in Northern Syria

Dunya didn't sleep the whole of the night. She made her WhatsApp picture a bleeding heart over the word *Halab,* the Arabic for Aleppo. A German woman she knew was circulating this message:

Hello, this is an urgent message from besieged Aleppo, buses are stuck since yesterday morning at check points, people's situation is extremely hard, because of cold and shortage of water and food supplies. Forced evacuation is suspended and people can't leave buses, we need to speak to as many journalists as possible to inform them and connect them to people, we need to talk to the UN too. Some of them on the bus have mobile phones, and they can speak to them, although all batteries are almost dead, if you can send them to as many journalists as possible, awake them [from] sleep if needed. As the situation can't hold till morning.

She felt fury mount inside her, and started texting. "Dumb asses go to kill tourists when the war is here."

The State Retreats

The Russian intervention shifts the war slowly in the Syrian regime's favor; in the first half of 2016, ISIS territory shrinks by 10 percent. Turkey moves away from its support for the rebel groups and starts staging incursions into northern Syria, creating yet another front of potential conflict with U.S.-backed Kurdish fighters.

The Islamic State leadership prepares its followers for more losses. As the territorial caliphate shrinks, attacks surge abroad: in November 2015, militants launch six simultaneous attacks in Paris, killing 350 people; in December 2015, Tashfeen Malik and her husband open fire on an office Christmas party in San Bernardino, California, killing 14 people. In January 2016, a suicide attack in Istanbul kills 13 people; in March 2016, three coordinated attacks in Brussels, two at the airport and another on a busy metro station, leave 32 dead.

In March, as Donald Trump campaigns for the presidency of the United States, he says on national television: "I think Islam hates us." In November, he wins. And promises to fulfill his campaign pledge of "a total and complete shutdown of Muslims entering the United States."

It is the first time in contemporary history that an American leader suggests Islam is an enemy of the West and that Muslims are not welcome in the United States, echoing two points often made by ISIS.

SHARMEENA, KADIZA, AMIRA, AND SHAMIMA

December 2015, Raqqa, Syria

KADIZA, TO WHOM THE HIGH SCHOOL WORLD OF BETHNAL GREEN NOW seemed the most elusive, distant memory, spent her days wandering listlessly through a dilapidated mansion in Mosul, trying to figure out who among the widows remained an ISIS zealot, who was disillusioned, and who was the former posing as the latter in order to snitch to the ISIS authorities.

Kadiza had married a Somali American not long after her arrival in Syria. For a time, they lived together on the edge of Mosul as he looked for work to avoid having to fight. Kadiza spent her days keeping house for her husband, cooking and cleaning. As a foreigner, she could move about with a degree of freedom, and was able to go out to the market and to internet cafés. Though she and her friends from Bethnal Green scattered after arriving in Syria, they kept in close touch.

By the time her husband eventually went to the front and was killed, Kadiza rued her decision to travel to Syria. The caliphate was not a land of honor and justice where Muslims could hold their heads high, where the call to prayer filled the air and the pavement was littered with roses. Instead it was a vortex of violence and corruption where men hoarded cars and women settled scores against neighbors and foes, as though it were one long mafia war. If she had stayed in Britain, she would have been studying for her A-level exams and thinking about which universities to apply to. In Syria, Kadiza was only sixteen years old, already a widow living among widows.

Some of the British women had become true believers. There was one girl from London who had brought her toddler son, and made him act in propaganda videos wearing combat clothes and an ISIS headband. The mother was active on social media, crowing over the beheadings of Western hostages and promising to become "da 1st UK woman 2 kill a UK or US terrorist!"

Kadiza thought these women were fanatics. She was petrified; she wanted to come home. Her family tried to counsel her from afar, helping with escape plans. As a widow, she lived in a women's guest house that was awash with intrigue, rivalry, and suspicion. She sensed the other women watching her carefully, suspecting that she wanted to escape. Rumors had spread that an Austrian girl caught trying to escape had been beaten to death. Especially frightening was the fate of another girl from East London who had tried to escape: the girl, married to an abusive ex-footballer, had gotten as far as a nearby village with her small daughter. Her husband tracked her down, had her prosecuted and imprisoned by a Sharia court, and took their daughter away, to be looked after by his second wife.

Kadiza spoke with her family back in East London with some regularity. They hadn't seen her in almost a year. They missed her, but sometimes their anger at her took over, and they shouted at her on the phone. She wanted to come back anyway. "I don't have a good feeling. I feel scared," she told her sister on the phone. "If something goes wrong, like, that's it."

Her sister reassured her that this anxiety was normal. She actually suspected that Amira, who was still loyal to ISIS, was trying to discourage Kadiza from escaping. She worried that Kadiza might have confided her plans to Amira and put herself in danger, should her best friend decide to turn her in. Kadiza said she felt a sense of dread. "You know the borders are closed right now. How am I going to get out? I'm not going to go through PKK territory to come out. I'm never gonna do that."

This part of the war was simple: the territory she had to pass through, to get out of Syria, was controlled by groups that hated ISIS; she thought they wouldn't hesitate to kill someone associated with the caliphate. Eventually Kadiza managed to move to Raqqa, still the capital of ISIS-controlled territory, where she hoped she could mount her escape under less watchful eyes. Umm Layth, the teenage blogger from Glasgow, lived in the same building, though she had stopped writing now that tech companies were finally patrolling ISIS content.

Kadiza's family, with the help of their lawyer, used cellphone tracking to identify her position within a five-hundred-meter range. The plan was for her to get into a taxi, which would be waiting at an appointed time and place. Back in London, her sister peered at a map of Raqqa, trying to explain the location to Kadiza over the phone. Right near al-Baik restaurant, she said. "How confident do you feel about that?" she asked, hoping Kadiza could store some trust in the plan.

After a long pause, her voice trembling and barely audible, Kadiza said, "Zero. Where's Mum? I want to speak to Mum."

RAHMA AND GHOUFRAN

February 2016, Sabratha, Libya

THE AMERICAN FIGHTER JETS FLEW OVER SABRATHA IN THE EARLY
hours of Friday, well before anyone would be stirring for the dawn
prayer inside the training camps on the fringes of the city, or in the
houses in the western and southern districts. In one of those houses,
Rahma and Ghoufran were sleeping.

The impact threw their bodies off the bed before their minds reg-
istered waking. Part of the ceiling caved in. Plaster started falling. The
air filled with smoke. Rahma opened her eyes and struggled to see
through the haze of gray dust. Her ears vibrated and she heard high-
pitched screaming as though from very far away. Then she realized
the sounds were coming from Ghoufran, across the room, pinned to
the ground, visible now through the dust, her eyes wild and crazed,
calling her baby daughter's name.

By dawn, there were men everywhere, surveying the damage done
by the American bombs. Large parts of Sabratha resembled a tropical
moonscape, all craters and palm trees. Some men came to take Ghoufran to the hospital. Rahma didn't know where to go. She sat for a
while in the rubble, holding Ghoufran's baby, just a few months old,
listlessly. A fighter came to tell her that Noureddine, Ghoufran's husband, was dead.

Later, one of the women lent her a phone. When she called Olfa,
the sound of her mother's voice broke through the shock. Rahma
began crying and speaking in broken sentences. Olfa couldn't under-

stand a word Rahma was saying. Her daughter was almost panting, and Olfa just caught snatches about planes and Ghoufran's husband being dead.

"If you're scared, just come. It's not far. Do you hear me, Rahma? You can come home."

"No," Rahma said, her tone suddenly calmer. "If my time has come, God has willed it."

Olfa winced. In the space of a minute, she had careened through her usual carousel of emotions: guilt, self-recrimination, and then intense frustration with her younger daughter, who—even now, even surrounded by death and destruction, with her sister in the hospital—clung to blindness.

May 2016, Mitiga Airport Prison, Tripoli, Libya

After the air strike on Sabratha, Rahma and Ghoufran were detained by the militia of the UN-backed government that ruled Tripoli, which had determined they were members of ISIS. They were taken to the airport prison. Rahma insisted that she didn't want to leave. She told everyone who asked—Olfa on the phone, the prison wardens, journalists—that she would rather stay in the Libyan prison, where she was treated with dignity, than return to Tunisia, to live in poverty at the permanent mercy of the police.

One afternoon, not long after they arrived at the prison, the guards brought the two sisters a little boy to look after. His hair was closely cropped; he had a round little nose and ears that stuck out. Tameem was two years old, and he was an orphan. His mother, a Tunisian woman called Samah, had died in the Sabratha air strike. She had given birth to Tameem in Turkey and they returned to Tunis when he was a few months old, but after endless middle-of-the-night raids by police looking for information about ISIS sympathizers, she traveled to Libya to join her husband. The baby's father, an ISIS militant, was nowhere to be found. He was presumed dead, but there was no body to prove it.

Samah's father, the baby boy's grandfather, lived in Tunis. The old man had lost multiple children by this point. His son had gone to fight in Syria a few years prior, and had been killed. Now his elder daughter was dead from an air strike.

Samah's father, back at his spare house in a run-down neighborhood of Tunis, was careful not to explicitly support his children's choice to join the militants. But he said, with something like pride in his voice, that many from the neighborhood had gone. "There are doctors who went, people who left behind millions and said, 'We shall go fight for God.' You see? Not just the unemployed, as you and I might say. People who were well off went for the jihad. As for me, I don't really get anything," he said, shrugging his shoulders.

He traveled twice to Tripoli, to try to bring his grandson Tameem home to Tunisia. The Libyan authorities were helpful, but the Tunisians threw up bureaucratic obstacles. "This could be any baby," one official told him. "How do we know it's a Tunisian baby? Does it have papers?"

Samah's father continued to travel back and forth to visit Tameem, who was growing bigger, and more and more unsettled in the prison. In the pictures he took of Tameem when he visited, the little boy looks impassive and blank. Many of the orphans in prison had been carried out of the rubble of air strikes. They wet themselves and grew withdrawn. At night they couldn't sleep.

Nothing in the world at that time seemed to make sense to Samah's father. What could you say about a world where your baby grandson was kept for months on end in a prison, because bureaucrats wanted to punish families for the path their children had taken? Tunisia's government, and many of its people, remained in denial about just how many Tunisian citizens had left to join the jihad, because this was an indictment of the state itself. Mohammed Iqbal Ben Rejeb, the man who started an organization to help Tunisians stranded abroad, whose own brother had left for Syria, warned that allowing these children to languish in Libya would just make everything go in circles, the future repeating the past. "What are they going to be when they get older? Doctors? Engineers?" he asked. No, he said, they would just form the next generation of ISIS.

Samah's father echoed this. "Even if al-Baghdadi dies tomorrow, someone else will replace him," he said wearily. "We ask of God peace, and that is all."

A Tunisian delegate traveled to Tripoli in April 2017 to visit the Tunisian women and children in Libyan detention, but failed to meet with them. Some of the children were detained alongside their mothers; Tunisian authorities floated a plan to repatriate the children only, which everyone refused.

In October 2017, after over a year and a half of negotiations, the Tunisian authorities allowed Tameem to come home. His picture appeared in a newspaper with his grandfather, both of them grinning and flashing a thumbs-up, the first photo taken of Tameem that shows him smiling.

The authorities in Tunis failed to bring home the other forty-four Tunisian children held in Libya.

BETHNAL GREEN

August 2015, East London

IN 2015, THE NATIONAL YOUTH THEATRE OF LONDON COMMISSIONED A play called *Homegrown* to explore the radicalization of British youth. The play was so abrasive it might have been flecked with shards of glass, but it was also self-contained and composed, in conversation with itself, invoking prejudice and raw youthful pain and then countering it. It was staged in a school, with student actors strewn across the audience and the theater, to impart a sense of a schoolyard chorus conversation. From scene 1, act 5:

> GIRL: Hey, guys. Today is super exciting because I've got three awesome hijab styles for you. Not only are they new looks, but they're a hundred percent pin free. . . .
>
> [I saw your dad on TV.]
>
> [Apparently you like *Keeping Up with the Kardashians*—I can't say that I do.]
>
> [People will either label you as traitors or children.]
>
> [I've seen you on Twitter.]
>
> [It's actually getting quite serious now.]
>
> [I certainly would never be brave enough to run away at sixteen.]
>
> [I heard you got sold.]
>
> GIRL: Okay, guys. Key here is to make one side longer than the other. Like there's not much in it, just a couple of centime-

ters—it makes all the difference between a horrendous hijab
and a hella fleeky one.

[A cynical, ideological terrorist group.]

[You're not a bad person.]

[I don't agree with your decisions.]

[You were looking for something to believe in.]

[What made you believe you were doing the right thing?]

The play conveyed what it was like to be young, Muslim, and
male, and to be humiliated by "random" police searches. It had young
people making beheading jokes; it included a devastating scene about
Mohammed Emwazi, who became the executioner Jihadi John, that
seethed with condemnation, empathy, and disturbing reality ("I know
kids like him"); it aired the indignation of Muslim girls who were told
that their religion was misogynistic; it showed that even teenagers
knew it didn't make sense for their government to be at "war with
radical Islam" while also "playing kiss-ass with Saudi businessmen." It
leveled painful jokes about liberal Islamophobia: "Who's more nervous
than a Muslim man on the tube? The *Guardian* reader next to him,
pretending to be fine." It encapsulated life as Sharmeena, Kadiza,
Amira, and Shamima had experienced it, as they struggled to make
sense of the noise that buzzed around them. It was also the story of
their peers who chose to stay behind, who continued to live with that
noise every single day.

The play was planned to debut at a school in Bethnal Green. But
the council at Tower Hamlets, the borough that oversees the area,
pushed the school to cancel. The National Youth Theatre (NYT)
found another venue, but there were further signs the play continued
to create unease. The police had asked to read the script, attend the
first three shows, plant plainclothes officers in the audience, and
sweep for bombs. The teenage actors protested, and rehearsals carried on.

Two weeks before opening night, the whole production was
abruptly canceled by the NYT, with no explanation. In 1968, with the
passage of the Theatres Act, the United Kingdom ended a 230-year-old

system of formal state censorship. Since 1968, no play had been banned by a theater or the police without clear indication that it might spark violence. A leaked email written by the NYT's director faulted the play's "one-dimensional tone and opinion" and accused the writer and director of an "extremist agenda." Various groups protested, from English PEN to the Index on Censorship, which said the government had "created an atmosphere" that made arts groups increasingly nervous to tackle controversial subjects, "specifically the question of Islamic extremism."

But it wasn't simply that plays dealing with Islamist extremism were hard to put on. Indeed, about a year later the National Theatre itself performed *Another World: Losing Our Children to Islamic State*, which included the stories of Kadiza, Amira, and Shamima as part of the narrative. But this production interspersed their stories with the points of view of U.S. generals and lawyers, and sawed off its nuance until nothing was left but the cliché it handed back to the audience: "We are just the same as you." If there was any truth to be gleaned from the stories of those girls, it was that their lives, worldviews, and experiences were precisely *not* just the same as those of the white, middle-class audience that turned up at the National Theatre.

Perhaps *Homegrown* was too raw and too unfiltered: it vented the views of the British teens without interrupting them to inject the views of American generals. It contained sympathy for the young man Mohammed Emwazi, before he became the ISIS killer Jihadi John. What could you do when you commissioned a play from young people, and they came up with this? How did you confront the disturbing truth that they felt sorry for him and despised him *at the same time*? Most of all, how could you allow them to reveal that while they rejected ISIS itself, they agreed with its overarching portrayal of the state of the Middle East and its apportioning of blame on Western state interventions and policies for that state? That, in fact, this view was so widely shared it could not in fairness be called the ISIS view at all, but the broad sentiment of many Muslim and Arab publics, in the region and in the West, that was simply articulated by ISIS with its own twist and political agenda.

As it turned out, you could not allow this to be aired publicly at all.

It was censorship, of course, but in the United Kingdom of that time, policing was an imperative over artistic freedom or even, really, freedom of expression. *Homegrown* was banned because it circled back relentlessly to foreign policy as the instigating cause of so much anger among young British Muslims. Its cast of characters seethed with so much grievance that you could not read it or sit through it and fail to understand how ISIS had recruited so skillfully; not because ISIS was especially clever, but because it knew its audience so well.

And though the CCTV image of the teenage girls gliding through the airport had transfixed the world, there was very little eagerness to truly understand *why* they had gone. Their disappearance raised many more questions than answers, but their story seemed to prompt one angry conclusion after the other, as everyone—the media, the police, Prevent officers, Muslim feminists, Western feminists, human rights groups—vied to impose their answers onto the girls' disappearance. To swirl in a morass of suppositions and half-truths seemed safer, in the London of 2015, than to hear what a youth theater group born and raised alongside those girls had to say.

SABIRA

Spring 2016, Walthamstow, Northeast London

AFTER THE ROUT AT THE AIRPORT, SABIRA SPENT WEEKS ENTANGLED with courts, the police, and counter-terrorism officers. It was a multi-layered institutional process that resulted in the loss of her passport, semipermanent surveillance, and the belated realization that—in the midst of her depression, and with the influence of Imran—she had very nearly demolished her young life.

As far as her view of Imran, it was as though he had suddenly been thrust under a glaring fluorescent bulb. What her own neediness and illness had obscured—his manipulations, his cunningly deployed charisma—now appeared obvious. On her backup mobile phone, a text came from him: "I miss you." She considered various retorts to this—*How is your wife? Thanks for getting my passport taken away!*—but decided none of them were worth the bother. One night that spring of 2016, Imran showed up at the door. She pressed herself flat against the hallway upstairs when she heard his voice. Her mother comported herself brilliantly, for once. "Don't you ever set foot in the direction of our house again!" she shouted hoarsely, slamming the door. Sabira felt the vibrations shaking through the wall.

She was obliged to attend the country's highest court to learn her sentence; her father accompanied her to the courthouse on the Strand, in London. Like dozens of other young women in Britain whom the authorities viewed as at risk of travel to Syria, the judge made her a ward of court. Sabira wore her hair down and a charcoal-gray dress and gray tights. She was grateful that everyone at the court treated her with respect and kindness, and that, apart from losing her passport and being barred from traveling, for a given period of time, to any Muslim country, the United Kingdom was giving her another chance. Had she been a young American woman in similar circumstances, caught by American authorities, it's likely she would have been prosecuted under vaguely defined statutes around "material support for terrorism" and been forced to serve a years-long prison sentence.

She spent weeks in email contact with various detective inspectors. She underwent psychiatric evaluations and endured visits from Prevent officers, who sat awkwardly in her living room and asked about Islam and where she stood with her religion. "What sort of Islamic thoughts do you carry in your head right now? What is your Islamic ideology at present, Sabira?" one of them asked her, sitting primly on the sofa in the living room, her language stilted, as though she were reading from a script. What to say to such a woman?

Sabira wanted to tell them she was fine, that she wasn't a mental patient, that a terrible situation had occurred—but given the simplistic questions they were asking her, she was certain they would never understand. If they wanted to know why she had tried to go, why were they asking about the "Islamic thoughts" in her head? Didn't they realize a naïve, broken-bird of a girl might follow a beloved brother to the very ends of the earth? Didn't they realize abused girls were easy prey for charismatic men with dubious intentions? Didn't they realize parents were sometimes hapless and didn't notice abuse under their noses, and even if they did, they were often too cowed and worried about what people would say to do anything about it? Didn't they realize that if her brother hadn't gone, she would never be in this mess in the first place, and had there been no Syrian uprising and no violent crackdown, he wouldn't have gone himself? How could she explain to this well-intentioned but extremely clueless and therefore potentially dangerous white woman in her living room that all these events were arrayed in her mind like the growth rings of a tree, that she couldn't separate out one ring and hold it up as her "Islamic thoughts"?

But Sabira responded with patience and humility, because she understood that both Allah and these people from the court and the police had given her a second chance. She talked to herself a lot, in those days. *Sabira, you're such an intelligent and clever young lady. How could you have allowed yourself to feel so small?*

Sabira's long-term goals had always been to work productively, marry a nice Muslim boy, and lead a comfortable life. These were the aspirations of most young women in her community, a great many of whom grew up in households that were poorer and even more exclusionary than Sabira's. For much of the 2000s and 2010s, due to austerity measures, the state cut programs that were intended to help less-skilled immigrants find work and integrate. This policy collided in the mid-2010s, around the time Sabira's life unraveled, with a wholesale shift in how the British government viewed and dealt with its Muslim citizens.

In 2015, the government redefined its thinking around counterterrorism, declaring that radicalism wasn't fueled by economic marginalization or political grievances, but by the ideology of conservative Islam. Prime Minister David Cameron set out the new approach in a speech that year: Britons who rejected "liberal values" were "providing succor" to violent extremists. Suddenly, wearing the hijab, being socially conservative, belonging to a family that hadn't yet made the transition from village patriarchy to modern independence—each of those traits marked a person as being extreme. And, warned Cameron, "the extremist worldview is the gateway, and violence is the ultimate destination."

By 2017, Louise Casey, an official overseeing integration, was arguing that "oppression of women in Muslim communities" was linked to extremism and Islamist terrorism. She went even further, blaming Muslims for the rise of the far right in Britain, outlining the causal relationship like this: Muslims' religious conservatism led to their poor integration; their poor integration together with their conservatism led to terrorism; their terrorism fueled the far-right and white supremacist movements.

Soon, there was almost no aspect of daily Muslim life and religious observance that was considered out of bounds for scrutiny by officials. Though most recent UK governments had resisted the European trend of banning face veils, by early 2016 both the ordinary hijab and face veils rose to become national security concerns. Cameron called on institutions like courts and schools to devise their own "sensible rules," while other authorities made clear banning face veils in certain spaces wasn't simply about sensible security, but also liberal empowerment. A top education official, speaking about face veils in 2016, said that "our liberal West values" must be protected and that "the Muslim community needs to listen," because British society has come a long way "to ensure that we have equality for women" and "mustn't go backward."

Amid all of these rows and interventions, officials clearly never considered that for a vast number of girls like Sabira, wearing a headscarf secured them freedom, autonomy, access to public space and education. But the hijab rows were never really about female equality at all. It was about how the state felt obliged, now that it had conflated Muslim conservatism with extremism, to nudge the community toward liberalism.

There is a necessary debate to be had about gender equality among Muslims. Britain's largely South Asian Muslim community is highly conservative in a way that often makes life unbearable for some of its young women, and to a different and less immediate extent, for young men. There are suffocating proscriptions around marriage, problems with forced marriage, domestic violence, stark double standards in the treatment of daughters and sons, and taboos around confronting and reporting sexual abuse. (Many of these behaviors are imported from South Asia and, interestingly, rejecting them has encouraged young people to seek religious knowledge and identity from urban, Mecca-trained imams.) But the possibility of shedding this atavistic conservatism while retaining religious values was lost in the acrimony, fear, and mutual suspicion that gripped the Muslim community.

Was it feasible to encourage people to reconsider inherited patriarchal tendencies while diagnosing these same patterns of behavior as pathologies that lead to bombings and beheadings? In January 2016, Cameron established a new fund for teaching English to Muslim women. He warned that those who failed language tests after a couple of years might be deported, because non–English speakers were "more susceptible to the extremist message coming from [ISIS]." The approach was something akin to integration at gunpoint: *The more English you know, the less likely your kids will be to blow themselves up.*

Would Sabira's mother, for instance, have been better poised to notice and deal with both her and Soheil's attraction to extremism had she been more integrated? Would the mothers, grandmothers, or older sisters of Sharmeena, Kadiza, Shamima, and Amira have been?

It depends on our understanding of integration itself. Immigrant parents were poorly equipped for the challenges of contemporary parenting in the urban twenty-first-century Europe. They behaved as though they were still back at home in Bangladesh or Ethiopia, where there was a surrounding cushion of extended family and friends supporting their parenting, casting a protective eye on all the children around them, because that is the way children had always been raised, collectively. In London, there was no such protection; there were gangs and knife crime, predators on Facebook and Instagram, whole collections of virtual and physical threats. These parents assumed the mosque and Quran classes were safe spaces, but the reality was that there were no safe spaces left, period, online or in the real world.

Add to this poverty and broken families, absent fathers, unemployed fathers, fathers who couldn't provide for and protect their families and marinated in that humiliation—realities that cut across all these girls' lives. Immigration often meant long years of separation that caused marriages to fail, as Sharmeena's parents' had; it meant marriages not surviving the strains of arrival, through which women often coped better and men languished in shame-faced, low-wage bitterness; it meant having to dedicate vast time and energy to basic things like securing the rent, navigating the health service, caring for ill relatives, all within a bureaucratic system that was foreign and confusing.

Parenting of millennial Muslims in the age of the War on Terror demanded levels of awareness that immigrant parents often didn't have the capacity for. Integration, then, in the context of *were you integrated enough to stop your kids from joining ISIS,* involved layers of proficiencies, abilities, awareness, and confidence that were gained from many different directions: socioeconomic advancement, education, language skills, access to adequately provided social services, involvement in public life.

But to the government, integration had come to mean acceptance of "British values," full stop. Britain's core national identity was enshrined in gender liberalism, women's physical visibility, an acceptance of homosexuality, and UK foreign policy, especially respect for Israel.

Because the state's understanding of integration was security-driven, it led to policies that increasingly aggravated the country's Muslims, who felt discriminated against, surveilled, and stigmatized. This was a political choice by the government, in the end; to this day there is no clear, established empirical research that shows why people commit acts of extremist violence or join militant groups. For every young girl or young man from a broken home who went to Syria, there were others from loving, intact families; for every one whose mother spoke halting English, there were five others whose mothers were native or fluent English speakers. The children of diplomats and consultant doctors had joined ISIS alongside the children of restaurant waiters and unemployed welfare recipients.

The thorny fact was that the *structural* factors that bred extremism—the Arab tyrannies and coups, Western wars and state collapses that extremists exploited—hardly lent themselves to counterterror policing in the West. These meta forces were too enormous, too profitable, and too endemic to even *acknowledge* as drivers of extremism. It was only the slighter factors, and indeed some made-up ones, that seemed feasible to tackle: getting YouTube to erase Anwar al-Awlaki, blocking encryption on messaging apps, vetting speakers at universities for "extremist views," discouraging boycotts of Israel or aid work for Syria, because these types of activism were portrayed as gateways to extremist views.

A local Prevent officer described with frustration his efforts to speak to British Muslims, especially men, about extremism. "You just get all these men droning on about 'the problem is your foreign policy,'" he said. To him, this was like complaining about the British weather: pointless. The country's foreign policy wasn't changing anytime soon, and those who opposed it—emotionally, practically, or legally—would find themselves increasingly squeezed by Prevent. Prevent now required doctors, teachers, and social workers to be on alert for signs of "extremism." If a family pulled their teenage daughter out of co-ed swimming classes, teachers were encouraged to consult Prevent guidance. A young Afghan British boy who attended school with a "Free Palestine" badge on his backpack had counterterrorism police show up at his door. "It's easier to speak to the women than the men," the Prevent officer concluded in the end. The women just wanted to stop their sons from going off to die, and were more cooperative. They would blame themselves in the end, anyway. The men, they just wanted to talk about *why* their sons were going.

Soheil's son was born in the early summer of 2016, nearly a year after he got married. In video clips, he gazed at his son with enchanted eyes, tickling his chin to coax laughter. He sent his sister photos every couple of weeks. Then one day, Sabira received a text message from one of her cousins: "Your brother's trying to contact you." She downloaded a new app and they managed to speak.

Soheil and their cousin Nadim were in the car together. The connection was unusually clear. It was the first time the three of them had been in one conversation together since the two young men had left, over a year and a half ago. Sabira wanted to be in the car with them so badly. She and Nadim had always been close. He always used to say she was the perfect model of ladylike deportment, and needled his sisters to behave more like her. "Ask Sabira whether she's still going to the gym. Ask Sabira whether her uncle and nan are still feuding. Ask Sabira whether her mother still speaks in proverbs." She updated the two men on everyone's mood, weight, proverb proclivity, social lives.

Two days later, she was in the car with her mum, driving to visit her father in Birmingham, when she opened an unusually long text message from Soheil. She had to stop reading after the first line: "Nadim is dead." He didn't say how it had happened. If it had been excruciating or swift and painless. Sabira's not-knowing changed quickly into a white-hot rage. She wanted to scream at him, *No! He was just in the car with you. I just talked to him. He was just alive!*

The memories flooded back. She thought of Nadim's throaty

laughter, his strange dislike of soda, the sweets he would pick up for her from East London, the goggle-eyed impressions he would do to make his little son crack up with laughter, his gentle insistence, when his sisters put on Bollywood movies, that such bright revealing clothes and dancing were, to his mind, just inviting temptation, the sad result of Indian Muslims mixing with too many elephant-god-worshipping, navel-revealing, white-people-ass-kissing Hindus. "It's no use me just going on about it," he would say to his sisters, sighing. "The modesty has to come from inside you. Like it's inside Sabira."

It was late morning; there was a milky sky and two hours of driving before them. Sabira grabbed at her mother's sleeve, saying, "We have to turn back." They pulled over at the next exit and her mother clasped the steering wheel and wept. Sabira's eyes were dry. She had found out first; she had to be strong for everyone.

After driving back to London, they walked into her aunt's living room without announcement. Sabira picked up the remote control and turned off the television. Her cousin, just back from the gym, wearing what passed for modest attire—tight leggings, a tunic that reached her mid-thighs but clung to everything along the way—looked up quizzically. Sabira found her aunt in the kitchen and led her into the living room and asked her to sit down. When she told them the news, she thought her aunt would collapse into bitter sobs and beat her chest. But her aunt's eyes shrank a little and went pebble hard. "I don't believe you," she said. "Tell Soheil to send a picture. I won't believe it until I see it."

It hadn't occurred to Sabira to suspect it could be false news. But in the contrast between her aunt, resolutely refusing to cry, and her own mother and cousin, grasping each other and sobbing, she saw that it was a bid for time. Without proof, her aunt could sustain denial. On a certain level, it was simply inconceivable: to have ended up in Britain, the daughter of a Pakistani transplant whose family had abandoned its farm amid the violence of partition, to have done your best to raise a happy son over a difficult cultural divide, to watch him increasingly chafe at feeling British in a way you never did yourself, even though he blended in better than you ever had, to watch that son retrace half of your own family's path eastward and end up fighting and dying in the Arab Levant in someone else's civil-territorial war under the banner of jihad. Was he a martyr who died fighting for the idea of a caliphate, a kingdom of heaven where Muslims could live in dignity under Allah's will? Was he a foot soldier in the Sunni Iraqi–Syrian jihadist insurgency that didn't want to be part of either Iraq or Syria, and rebelled against those regimes? Was he both? *Could* he be both? What was the legacy of his death? Did it mean she had raised her son with a heart that burned against injustice, or that she had let him down, not noticing that he was being preyed upon? It was too much for her to bear. "I need a picture," she repeated flatly.

"Really? Should I actually send u a pic?" Soheil asked, when she managed to message him later. Sabira replied, *"Auntie needs an explanation. Just send."*

The picture. It was night when he sent it. She could see the moon from her bedroom window, bloated but not yet full, pouring light out onto the street. For a split second, she thought Soheil had sent the wrong picture. The image looked like the mangled Syrian bodies they had gathered around their phones to look at together over eighteen months ago, back when the Syrian war was beginning. But this wasn't an anonymous victim. It was Nadim, with fragments of his face and left shoulder missing, bits of bone sticking out, ash caking his remains. She could not understand what had done this. Had bullets gone into him? The picture seemed to emit sound, an unbearable shrill screaming like a siren. Sabira felt disoriented, her hands acting of their own accord as they slammed the phone facedown against the bedside table.

IN OCTOBER 2016, SHORT MONTHS after his baby was born, eight months after Nadim's death, Soheil was killed by a sniper shot to the head during an extended fighting campaign outside Manbij. An instant kill, apparently, his wife said later.

"Don't you want to leave, now that he's gone?" Sabira messaged her.

"No. I'm not getting married again. There's no one for me after Soheil. But I don't want to ever leave. I'm waiting for the afterlife, where we can be together."

The family's mourning for Nadim bled into their mourning for Soheil, a period of counting days: the seventh day, the fortieth day. They moved through these time markers physically, as though passing beads along a prayer rope. Sabira floated through many of those days barely alert, so often astonished that everything outside remained un-altered: the alleyway shortcut that led straight to the Victoria line sta-tion, the ivy that crawled from their neighbor's trellis onto their fence, the bluebells that ringed the cricket ground.

Over a year earlier, before the travel disasters, Sabira had signed up for a professional course in play therapy. She was patient with chil-dren and loved being around them. She loved their quirkiness, their little vulnerabilities, their innocence. When the course began in late 2016, when she was stunned by grief, she went out of a feeling of me-chanical obligation, but she was quickly engrossed in the coursework, the theories about family structures, the myriad ways something as simple as play could be used to help children deal with small fears and major damage. There was a clinical observation once a week that Sabira always looked forward to. She liked how present it required her to be, watching the children's behavior for signs, anticipating the reac-tions of the trained therapist.

Most of all, she liked how productive it made her feel, being in that room, helping make a difference in those children's lives. She liked walking in each week and having the children rush up to her. She liked being an example, with her hijab and abaya, of a strong Muslim woman. She had long since dropped the extremist al-Muhajiroun women, whose attitudes around "free mixing" would have made her work impossible. She wanted to be productive and contrib-ute to society, like the Prophet Muhammad's first wife, Khadija, who had been active as a businesswoman. That fact was part of a side of early Islam she'd certainly never heard about when she moved in the al-Muhajiroun circles. Islam was too big a religion for such constraints against women, and too noble a religion to countenance viewing non-Muslims with contempt, she thought.

She started listening to Islamic talks on YouTube again and read-ing the Quran before bed. It was strange thinking about the future, thinking about her *iman* and responsibilities to Allah. It was through all of this that she had decided to put the hijab back on. She listened to the various scholarly positions; she read and reread the sections of the Quran dealing with modesty. She decided that covering more fulsomely was what Allah asked for, and she felt a calm, satisfied peace for choosing this herself, in the path of pleasing Him.

She didn't feel even a beat of resentment when pulling on the hijab in the mornings. Best of all, she no longer felt herself superior to Muslim women who didn't wear it. Now she viewed it as her individual choice, and felt no disdain for girls who wore turban-style hijab or bandanna-style hijab or hijab over lacquered faces and blatantly sexy outfits. No one was perfect. Everyone sinned differently. For herself, she felt blessed from the very first day she put it back on. The massive drop in daily comments, come-ons, harassment, eyes perving their way up and down her body: it was just a fact. Thanks be to God that she had the choice, and had found her way back to the choice.

Sabira looked back on the summer of 2015 as a period of delirium, and felt acute shame for her recklessness and naïveté. It still hurt her when the newspapers mocked all the young men from Walthamstow who had gone, like her brother and Nadim. She would never denigrate them like that, because she knew why they had gone. The newspapers only cared about who had brainwashed them, never about what they had gone to fight *for*. In September 2016, Anjem Chaudry, the dark media narcissist whose group had led Soheil and Nadim to Syria, finally went to prison. The *Daily Mail*'s triumphant headline hinted at how the paper had enjoyed the chase while it ran: "Nailed at Last! For 20 years, hate preacher on benefits laughed at Britain as he spawned terror worldwide. Now, after vowing allegiance to ISIS, he faces 10 years behind bars."

She found out later, through a friend, that a group of more than twenty British Sudanese medical students had traveled to join ISIS during the summer of 2015. Reading about these young people made her own mistake a little lighter to bear. They were respectable, educated, affluent children of consultants and doctors and diplomats; if young people like this could be drawn to the caliphate, was it any wonder Soheil had been drawn in? That she had allowed the idea to flicker in her mind?

Sometimes, in the evenings, Sabira scanned the news reports on-line. How easy it was to call these people "a waste of space" or call their religion demonic. But if someone were to create a memorial wall of all the hundreds and thousands of bright, educated, promising, big-hearted young people who had gone to Syria, would it be possible to look into their faces and not see something to learn from? But it was a mirror that no one really wished to look into.

The only face Sabira wanted to see was her brother's, staring back at her in the little frame of her nephew, who was his carbon copy. But she had resigned herself to missing even this.

EMMA/DUNYA

January 2017, a Village in Northern Syria

TODAY WAS HER BIRTHDAY AND SHE WAS CREEPING TOWARD THIRTY, penniless in a Syrian village. She put on Sting's "Desert Rose," the song that almost always made her feel better; she ate the chocolate brownies the family she was staying with had bought for her. The generator went off with a loud, sad clunk, taking the Wi-Fi and the small electric heater with it. She sighed and started pulling extra socks on. The cold made her digits numb and sapped her will to get out of bed, even for meals. Without the internet, she felt like Tom Hanks in *Cast Away*. Unlike most nights, she had remembered to fill her hot-water bottle before the generator gave out, and she pressed her toes against its womb-like heat.

Sometimes it felt like she would be the last German woman left in all of Syria. She knew of many others who had managed to cross the border into Turkey, but while the German consulate in Ankara said repeatedly it was working on her case, no help ever materialized. The idea of winging it, just walking or driving up to the border and handing herself over to the Turkish authorities, this frightened her, even though it was probably what others had done. What if they threw her into a filthy detention center where she had to spend weeks sleeping on a dirt-encrusted floor and eating gruel, surrounded by drug addicts and prostitutes? What if they interrogated her for hours à la *Midnight Express* before turning her over to the German authorities?

Then there was the problem of her cats, only slightly less complicated than her own situation. The cats would have to stay in Turkey for a period of three months, receiving their shots and being cared for by a vet, before they could qualify for health checks and an official pet passport. Whom would they stay with? She didn't speak any Turkish and didn't know a soul in Turkey, apart from the Syrian FSA men who had helped her out, who traveled back and forth across the border.

There were people who wanted or needed information from her. Journalists who had her WhatsApp number and called with questions; intelligence agents who showed up at the house pretending to be local NGO workers or municipal police, as though she couldn't figure out immediately who they were. Some of these people promised to help get the cats out and find them lodging. One texted to tell her there was a Facebook page popular among cat owners living in a smart neighborhood in Istanbul—Cihangir Cat Lovers, it was called—and suggested she post a request there. She balked: "I can't tell anybody 'please let us meet at the Syrian border because you have to take my cats from there.'" Even if someone could arrange to get the cats to Istanbul, she was still uneasy. "I don't like to give them away to strangers from Facebook. But when I was thinking I have to leave them in turkey for three months I start crying like a baby 😭😭😭😭."

The family she was staying with were the most prominent clan in this small village in northern Syria. They lived together, three generations, in a communal home, and allowed Dunya to live with them out of kindness, though when she was able to offer them little payments, they gratefully accepted. They were firm supporters of the Free Syrian Army, and also deeply religious. There was no drinking. Dunya wore her hijab when the men were present. As far as she could tell, the men of this village had married their wives when they were young, arrangements that were deemed propitious to village relations. Everyone seemed tolerant of the fact that now, years and many children later, the men were looking for second wives.

The matriarch of the family was extremely kind, and treated Dunya as one of her own daughters. She poked her head inside the room if she didn't emerge, tended to her when she got sick from bad kebab or had chronic chest colds. If Dunya felt too ill or too depressed to come out, the matriarch sent one of the children into her room with a plate of doughnuts or sweets. It was the first time a family had properly looked after her, and their care made Dunya feel both ashamed of being a burden and disinclined ever to leave.

She spent hours on her own. On any given evening these were the thoughts that might be flitting through her mind: how exciting it would be to go shopping in Manhattan and how utterly unlikely it was to ever happen, due to her stupidity and Trump's election; how she had to be strong and not give in to desperation because she had made a bad decision and had to handle the consequences; why some women looked better than others in hijab; the wisdom of that Syrian poet Nizar Qabbani, who realized that love could transform and that the key to happiness was allowing your heart to choose. Qabbani, she thought, understood desire as no one else did. He wrote that "the female doesn't want a rich man or a handsome man or even a poet, she wants a man who understands her eyes if she gets sad, and points to his chest and says: 'Here is your home country.'"

Like her mother before her, she hated men; she felt herself done with them. She contemplated baking a cake in the shape of a man and eating it slowly, limb by limb. She changed her WhatsApp profile picture obsessively. It was a better barometer of her moods, aspirations, desires, and regrets than any words she could articulate. In the span of one month, it featured her mother, herself as a baby, a BMW at sunset, the sloth from *Ice Age,* peach Nike sneakers, cuddling penguins, the Taj Mahal bathed in moonlight, Homer Simpson hoisting a "The End Is Near" sign, Syrian children in a field waving their national flag, a stark Arabic "I Hate You," pouting selfies with flowing lustrous hair, pouting selfies with hijab, SnapChat selfies with mouse ears, a beach in the moonlight, "Whatever," "Sometimes you have to forget what you want to remember what you deserve," a fighter on a battlefield cradling a cat.

She mostly daydreamed about what her life would be like back in Germany, once she served her time in prison, which would surely be required. She wanted to go off religion for a while, to take off her hijab and have a normal European life again. She would always be a Muslim, and eventually she would cover again. But you couldn't walk into a bar or sit around smoking shisha with a headscarf, and she wanted to do those things. She wanted to take Arabic classes, because she remained in love with Arabic, the language of the Quran and Umm Kulthum.

ONE NIGHT THE NEARBY SHELLING by the YPG was so loud the windows rattled continuously. She wished they would just shatter and be done with.

The YPG was a Syrian Kurdish militia closely linked to a group that the United States considered a "terrorist entity," but now, recently scrubbed and rebranded as the Syrian Democratic Forces, the militia was working together with the American and European militaries to dislodge the Islamic State from the areas around the east and northeast, now edging closer to Raqqa. Dunya jumped up to wash off her face mask, in case the generator went off. It was black, made of something tar-like, and she needed the light to get it off. Now that she had escaped from the caliphate, Dunya devoted herself to wellness. She made scrubs out of salt and honey, masks out of almonds and olive oil, and found that organic self-care could reliably fill a long stretch of the average day.

As for the war, it continued as the backdrop. Dunya now experienced the fighting primarily through sound, and had developed an aural catalogue of expertise: the Russians dropped what she called monster-bombs, relentless rounds of seven booms, always seven, flying away and swooping back after ten or fifteen minutes for another round; the Syrian regime bombers were erratic and bombed indiscriminately, often hitting civilian areas and shopping centers and hospitals; the American planes, at least at that time, came in for discrete strikes.

A friend texted to ask her how she was feeling. She replied, "Damn YPG. The whole morning only boom boom boom and now again 😒."

They messaged for a while about the bombing, and then moved to discuss makeup.

"i hate the daily mascara struggle in Germany. looking like a panda every morning 🐨 i think about false 3D lashes."

"not sure they're halal? 😬."

"yes right because of the glue and the hair maybe the water dont arrive every single lash."

The Muslim internet was divided as to whether fake eyelashes were religiously permissible. She watched *CSI Miami*, *CSI New York*; she memorized the specs of the new BMW 6 series. She read poetry and, along with the politically active household, followed the continual emergence of new rebel groups morphing from old ones. She could hold her own in a discussion about their varying tactics, and to what extent religion was a genuine or instrumentalist aspect of their military and political vision.

She heard from Selim only sporadically. He couldn't get out of Raqqa on his own, and she was in touch with other ISIS fighters who were trying to help him escape. The German journalist who had helped coordinate her escape refused to help Selim; the journalist said he was too indoctrinated and could pose a danger to any Syrians that might try to get him out. She decided it was time to contact his family; whatever had transpired between them in the past, they deserved to be updated on his situation.

She thought of how she had once imagined they would have children together. She thought of the night their very first cat, ill from something toxic it had eaten outside, died in Selim's arms. Selim had stayed up for hours stroking its head, and cried when it finally stopped breathing. She prayed that there would be one last time to see her husband again, so she could explain why she had left, and ask forgiveness for everything.

October 2017, the Same Syrian Village

She was still in Syria when the caliphate started to crumble. The Islamic State faced an onslaught from every direction—from coalition forces, from Kurdish fighters and the Iraqi army, from the Assad regime, from the Iran-backed Shia militias. Fighters and their families were escaping everywhere, turning themselves in, trying to evade capture. She thought of how her husband would be treated. Would anyone stop to ask when he had come? To take his measure based on his date of arrival? Although the life of the false caliphate spanned only two short years, it mattered deeply when a man had arrived. Was it in the early days, when the war seemed just and right? Or was it later, when it had devolved into an orgy of spectacular violence?

The best men came early and died fast. They were the men of the purest ideals and conviction, who came to fight for God. Had they known how it was going to turn out, they wouldn't have come. The men who came later, responding to the siren song of the violence, were the mercenaries and the riffraff, the vulnerable converts and the lost souls, the thugs in search of a cause, the petty gangsters and the drifters, seeking redemption, identity, meaning. These were not men on whose shoulders you could build a society.

NOUR

NOUR STARTED AWAKE WITH THE FIRST BANG. IT WAS LATE SPRING OF 2016 and her window, overlooking the street, was open a crack, so she could hear the police shouting as they pounded against her front door. She locked the door to her bedroom, panicking; she needed to hide her mobile phone before they got to her.

The police were in the hallway now, demanding that she open the door. "I'm just putting on my headscarf," she called out, fumbling with the wardrobe, where she stuffed the phone, wrapped in a sock, into a mess of clothes.

"Come out, Nour. We're done with you. Your case is closed. We just want to know where your husband is," the officer said.

Nour unlocked the door and stepped out. She explained that she was in the process of divorcing her husband Karim and was no longer in regular contact with him. They shouldn't have any reason to be bothering her. They asked to see her phone, and she said she didn't have one. "All right," sighed the officer. "Let's go back to the station."

It was barely past dawn as they drove through the streets of Kram. At the station, the officer resumed his hectoring. He kicked the legs of her chair so that it skidded back. He threatened to make her life excruciating unless she handed over the phone. All this she took impassively, but then, later in the afternoon, the door swung open and they marched in her father. He was in his early fifties, but years of labor had made him hunched and creased as though he were two decades older. This was their leverage: they ordered her father to deal with his daughter, or else they'd make life hell for the whole family. Her father looked ashen and gripped the sides of his chair. Nour rose and said she would go get the phone.

Her mother was chopping vegetables in the kitchen when she came back home to retrieve the phone. Nour kissed her mother on the forehead before the officers escorted her back out to the waiting car. At the station, they offered her lunch—a cheese sandwich with harissa, pushed across the metal table. When Nour turned on her phone, she discovered that everything had been wiped: her apps, Facebook, Telegram, WhatsApp. Her resourceful younger sister had acted quickly.

The police asked her to reinstall her Facebook account, and she obliged. They went through her timeline, and didn't find anything there, and then started on her Friends list. There were some Salafi girls there, and the police asked who they were.

Like many conservative young women who chose not to work outside the home, or who couldn't find jobs because of their face veils, Nour was trying her hand at running a clothing business from home, selling modest Islamic robes. During the early heyday of Salafi activism that followed the 2011 revolution, niqabi women had organized to demand the right to attend university classes with their faces covered. There was little political support for this unsettling demand, which fused a progressive impulse (women's access to higher education) to a highly orthodox one (the divisive, unpopular face veil). In Tunisian society, the notion of Salafi feminism seemed outright laughable. There was no political current that saw any benefit in grappling with these young women's demands. Ennahda refused to engage with any niqabi discrimination issues—a fact that young protesters held up as proof of the group's excessive caution—and it stayed silent throughout, even when the dean of the Faculty of Letters, Arts, and Humanities at Manouba University slapped a niqabi student for covering her face. But in part, the niqab wars were about pushing the boundaries, a way for radical, antiestablishment young people to see how far the new political sphere would accommodate and include them.

Bourguiba's legacy as "liberator of women" had been revealed as a comprehensive success, with unexpected ramifications. The rise of women like Nour and her Salafi sisters showed that the religious women of Tunisia had internalized the message of independence. Now, they were exercising their newfound freedom to request a very awkward thing: that society include and accept them in the framework of a highly conservative, orthodox vision of Islam. What to do with willful women like this, who started as strong-minded girls determined to wear the hijab, impatient for society to catch up with them? Politicians scarcely knew how to respond, let alone the police, who looked at a woman like Nour and, truth be told, just wanted to beat the disobedient piety out of her.

"They buy stuff from me, they're my customers," Nour said, in answer to the police's question about the Salafi women. They found an older Facebook account that belonged to her, and scrolled through that timeline. One of them looked through the older posts and status updates, and exhaled loudly. He held the screen up in front of Nour's face, within an inch of her nose. "Exactly what does this mean?" She had posted, *"There is no God but God, and Mohammad is his messenger,"* and underneath it, *"my last words before death."* "You want to be a martyr, huh?" the policeman said.

Another officer walked in with a sheaf of papers. It was a list of girls, with photos and names. They asked Nour to go through the list, and asked if she knew any of them. Those who she knew had been arrested before, she pretended not to know. She didn't want them to go through the same hell again. Those who she knew hadn't been arrested yet, she admitted to knowing.

Nour asked if she could go home, but the officers pushed the untouched sandwich toward her and told her not yet. Around the time for the evening prayer, they brought her little brother to the police station and sat him down in the corner. The officer tossed the list in front of her again. Her brother edged back into his chair, as though making himself more compact. Seeing his well-worn, faded FC Barcelona T-shirt in the interrogation room made her feel faint. When the officers demanded that she look at the list again, she told them she wouldn't do it until they took her brother home.

The interrogation room was small and windowless, with a stained linoleum floor. Before the revolution, the security services routinely

raped and assaulted women suspected of ties to the religious opposition, interpreting "ties" as broadly as possible. It was meant to be different now, now that Tunisia was a model of democracy. Nour sealed
her mouth shut, refusing to speak until they took her brother away.
About an hour later, the door opened again, and the interrogator
pushed another woman into the room. She attended the same mosque
as Nour, in Kram.

"When did you first meet her?" The interrogator started, as usual,
from this premise.

"Don't know her at all," Nour replied, lying.

"You don't know the guests at your own wedding?"

"My parents invited lots of people."

"Does she share your ideology? Was she happy when policemen
were slaughtered? What are you, Nour? Are you al-Qaeda? Ansar al-
Sharia? Jabhat al-Nusra? Daesh?"

Nour wondered if the officer even knew how these groups differed
from one another, and if he didn't, as seemed the case, why he was
even a policeman. If all the police did, apart from taking bribes, was
hunt Islamist militants, shouldn't they have some basic knowledge
about different factions? Apparently even this was too much to expect.

It went on like this for about fifteen minutes. The girl shuffled
back and forth against the wall. Nour feigned peering at her, as if she
were making a genuine attempt to recognize her. The police hustled
three more women in, with the officers demanding that Nour say
whether she recognized them and Nour pretending not to know them
at all.

Around 10 p.m., after a full day of interrogation, the police put
Nour in a van and drove her to al-Gorjani, the detention center where
terrorism suspects were handled. Tourism had evaporated in Tunisia
after the terror attacks the past year, on the beach in Sousse and a
museum in Tunis, giving the police ample reason to pursue extremists. But in reality, they used the terror threat for much vaster purposes: sweeping up anyone with suspicious connections, or anyone
simply in contact with those people. The Tunisian police were predis-
posed to abuses, and then they were given a task that invited abuse:
fighting terrorism on a nationwide scale.

This new holding room at al-Gorjani was slightly larger, and included a random assortment of women: a teenager, a wife of an Ansar al-Sharia member, and a woman who explained in bewilderment, "All they found was photos of bin Laden on my phone, that's all." They all sat on the floor, legs outstretched; two of the women were pregnant, and kept moving wincingly from one position to another.

The days began blending into one another, the sameness of the light and the sameness of the noises interrupted only by interrogations. The questions were the same too: "Are you with ISIS?" "Do you prefer al-Qaeda?" "Do you believe in the nation-state?" "What sheikh do you follow?" Nour wanted to stay completely silent. She wanted to be so quiet that her silence would amass into its own force and devour these men. But she was afraid they would beat her, so she spoke only to deny everything, and it always ended up the same way too: "Stupid *takfiri* bitch, you'd have us all killed!"

The police varied their routine, trying to come up with new ways to scare her into talking. One day they brought a young man into the room, a detainee, and punched and pummeled him until he crumpled to the floor, covering his face with his hands. Two officers kicked him until one eye caved in and blood was everywhere. As he grabbed his eye and turned away, he left a bloody handprint on the wall.

Nour slept on the soiled mattress on the floor, breathing the stench from the toilet in the cell, with an arm flung over her eyes to blunt the fluorescent light that blazed on, day and night. Lunch was cold tomato water with a few peas floating at the top.

One day, early enough that the morning was still cool, a new interrogator arrived with a file of papers, containing records of bank statements and transfers. Nour didn't know what day it was anymore. That morning at dawn, a prison guard had stopped her and the other women in the cell from praying together. Now they had to use a pantry with filthy mops at the head of the hallway, praying one at a time. The room where the new interrogator took her was in a different part of the detention center, a wing that was cleaner, with proper offices and desks and computers. The new interrogator had everything in hand, and Nour's lies felt heavy and leaden. He had a computer screen that was somehow connected to her various accounts. He could see the messages, as though her phone was on his screen, and he pointed to a Telegram message from her husband. "What are you planning, Nour? Are you planning something here in Kram? You want to kill someone?"

She didn't know whether to say the money that Karim sent was just for her and the baby, or to deny receiving it at all. She said she thought her husband was dead. She had asked for a lawyer two days prior, and they had allowed a man sent by her father to visit her. But when the lawyer asked for her file, the police said no, and when he protested, they laughed and said, "Go complain to the security chief, if it bothers you."

Nour lost track of how long she had been at the prison. One night, one of the officers brought a young woman into the room. Nour remembered her distantly from Kram, a girl who had gone to Libya the previous summer. She was another attempt at leverage. "Talk to us about your husband, or this girl will sit naked here the whole day," they said.

She didn't think they would actually do it, or do it the way they did. Four men pounced on her at once, ripping at the girl's clothes. The girl screamed and stumbled back. Nour sprang from her chair and tried to push the men off her. They pinned the girl's arm back to wrest her shirt off. Her skin was so pale that everywhere they grabbed erupted into red splotches. They grabbed as they went along, pinching at her skin, tearing at the girl like wild dogs.

They held that girl from Kram for a week. Another girl was brought in for smoking a joint in the street. The security services often arrested activists, religious and secular alike, on drug pretenses, sometimes detaining them for as long as a year, simply for possession of marijuana. It was a clean way of keeping the opposition in check without seeming authoritarian before the international community.

One afternoon they allowed Nour's father to visit. He whispered to her, in the little room reserved for visitations, that if they paid the lead officer two thousand dinars and changed lawyers, Nour would no longer be a *takfiri* terrorist charged with being a member of Ansar al-Sharia and al-Qaeda and with aiding a member of the Islamic State. Neither Nour nor her father knew it, but the bribe the officer had asked for was modest; depending on the type of case, police usually demanded between three thousand and twenty thousand dinars in terrorism cases. With so many women detained simply for being "in contact with jihadists," on top of the thousands of others arrested on suspicion of actual militant activity, the police had a generous inmate pool to squeeze for cash. Recommending a new lawyer was a popular way of dealing with this: the new lawyer would incorporate the bribe into his "fee," and then divide the money with the police.

The corrupt, extralegal way it dealt with those accused of extremism was classic to the Tunisian state. If the extraction of a bribe had triggered the Tunisian revolution—the immolation of the fruit seller Bouazizi back in December 2010, the moment that shook the Middle East—then it felt, certainly for women like Nour, that events had come full circle. Perhaps for others a great deal had changed, but for her, the story of the new Tunisia as it was being written was the old story she already knew.

Three weeks into detention, Nour had lost weight and had scabs on her legs from the bug bites. She had not seen her daughter since her arrest. The final day, they brought Nour's mother to the station. She was wearing a pale blue headscarf and the one coat she had for formal occasions, and grasped Nour's father's hand as she entered the room.

"Enough. It's enough, now."

Once her family paid the bribe and changed lawyers, the police dropped all charges against her.

NEAR CARTHAGE, NOUR SAT AT a café with her sister and a friend. The sun cast long shadows on the ground and they drank their coffee slowly. She saw a man looking at her intently and then speaking into his mobile phone. He didn't take his eyes off her. She grabbed her handbag, rose, and signaled her sister to leave the café. They walked quickly along the main street and then turned down an alleyway. A car pulled up alongside her, and one of the policemen who had interrogated her just short months before leaned his head out.

EPILOGUE
AMONG THE DISSEMBLERS

She herself is a haunted house. She does not possess herself; her ancestors sometimes come and peer out of the windows of her eyes and that is very frightening.
—ANGELA CARTER, "The Lady of the House of Love"

Cities die just like people.
—KHALED KHALIFA, *No Knives in the Kitchens of This City*

THE FINAL TIME I MET NOUR WAS AT A CAFÉ NEAR AVENUE BOURGUIBA, nearby where she works in a shoe shop. The café has multiple televisions, all set to the Rotana music channel; the music network is partly owned by a wealthy Saudi, and reflects the confused ways in which Saudi money reaches around the world, whether funding jihadists in Syria or pop music sleaze on television.

It is early 2017, and it has been over six months since Nour's release from jail. She looked radically different from any of the previous times we had met. She wore a lavender wool sweater over dark skinny jeans, her nails were long and French-manicured, and her hair, which I was seeing for the first time, was lustrous and wavy, shot through with flecks of gold. Her makeup was like that of a well-groomed American college student: natural but filled-in eyebrows, subtle mascara, a sweep of bronzer. She was so easy to look at that I found her more appealing and sympathetic than on previous occasions. This reaction may be natural enough—we sympathize more readily with those who look like us—but it made me feel guilty. Nour the almost-model, with eyelashes that swept up and down like butterfly wings, should not seem a more defendable girl because of her new, more liberal, lacquered looks. It was also true that she seemed more open in this guise. She smiled and talked more, but perhaps that was part of the role she was inhabiting.

Nour told me she had stopped going to the mosque on Fridays, stopped seeing the group of Salafi sisters. Some of her friends had gone to Libya to join their husbands, who were still fighting with an ISIS faction there. I asked her what it felt like to look completely different on the outside than she felt on the inside. Her eyes welled up with tears as she looked out at Avenue Mohammed Cinq, the Tunis thoroughfare modeled after the boulevards of Paris. "It is like living a lie," she said.

We sat on the second floor of a bustling art deco café, the tables around us filled with old men in tweed caps smoking, young people eating French pastries, couples with their heads bent low in conversation. At one point, I asked her if she supported what had transpired in Paris in November 2015. I said they were just regular people who were killed, nodding at the tables around us, people just like this, many of them Muslims. She shrugged. Of course she supported the attacks. "They kill our people. They don't play by the rules. Why should we?"

July 2017, **Ain Issa Refugee Camp, Thirty Miles North of Raqqa**

It was near midnight as they set out from the refugee camp, Ayesha with her three children, the dour Turkess with her two, with Ayesha feigning a broken foot that was, at moments, remarkably easy to walk on. They bribed the driver with cash they had managed to keep when they fled Raqqa, and which they supplemented by selling the diapers the Kurds had given them in the refugee camp. Their fighter husbands were in prison, and who knew what the Kurds planned to do with them. The only thing to do was disappear, to get as far as Manbij and then the Turkish border, to disappear into the cities of southern Turkey as though it had all never happened, as though the caliphate had been a dream, a whisper as corrupted as the Satanic Verses themselves.

Ayesha had hatched the plan. She had flirted, bribed, and wheedled her way into the graces of enough men at the refugee camp to slip out without anyone raising the alarm. She was a Syrian woman who was slim and attractive in a charismatic rather than pretty way, with a teacher-like manner that had a way of making people do what she said. The Turkess had no such abilities or charms. She was short and stooped, with features that were now permanently pinched, the result of trying to hide how much she despised the people around her. The Turkess had asked to join Ayesha's plan out of desperation: her ten-month-old daughter's stomach was as bloated as a basketball, and the Kurds weren't taking her to a hospital. Not that there was any functional hospital to be taken to. Not that with the final assault against Raqqa unfolding just thirty miles south, an ISIS baby with a swollen belly was anyone's priority.

The rest of the ISIS women watched them leave, silently. They were living ten or twelve to a room, the kind of proximity that bred pique and occasional hatred, and the feeling of not being entirely disappointed that God had not seen fit to send clouds across the bright full moon that night.

As the two women and their children drove away toward the Turkish border, they passed through the first two checkpoints smoothly. At the third checkpoint, their driver assumed a tired look, spoke in Kurdish, and was waved through. The van's windows were tinted, and no one asked him to open the doors.

Ayesha was just starting to relax, feeling satisfied with her resourcefulness—she was so unlike the other women, passively content to be corralled up at the refugee camp awaiting their fate—when they arrived at the fourth checkpoint. She couldn't understand the Kurdish they were speaking, but she knew that the conversation was taking too long. The driver was waving his hands. The soldier at the checkpoint kept repeating one word: maybe *open*, or *hurry*, or *now*, something like that, because the driver got out and pulled the van door open. The checkpoint was nothing more than several enormous concrete slabs arranged irregularly, so that any car would have to slow down and maneuver around them. Ayesha focused on the slabs, cradling her foot.

The soldier peered in at them. Ayesha wished for a moment she hadn't brought the Turkess, who could never pass for a Syrian Arab or a Kurd, and whose inclusion had necessitated a van. She might as well have brought the Russian woman who looked like Michelle Pfeiffer, who was so absurdly beautiful her face disrupted whatever space she occupied. Ayesha and her kids could have fit into the back of a regular car and been plausibly asleep, the driver's family, maybe. But with the Turkess along, there was no mistaking who they were: ISIS women in flight. What else would a parchment-pale Turkish woman be doing in the hinterland of Syria as the caliphate collapsed?

The soldier gestured at them to pull over and made a call on his cellphone. It was over. Kurdish soldiers escorted them back down the same road, past the same destroyed buildings glinting in the moonlight. Within an hour, they were back at the camp, and Ayesha, the Turkess, and their children filed back into their quarters. Back to the squat toilets and concrete rooms, one starch-laden meal a day, back to the flies and the hate-drenched stares of the *awam,* the ordinary Syrians, who looked as if they would like to plunge knives into them right there. Back to having to confront the reality that many people didn't care at all if you were sorry, that most of them didn't believe you anyway, and that even if they did, they still wanted you to pay.

THE SEA OF WHITE TENTS stretches out across the desert, dotted with giant red cisterns of water. During the day the temperature often reaches 115 degrees; at night the sky is littered with stars and there is a cooling breeze, but mosquitoes prey on bodies that lie unprotected under the tarpaulin. At the center of the camp there is a market, heaps of used clothes and shoes laid out on tarps, refugees combing through them as much for something to do as for need of an extra faded T-shirt. There is a ramshackle row of covered kiosks selling foil-wrapped cookies, french fries, and ice cream.

American and British special forces and officials stride about, mostly not in uniform. They are setting up outposts across this northeastern stretch of Syria called Rojava, land that is administered by the Syrian Kurds, outside the reach of the regime. The U.S. bases that house the security officials, intelligence officials, diplomats, and the United States Agency for International Development (USAID) are so new that they don't have names yet, just GPS coordinates. No one knows how long these bases will stay—whether the United States is just helping prosecute the final phases of the ground war against ISIS and interrogating captured fighters, or whether it intends to stay and permanently occupy this part of Syria. Whatever the plans are, the scale and purpose of the American presence is barely disclosed to the media, rarely discussed by politicians, and, as such, remains largely outside the bounds of public scrutiny. This is not Iraq in 2003, when American officials flaunted their administrative occupation of Baghdad and held court in the Green Zone, wearing crisp khakis, dreaming up anti-smoking campaigns for Iraqis over cocktails and pork hot dogs flown in by Halliburton, only belatedly realizing there were problems when Sunni insurgents began planting roadside bombs under their military convoys. It is said that the Americans, unlike the British, don't know how to do empire because they lack subtlety and institutional memory. Their discretion in eastern Syria suggests they are learning.

The camp has only one permanent structure: a low-slung, four-room cement shelter. It buzzes with flies and is covered with dust, but it boasts actual walls and an actual roof and sits in close proximity to the makeshift showers, the pit toilets, the feeding hall, and the kiosks. In the eyes of the camp's seven thousand tent-housed inhabitants—mostly civilians from the eastern district of Raqqa, streaming up as Kurdish fighters clear ISIS from the city—the shelter is a luxury hotel. It is here where the ISIS women reside with their children, in comfort and privacy, protected from the sun, the mosquitoes, the nightly arguing of neighbors wafting through the tents.

Everyone in the camp has arrived after enduring weeks and months of bombardment, the eerie permanent tinnitus of hovering drones, which can itself drive you mad. They now spend their hours dazed, lying listlessly in tents or wandering about the camp. The camp is Raqqa transplanted about thirty miles north, but whether it is liberated Raqqa or reoccupied Raqqa, no one quite knows.

The entrance is strewn with trampled strips of black cloth, the black abayas and niqabs that women fleeing the city have discarded and shredded upon arrival. The refugees believe they have escaped the Islamic State, and women are now dressing as they used to, in long sleeves, long skirts, and headscarves. But then the ISIS women appear in their black niqabs, just as they wore them on the streets of Raqqa, wraiths floating through the camp, stark against the chalk-white earth. Sometimes the refugee children cower when they see them, and clutch at their mothers. But as the days pass, the children absorb the changed circumstances. They hear from the adults that they are safe, that the black-robed women no longer have any power over them. The children then become emboldened. They start throwing stones at the ISIS women as they line up at the cisterns for water, or sidling up to them at kiosks to demand money.

In the guarded compound where the ISIS women stay, the Kurdish soldiers run what might be called a deradicalization program or an indoctrination program, depending on your perspective. Whether these ISIS women are civilian wives or female jihadists in their own right is a question no one feels ready to answer.

Commander Salar is a senior member of the Syrian Democratic Force, charged with the security of Ain Issa refugee camp and the ISIS women detained there. He has observed the women since their arrival and does not consider most of them combatants, or even especially dangerous. He sees them as civilians who went down the wrong path. He was well positioned to know the difference between these women and women actively involved in war. In the SDF, he is a commander to women fighters who clip their long hair back and sling rifles over their shoulders and go to the front, just like his men.

Salar grew up in Syria among Kurdish families who split down political lines as the civil war unfolded: daughters who joined the PKK, sons who went to ISIS out of despair at the Kurds' "failing national project." There are many paths to militancy, he has seen, that aren't about militancy per se. Often the militancy is a reaction to repression and broken aspirations and false hopes, a disavowal of circumstances that feel unbearable. "These women, most of them aren't even ISIS, really," he says. "They were tricked and cheated into coming here, out of some belief in true Islam."

But at present, he is not concerning himself with these questions. His job is to offer the most humane, international-norm-abiding detention possible in the middle of this desert heat, in order to further the Kurds' dreams of retaining this patch of Syria as an independent statelet. Kurdish fighters have kept the Assad regime out of this large eastern stretch of Syria for years now—it is a de facto, temporary autonomy that makes genuine autonomy feel tantalizingly within reach. Like all his soldiers, Salar manages a close shave every single morning despite the lack of electricity and running water. The clean shave is ideologically necessary, signifying the militia's fierce secularism, or at least its fierce commitment to the personality cult of its leader, Abdullah Öcalan, a Turkish Kurdish separatist who is interned in an island prison in the Sea of Marmara.

Most American press accounts of the battle for Raqqa in 2017 feature convoluted, acronym-heavy descriptions of the SDF. It is usually described as a Kurdish and Arab military force, with links to the YPG, which is the military wing of the PYD, which is in turn linked to the PKK, the Kurdish militant separatist group classified as a terrorist organization by the United States and Turkey. Despite these contortions, which are meant to paper over awkward political realities, everyone here calls the SDF "the Kurds," and their allegiance to PKK leader Öcalan is everywhere on display. His mustachioed picture hangs from lampposts in towns and in offices in this eastern part of Syria.

Every morning, Commander Salar plays Arabic pop music for the ISIS children, featuring the throaty, luscious voices of Lebanese and Egyptian divas. The children cluster around the soldiers, their hair hopping with lice and matted to their scalps, shrieking offendedly, "*Haram!*" "You're a *kafir*!" four-year-old Abu Bakr shouts at him. Commander Salar plays an ISIS *nasheed* next and the children relax. The Kurds play the pop music every morning. After about a week, some of the ISIS women stopped covering their faces and hands, and stopped wincing at having to speak to Commander Salar. "Their husbands told them we'd behead them. It took a little while for the shock of their reception here to wear off," he says. Eventually the pop music becomes ordinary to the children. But they continue running around in the dirt playing their "*Allahu akbar!*" shootout games.

Some of the ISIS women have taken wildly circuitous routes to arrive here, hoping to avoid falling into the hands of the Iraqi forces battling ISIS to the south, inside Iraq. Accounts are already emerging of atrocities committed during the retaking of Mosul, of Iraqi forces executing civilians for simply being Sunnis who stayed behind, set- tling old scores in the name of exterminating ISIS. The ISIS women who end up in the hands of these forces, the rumors hold, are being forcibly divorced from their husbands, often raped. For now, they are safer in the hands of the Kurds, though the bar for their treatment has been set very, very low.

Now that al-Baghdadi's aspirant state is crumbling, it is expedient, indeed a matter of survival, for its fleeing ruler-inhabitants to declare to have never believed in it. The fall of every empire is accompanied by such a rush of candor and soul-searching, and because every em- pire's fall necessarily reflects a decayed inner core, it is the hard work of time to tell whose tales of regret are genuine and whose contrived. For now, the truth can be gleaned mainly from the children of Ain Issa. Their parents' devotion to ISIS, at least at one time, can be read in their style of play, and in their names like Jihad and Abu Bakr— though the mother of four-year-old Abu Bakr is now quick to say, "After Abu Bakr al-Siddiq, of course," the companion of the Prophet Muhammad, not al-Baghdadi.

Nearly all of the ISIS women detained in this camp claim to be victims, dissenters at heart who were forced to stay in Islamic State territory because getting out was impossible. They cite happenstance and conniving husbands and bad roads for how they ended up with ISIS. They admit they were originally true believers in the state- building project, but maintain that they quickly lost faith when they saw it was a miserable, vicious lie.

The civilians in the camp don't buy it for a second. Neither do some of the officers and staff who are tasked with looking after them. "They are liars and daughters of dogs," a local Syrian working for the United Nations High Commissioner for Refugees says. "If it was up to me, I would kill them slowly. I would cut their fingers off and then their arms and then their feet."

Some of the ISIS women hold themselves with the arrogant mien of recently deposed rulers. Others are humble, shoulders stooped, aware they must carry the weight of their choice, however disastrously it turned out. If the courtyard of the women is a microcosm of the Islamic State in exile, then the wider camp is the future of Syria, teeming with questions of complicity and regret, everyone competing for a share of victimhood.

AYESHA, THE WOMAN WHO FAILED to escape the camp, glides around with the air of a beleaguered exiled aristocrat—as though she were a White Russian washed up in Paris, a post-Shah Persian in Kensington—keen to establish that her current status doesn't reflect her proper station in life. "My uncle has a flat near Hyde Park," she announces, offering a cigarette with a conspiratorial look. "It's okay, we can smoke in here."

She is everywhere at once, batting her eyelashes at the guards (at 10 a.m. she already has impeccable smoky eyes), ingratiating herself with the kiosk vendors. It emerges that she attended Homs University at the same time as Mahmoud, the journalist who has accompanied me here from Iraq, and she trades stories with him about mutual acquaintances ("Do you remember that Palestinian girl, the fat one, who studied English lit?"). The children are sharing a bag of sweets, and she pockets one for later. "I can't smoke and have anything in my mouth at the same time," she says daintily.

At university, Ayesha also studied English literature. "We did everything—poetry, criticism, translation," she says. She read Shakespeare and Christopher Marlowe, Dostoyevsky and the *Iliad*. She had romantic dreams of a husband who would be sensitive to her "needs and feelings," but ended up marrying an unimaginative engineer named Mohammad, with whom she was unhappy. "He wasn't attractive at all. He looked exactly like him," she says, nodding at her oldest son, Mohammad, who moves around the room with a slight shuffle, due to having only one flip-flop.

The couple lived together in the capital, Damascus, with their children. A few months into the uprising against Assad, her husband was killed by a sniper shot to the head while praying at the mosque. As a newly single mother, Ayesha taught English to support her children, relied on neighbors for babysitting, and suffered from the uniquely lowly position occupied by widowed or divorced women in traditional societies. Eventually, Ayesha decided to move near her sister, who was living at the time in Turkey. The direct northern route she would normally have taken, she says, was blocked because of the fighting, and she had to travel circuitously east across the country, to approach the Turkish border north of Raqqa. She happened to overnight in Raqqa, staying with a teacher friend. "And in the morning the ISIS police came to the house, and told me it is forbidden to live in the Land of Unbelief," she says. "I was forced to stay."

Getting stuck in Raqqa, however, reversed her fortunes. "The first time I saw him, I thought I was dreaming. He was tall, handsome, thick hair, wide shoulders. . . . He was living in the house next door all alone, with no woman to even make him tea! I made him a tea and had the children take it over next door. He asked them, 'Where's your father?' And they said, 'We have no father!'"

The man next door was Moroccan, a gold trader from the medina of Tangiers, who was "persuaded by Facebook friends" that Assad was killing Muslim women, that he should come to their aid and join the fight; that he could practice his Islam freely in Syria. One day the Moroccan man took Ayesha and her children to the park for ice cream, and there, among the trees, confided that he wanted to flee. "Where is this Assad that I came to fight?" she recounts him saying. Also, the ISIS salary was measly; he complained it could be wiped out by buying just one pair of shoes and a pair of sunglasses. Despite all this, the Moroccan proposed. If they were stuck, they might as well be stuck together. Who was to say you couldn't find love in a time of brutality?

Under normal circumstances, a handsome single man would have commanded a younger, less constrained bride than a widow like Ayesha with three children. Ayesha was love-starved enough to consider herself fortunate. "All my life changed after that," she recalls rapturously. "When you finally feel someone loves you. We stayed up all night laughing, smoking . . . looking into each other's eyes. We both kept saying to each other, 'I wish I had met you earlier!'"

Ayesha seems aware that parts of her story sound implausible, and she moves briskly on to other topics where she sounds more persuasive:

"ISIS was really preying on young Europeans' vulnerabilities, the ones who already had problems with their families. They were very clever to prey on the Europeans like this." She mentions that a journalist who works for a Dubai-based television network recently visited the camp, and wonders what has been said about her and the other women.

"Nothing very positive," I tell her. "She wrote about how you complained that your husbands spent too much on makeup for sex slaves."

"Really?" Ayesha looks crestfallen. "But she was so nice to us."

Oddly, despite her excellent English, her wily escape plans, and relatively sophisticated education, she is the least good at projecting any shame or regret.

She says things like "They never serve fish here. Not even fresh vegetables."

As her kids surround her in the concrete room where we are talking, they appear conspicuously cleaner than some of the other ISIS women's children. Their clothes fit, her daughter's hair is cropped short to avoid lice, and her baby sleeps quietly in a car seat, in a clean diaper. Earlier, one of the other women's toddlers had wandered into the room and squatted, emitting a stream of diarrhea across the floor.

"Why don't they have diapers?" I asked Commander Salar.

"They have enough diapers for two months," he sighed. "They sell them for money at the kiosks."

The camp is starting to receive visits from international aid groups, military intelligence officials, and journalists. Everyone has a few euros in their wallet and will feel sorry for a diaper-less baby forced to poop on the floor.

"Have you met Hoda yet?" Ayesha asks brightly. When the company of the ISIS women grows unbearable, she calls on Hoda, a nineteen-year-old Indonesian, who, along with the rest of her twenty-two-member family, lives in a capacious tent at the head of the camp. The tent is organized carefully, with separate areas for tea making, cooking, and sleeping. There's a recycling corner, piled high with empty water bottles. It is cozy and tidy, a reminder that people seem to do very different things with nothing.

Hoda has smooth skin, a delicate nose, and speaks quickly, smiling often. Back in Jakarta, she had been a normal high school student, pious and inquisitive, and like a true millennial, felt the most alive and comfortable while online. It all started when she encountered a Tumblr blog called *Diary of a Muhajirah,* written by a Malaysian woman who called herself Bird of Jannah. She was like the Asian version of the Scottish Umm Layth, the blogger who transfixed the London girls.

Bird of Jannah was a doctor who traveled on her own to Syria in 2014, with the eventual support of her parents, to work and contribute to the project of Islamic statehood. She chronicled her experiences on her blog, detailing the free health care, education, jobs, and largesse that were on offer in the Islamic State, calling on fellow Muslims to join her. She posted still-life photos representing herself and her new husband—a stethoscope with a Kalashnikov—and wrote amusingly of the foibles of communicating with him through Google Translate.

Back in Indonesia, Hoda's father was desperately in debt. The family was tense with worry. Hoda thought she had found the solution. She told them about a place in Syria where devoted Muslims were building an Islamic state. She contacted ISIS officials through Bird of Jannah, and received assurances that they would cover her father's debts. Health care, their travel costs, housing—everything would be paid for. They all packed up, her parents and two sisters, aunties and cousins and uncles, all twenty-five of them, and headed for Turkey. Commander Salar says Turkey, which initially supported the uprising against Assad, covered the family's travel costs from Istanbul to Raqqa.

What about the gory and violent acts the media showed ISIS committing? The beheading of the aid worker Alan Henning, and the reports of Yazidi women being forced into sex slavery? Hoda bows her head. "Do you know what it's like when you love the idea of something so much you're willing to overlook the bad in it?" The truth that lurks behind her sentences is that if the Islamic State had actually formed a proper state, if it had upheld its obligations, behaved justly, and provided its citizens with security and livelihoods, the violence might have been forgiven—regarded as a means to an end, the brutality required to achieve independence. Hoda and her family seem guileless to the point of dangerous naïveté, the kind of family who'd be the first in any town to fall for the local pyramid scheme.

Once the family was in Raqqa, ISIS fighters quickly tried to hustle the men in the family into military training. "Fight? No one said anything online about having to fight!" Hoda recalls. They were all indignant. The men refused to be trained, refused to go to the front line. Meanwhile, Hoda and the women were confined to a dormitory, waiting to be housed. Getting anything out of the Islamic State, she soon found, was like trying to cajole a drug cartel into following the rule of law. ISIS kept coming up with reasons why Hoda's family didn't deserve anything. "They called us hypocrites and cowards, because our men wouldn't fight. They said to us, 'What have you done for the State? What have you done for Islam, that we should support you?'"

Hoda spent her days writing argumentative emails to the Islamic State authorities, laying out why her family's demands were legitimate. She tried exegesis. She tried being litigious. Nothing worked. She befriended only civilian Syrians, rather than ISIS women, because she found the latter overwhelmingly catty and prone to shrieking and gossip. The Islamic sisterhood that Bird of Jannah had so movingly described seemed, in reality, more like an especially vicious season of *Real Housewives.* She felt bad for her *madani* friends, the civilians. They lived in a state of permanent fear, and the ISIS municipality also charged them three times more for electricity.

Worst of all, though, were the coarse and pushy fighters trying to pick them up all the time. They would come by or send emissaries asking Hoda and her sisters for marriage. "They would want an answer that *same* evening! Isn't that silly? They would say, 'He's from this or that place.' One sentence! Not even, 'He's an architect or a doctor'!" she says, her face puckering in disapproval. "The men, they were just completely obsessed with women. They talked about women in their chat groups, on the street, walking with my dad, they would stop him and ask us, 'Do you know anyone else who has daughters for us?'"

The men in Hoda's family eventually went to prison for refusing to fight. One uncle disappeared, and another died in an airstrike. The others spent three months in detention while Hoda worked the internet, trying to get help. She contacted the Indonesian embassy in Damascus; she sent messages to Raqqa Is Being Silently Slaughtered, a clandestine organization that sent news of ISIS atrocities into the world. Twice they hired smugglers to get them out, and both times the smugglers abandoned and robbed them before the border. The third time, the smugglers stole their cellphones, but at least got them across.

Hoda and most of her family no longer wear the black abayas. They are back to the pristine white hijabs favored by women in Indonesia; they attract less attention when they leave the tent to collect water or food. At one of the cisterns in the center of the camp, people stop to chat under a sky that is starting to blush at the horizon; more people slowly come out of their tents to talk and stroll in the precious two-hour stretch of time, before and after sunset, when the heat gradually softens and the mosquitoes do not yet prey.

NAHLA AHMED, FIFTEEN, LIVES IN one of the tents along with her brother and parents. The family is from East Raqqa. Her father had worked odd jobs as a handyman and kept a few sheep; they were the sort of people who couldn't afford to flee anywhere at all. Nahla says the women in the cement compound were ISIS "punishers," and swears she recognizes them from Raqqa. Once they cut up one of her flip-flops because it wasn't black. That was back in the early days, before the cages and the crucifixions, before the militants' methods became like those of Mexican drug cartels, who sent threatening messages with mutilated corpses in conspicuous public places.

Nahla's cousin was an electrician at an auto repair shop in Raqqa. One day an ISIS commander pitched up with his car and demanded it be fixed immediately. Under the two-caste system of ISIS rule, militants and their families always jumped to the front of the line. Her cousin told the commander to wait his turn. For this, he was beheaded. By that evening, everyone in the neighborhood, including the young man's new bride, had heard the news. When I ask if Nahla thinks any of the ISIS women in the camp might have also suffered at the hands of men, men rabid enough to execute mechanics for minor impudence, Nahla narrows her eyes and laughs. "Have you ever heard of a criminal admitting his crime? They have no other choice than to say these things to you."

Other women from nearby tents have dropped in to visit Nahla.

They talk of something they call the biting machine: a device with grips of serrated metal used by ISIS morality enforcers to punish women for dress infractions. The biting machine, they say, was whipped out and clamped onto a woman's breast, inflicting a pinching bite. The descriptions of the machine vary widely and keep to the tones of a dark fairy tale: "It had terrible sharp fangs" or "the sharp teeth of a small shark." Nahla's friends are settled on the floor of the tent, nodding their heads at the accounts of the biting machine, which seems a figment of a collective imagination turned gothic.

They describe punishments I have never heard of before: rubbing severed heads up against the bodies of women; grilling people alive in hot oil; holding women in cages in graveyards from nightfall till dawn. Did these things actually happen? It almost doesn't matter. Their stories reflect the point at which the human mind can no longer tolerate the scope of actual violence and trauma to which it is exposed, and so the mind begins to disassociate, inventing darker, ever more grotesque tales in order to make the daily ones seem more tolerable. As we're talking, Nahla's older brother lies motionless on a mat, his back to the family, his face inches away from the tent fabric. He stays that way for a very long time.

Around two hundred new people arrive at the camp every day. That evening, a man approaches the entrance carrying an injured child. He has walked the thirty-mile stretch from Raqqa. His red plaid shirt and long beard are caked with dust. His eyes are hollow and he takes slow, halting steps, holding the child with outstretched arms, as though he has reached a place of safety, as though there were someone there to take the child.

AS AYESHA AND THE TURKESS are mounting their escape, Commander Salar retreats to the two-story, gutted-out municipal building in Ain Issa where he and his soldiers sleep. It is guarded by several rows of concrete barriers, whorls of barbed wire, and numerous checkpoints. A generator powers a television set that is tuned to a Kurdish network. Soldiers file in and out, arranging themselves on the cushions that line the walls.

The ISIS women's situation preys on Salar's mind. Their presence in the camp is disruptive and precarious. He smokes cigarette after cigarette. "Some of these women have already been on television. Why aren't their governments asking about them? Why don't they take them back?" he says, shaking his head. "What am I supposed to do with them?"

The fact is, no country wants its ISIS citizens back. To afford them due process is costly and time-consuming; evidence is often inadmissible or hard to come by. This makes it difficult to prosecute every ISIS woman or fighter who has committed atrocities, and the risk is that courts will have to allow many to go free or to impose light sentences. But equally there is no mechanism to account for the violence and coercion many members endured themselves at the hands of the group. How to sieve out the regretters and the dissenters, those who were appalled at what they found in the Islamic State and tried to escape but could not? Most Western countries have been content to make their ISIS citizens the problems of others—the Syrian Kurds, the Iraqi Kurds, the Iraqi criminal justice system. To inflict this on fragile countries already deeply securitized and struggling to recover from years of war is immoral; it also runs the risk of allowing ISIS members, men and women alike, to receive vengeance-as-justice or perhaps even worse, no justice at all.

It was perhaps clear from early on in the conflict that Western nations had ceased viewing their ISIS citizens as their citizens at all. States like Britain, France, and the United States passed on "kill lists" early in the war to the Iraqi military. A British official said openly that "unfortunately, the only way of dealing with them will be, in almost every case, to kill them."

"It's too difficult to take them back," I say to Commander Salar. "Would you do it?"

"If they were mine, yes. I would take them."

ONE OF THE ONLY ISIS women at ease in the camp is Khadija Omri, twenty-nine, a sturdy and olive-skinned Tunisian. She understands that the civilians in the camp see her as a blight, and that she has the

first thirty seconds of each encounter to conquer that. She often manages to. Commander Salar has a high opinion of her. "She's the intellectual among them, the only one who's really thought through what
happened." When the soldiers need to convey directives to the ISIS
women, they talk to Khadija.

Khadija grew up in a dense, conservative neighborhood in Tunis,
in a large, tight-knit family that was both pious and worldly. As a teenager she spent her time doing hip-hop dance and theater. Her brothers
left for France as soon as they could, knowing there was no future for
them in Tunisia. Their neighborhood was full of young men with no
jobs, who sat around "helping" at kiosks selling tissues and nuts. For
her brothers, turning their backs on Tunisia paid off: one became a
successful chef, the other a prominent kickboxer.

Khadija married a distant cousin, Mohammad Ali, who had a university degree in mathematics and was trained as a teacher, but who—
lacking the right connections in the corrupt political system—sat at
home, jobless, for a full six years. When they got married, he started
working on construction sites, making little more than what an accomplished beggar might earn on a good day. One day, an old friend
from university saw him working as a laborer and pulled him aside.
"How come your situation is like this? Why don't you pray more, and
spend some time with us?" That's when Mohammad Ali fell in with a
local group of jihad-minded Salafis. He gave up on any prospect of a
future in Tunisia and decided it was his duty to fight for God in Syria,
to lend a hand to the brothers trying to establish a state.

When Mohammad Ali left Tunis in late 2013, there was no ISIS
yet. Just Jabhat al-Nusra and other rebel groups who were fighting
back against Assad. Khadija eventually followed him, against her family's wishes. She traveled with her one-year-old daughter, and was
pregnant already with her second. A few short months after her arrival, Mohammad Ali was killed fighting against the Free Syrian Army
in Aleppo.

Like others, she ended up in a Guest House for Widows. The
house matron was a brutal and powerful woman, the daughter of Abu
Luqman, the ISIS Emir of Raqqa. If a widow offended her, she would
ban her from the common rooms in the house, and keep her locked up

in a small room with her children the whole day. Food would be passed through the door. She refused to refer to Khadija's daughters, Barra and Sajida, by name, and designated numbers for them, 99 and 88, instead. When a young British Somali woman hurt her foot, the matron accused her of faking injury and refused to take her to the hospital. When her husband, also British, returned from his military training to pick her up, she could barely walk. He filed a negligence complaint that went nowhere. A Syrian woman went into labor in the middle of the night, and the matron couldn't be roused to take her to the hospital. The woman gave birth in the bathroom. Her baby didn't survive. "By then, I hated the State," Khadija says.

By the time Khadija remarried, in early 2015, the cities ISIS controlled were littered with men who had been seriously injured in battle and were handicapped at home, addicted to opioid painkillers. Some were organizing a rebellion against Abu Bakr al-Baghdadi. They would write openly on Facebook about the injustices and brutality they saw around them, sharing posts by prominent Islamist scholars speaking out against ISIS. They wrote, "We are here on the ground and we can tell you there is no way the Prophet, peace be upon him, would do something like this, the things that we are seeing."

At first, Khadija and her second husband, Abdi, didn't trust each other enough to reveal their real views about ISIS. He worried she might betray him if he told her what he really thought; she worried the same. In their circle of Tunisians, many men had been executed for refusing to fight or trying to escape. Some Tunisians tried to move to the distant countryside, where ISIS had little or no presence.

Eventually Abdi and Khadija came to understand they had the most important thing in common—their only aspiration was to get out of ISIS territory alive. Abdi forbade her from talking to any ISIS women and from going to the mosque. "He didn't believe it was Islam anymore, what they were doing," Khadija says. In the end, they moved to Mayadin, one of ISIS's most important strongholds near the Iraqi border, and Abdi joined a gang of fighters trying to raise money to escape by stealing ISIS cars and selling them in nearby rural towns. In those final weeks, Khadija witnessed things that would remain lodged in her mind until her time on God's earth was over. Not long after she gave birth to her first child with Abdi, Khadija and a friend visited an acquaintance's house. There was a Yazidi girl there, from Sinjar, being kept in the family as a slave. Her eyes were dull, as though she were anesthetized. When she saw Khadija, she jumped up and asked if she could hold her baby. Once the infant was in her arms, she cradled it to her chest, rocked back and forth, and cried silently.

"What's with this girl? Did her baby die?" Khadija whispered to her friend. The friend explained that the Yazidi girl had recently given birth and that her ISIS captor had taken the baby away and given it to his infertile wife. Khadija even heard tales, as the city was close to crumbling, of a brothel off Tal Abyad Street. It was a house where fighters visited kept women, because they were tired of polygamy and squabbling co-wives, tired of the WhatsApp groups with pictures of Yazidi girls for sale, tired of having to bear responsibility for a woman through formal possession and subjugation.

"A lot of us left our families and came to this place, because we wanted to live in a country that follows the real Islam," Khadija says. "I lived under the Islamic State for four years. I didn't see a single thing that resembles real Islam. All they cared about was women, pleasure, money, and power. Many of the Tunisians, we doubted whether Abu Bakr al-Baghdadi even exists. If he does, why doesn't he show his face?"

There are Kurdish soldiers continuously passing through the cement room where Khadija sits, recounting these stories. One young man stops and says to her, "If it was so bad, why didn't you leave earlier? How do we know you're not just saying these things now that ISIS is defeated?"

"I will speak for myself," she says. "If ISIS was real, I would not have left it. I would've preferred to die there, rather than leaving. But it was not easy, leaving the State. If you disappear even for a little while, everyone starts asking about you. Everyone watches you. It was almost impossible. Even my husband feared speaking to me about leaving, at first."

In June 2017, they managed to get smuggled out. In the smugglers' safe houses, there were anxieties about crossing, fears of getting raped by the Kurds or the Iraqi army or Assad's military. Soon after they reached the border, they were arrested by American and Kurdish soldiers. Khadijah wept, convinced she would be raped. But the Kurdish soldier next to her in the car squeezed her hand, and told her to calm down. It was the month of Ramadan, the heat bearing down like a furnace, and at dusk, the Americans brought them food and drinks. An American soldier brought her something to lay the baby down on. "How come he did not rape me? It completely changed the way I thought." She felt humbled that unbelievers would treat her with such decency.

Khadija likes walking near the kiosks and talking to other women in the camp. She is hungry to speak and be spoken to. Life in the camp would be easier if she stopped wearing her black robes, but she clings to them, defensive about their meaning. "Let me tell you, this is not ISIS clothing! This is the clothing of the wives of the Prophet, the clothing of the women of Islam. It is an Islamic outfit. I have also heard that the queen of England wears dark clothing and sometimes covers her hair. Is this true?"

I don't have the heart to tell her yes, but only when she is driving her Range Rover around the highlands of Balmoral.

THE COALITION OFFENSIVE TO RETAKE Raqqa is razing the city to the ground. The American, British, and French planes strike thousands of times, deploying tens of thousands of rounds of artillery. These strikes are conducted by a command center 1,200 miles away in the Persian Gulf state of Qatar, based on scant seconds of observation and often outdated intelligence. Journalists who visit sites of coalition strikes in Iraq find that one in five result in civilian death, a rate thirty-one times that acknowledged by the coalition.

In Raqqa, the U.S. military operates on the belief that Raqqa is no city for civilians anyway; that to be in Raqqa is to have asked for death. The city is pulverized, street by street. Raqqa, like much of Mosul, becomes a city of rubble.

At the Ain Issa refugee camp, the night is sometimes quiet, sometimes punctured with the sound of aircraft. They are soaring toward Raqqa city, just thirty miles south of the camp, where we sit outside

EPILOGUE: AMONG THE DISSEMBLERS 315

under the dark night sky frantic with stars. It is the closest I have been to Amira, Sharmeena, and Shamima in the months and year that have passed since I went in search of them. Since arriving, I wonder if they will have tried to escape among the final exodus from the city. Could they not have slipped in among the women who made it to this camp?

HAJAR. THE NAME MEANS ONE who migrates, and it is apt for this woman, her eyes roaming and hard with contempt. Hajar is in her late twenties, with skin white and translucent like paper. She is reluctant to talk, because she is the only one of these women who is neither regretful nor willing to lie. Commander Salar says her father-in-law is an important senior ISIS figure and that during the first few days of her detention, Hajar threatened his men with torture and beheading, were they to harm her. That was two weeks ago. In the interim, no one has come to rescue her, and her tone is softening. Salar says she won't speak to anyone, but tells me I'm free to try, as she is free to continue saying no.

She wavers for a second, deliberating whether to speak to us. Mahmoud, who accompanies me, is a Syrian Kurd, and I realize she wants to ask him for information. To the ISIS women, every Kurd they meet is a YPG soldier. To Mahmoud, every ISIS woman is a liar.

She does not know that Mahmoud is from Ain Issa itself, the town that houses the camp. That he moved there from Homs to teach school, contending with the domineering local Ba'ath Party members. That his son was born in Ain Issa, that he and his wife bought their first house there, a house he eventually had to flee with his little son on his back, leaving everything behind. The three of them had to travel through a snowstorm across the mountains into Iraqi Kurdistan; his son was almost lost on the way. The very morning I met Mahmoud, he returned to the Ain Issa house for the first time after three years away. It was pocked with bullet holes, one corner of the roof collapsing over the living room. He peered through the bars on the door and pointed at the flowered red cloth his wife had hung at the end of the corridor because she said it blocked smells from the kitchen. "It's still there," he said, smiling broadly.

Hajar's older children are lost, or at least lost to her. She left them with a neighbor to go collect her husband's ISIS salary in Raqqa, and then she was captured by Kurdish fighters en route back to Mayadin, where they were living. She had her baby, Jihad, with her, but has not been able to speak to her son and daughter. They are seven and five.

"If someone was killed, would they burn him?" Hajar asks Mahmoud. She is really asking, *If Kurdish soldiers killed my ISIS fighter husband, as I suspect, would they then have thrown him into a ditch or set him on fire, or wrapped him in a shroud and given him an Islamic burial?*

Mahmoud recoils at this question. "Who knows? Last week they burned an imam to death in front of his mosque." He is really saying, *How dare you impute such a punishment to us?*

"ISIS?" she asks.

"Who else? No one else burns but ISIS."

"I am asking about the Kurds. He was taken by them."

"No, they don't kill detainees. They are organized. They take the injured to hospitals."

"I asked one of the commanders," she says, nodding her head toward the outpost where the Kurdish soldiers sit. "He told me, 'Your husband is in hell.'"

"We don't know where he is."

"I need to know if he is alive or not. And I need to know what will happen to me. Do you know? Will there be a court hearing for the women?"

Hajar. In a sense, she is the ISIS woman I have been waiting for, all these months and years. A true believer; a real female jihadist. Not some fatherless teenager groomed and manipulated by slick propaganda. Not some lost soul who fell for a smooth-talking brother with pious swagger. Not some naïve, forlorn sister following a brother, a loyal-to-a-fault wife following a husband. Not some narcissistic drifter looking to rebel and live in comfort on the pain and misery of others. Not some mentally unstable divorcee. Not some sincere but insufficiently skeptical believer who thought a kingdom of heaven, forged in the middle of bloody war, would save her husband or family from debt and joblessness.

Hajar is none of those things. She believes it all. She believes in the coming apocalypse that al-Baghdadi prophesied and the already apparent signs of the end of times. Her language is replete with scripture about the land blessed in the Quran itself. She says, "There will be a lot of blood. When you walk, you won't find a place to put your feet, there will be so much blood." Hajar is meant to be the personification of the apocalyptic darkness at the very heart of ISIS, stripped of explanations and grievances and justifications.

But even Hajar has a story, and it is the story of Syria itself: the authoritarian rule of the Assad dynasty, and the lengths it has always been willing to go—massacres, oppression, and bloodshed—to retain absolute power. Hajar was born in 1990 in the city of Hama, to a mother and father who had lost their spirit and dignity well before she was even born. She is the daughter of a family, like so very many others, whose early inheritance was loss.

When the city of Hama rose up against Hafez al-Assad in 1982, Hajar's father dropped out of the military to join the revolt, as did most of the men of the city, including many who had nothing to do with the Muslim Brotherhood. When Assad dispatched his troops to raze the city, four in Hajar's family were killed: two paternal uncles, one maternal uncle, and a cousin. The cousin died stupidly, shot in the back while riding his motorcycle.

Hajar's father had been training to be a pilot, but after the massacre there was clearly no future for him in the military. For a long while, he stayed at home, depressed, and then finally set up a shop selling doors and windows. Hama in those years was a traumatized city. Its residents walked through streets cleared of the corpses, past new busts of the president emblazoned, insultingly, with the creed of Islam, *There is no God but God, and Mohammad is his messenger.* There was a cemetery not far from the playground near her house, where many of those killed in the uprising were buried. Her family, she recalls, were devastated by the events. "Many of their relatives were killed, many went missing. There were some people we knew who stayed in prison for twenty years. My parents were very angry."

Mahmoud listens to Hajar impassively. Being asked about Hama, about the past, has relaxed her and she is now speaking more openly.

She describes her family as "committed, not extremist." Mahmoud whispers to me, "No one in Hama is moderate! Their moderate *is* extremist."

Hajar grew up wanting to be a doctor, but her father ended her education early and asked her to get married. "I didn't want to, but I agreed for his sake. I had to obey him." She was a young mother and housewife when events in the poor southern town of Dara'a sparked the 2011 protests against the government, now in the hands of Hafez al-Assad's son, Bashar.

Hajar's father came alive again, as though awakened from a three-decade stupor. "We thought this time, Bashar would fall quickly," she says. "We never thought there would be so many factions, that it would expand and expand." Every day, her father left the house, helping the wounded. The Syrian military raided their house daily, usually around five in the morning. They came with armored vehicles and tanks. They brought green passenger buses and rounded up men, cars, motorbikes, indiscriminately. "Assad or I burn the country," the president declared, meaning, *It's either me or destruction.*

And what it meant for Syrians was this: 500,000 killed, 11 million refugees including the internally displaced, cities of rubble. Young men and young women with stellar educations, who once dreamed of cosmopolitan careers and happy families, now impoverished and stateless, focused only on subsistence.

It is arguably the most defining conflict of our time, and yet, has there ever been a modern conflict so readily misunderstood? The Syrian civil war, now drawing to a close, is most often viewed as a sectarian war between Shia and Sunnis, a proxy conflict between Iran and Gulf Arab states, and a contest for the upper-hand among those Arab states themselves. Those who wish to excuse America's role in exacerbating the conflict call it a war of Iranian aggression, abetted by Russia; those who wish to challenge U.S. hegemony minimize Assad's war crimes and paint his opposition as al-Qaeda fanatics.

All these descriptions carry whispers of truth, but they elide Syria's many other divides—the fractures among Syrian Sunnis themselves, along class and geographic lines, degrees of religiosity and secularism; the frightened early turn of Syria's other religious minorities, the Christians and the Druze, in favor of Assad, whose decades of familial authoritarian rule seemed safer than any alternative that might replace it; the decision of millions of Syrians to simply stay put, not out of loyalty but because they wearied of fighting, or chose the regime as a lesser evil.

Then there is the fluid nature of the opposition, which includes men like Hajar's husband, so intent on bringing down Assad that they moved pragmatically between whatever groups seemed best poised to accomplish that goal. Hajar's husband started out with the CIA-backed Free Syrian Army, then moved to the Nusra Front, which was called an al-Qaeda affiliate. Then, finally, to ISIS.

One day Hajar's father left the house, as usual, to organize with other men in the city. He never returned. Two months after he disappeared, a man called Hajar's mobile phone, claiming to be a friend of her father's from the FSA. She asked to speak to him and the man told her it was not possible, that her father was injured. But she never saw him again.

IT WAS IN AL HOL, on the western flank of Syria, about two hundred and fifty kilometers west of Ain Issa, in that fetid, freezing camp brimming with people, that Shamima Begum surfaced again, in the eyes of the world. "I'm a sister from London, I'm one of the Bethnal Green girls," she told the British journalist who found her, and splashed her face and interview on the front pages of *The Times*.

AT THIS POINT, THREE OF the Bethnal Green girls—Amira, Shamima, and Sharmeena—were still alive. A month earlier, in late January 2019, as the Syrian Democratic Forces pressed down on the final remaining sliver of territory ISIS held in southeastern Syria, in an area known as Baghuz, the girls weighed what to do. The husbands of Amira and Sharmeena had been killed in previous bouts of fighting. They were single and alone, but still zealous and determined to stay with the caliphate to its final end. The winter was freezing cold and they were now continually on the move, scarcely eating, sleeping under trees. Shamima's husband was still alive. He still believed, for no reason seemingly beyond blind faith, that the group might prevail.

SHAMIMA HAD TWO CHILDREN AND was heavily pregnant with her third. Her young daughter and son were sick, but it was difficult to be seen by a doctor; the hospitals in the areas where they were staying, around Mayadin and Hajin, were overwhelmed by people with war injuries. They turned away even people whose bodies were cut up by shrapnel. There was no medicine left. Her young son died first. That was when Shamima knew that she had to try to get out, for the sake of her daughter and her unborn child. She joined the crowds moving away from the fighting, streaming toward the territory held by the militias fighting the latest dredges of the Islamic State. Her daughter, increasingly ill, died before they reached the camp at Al Hol, where ISIS families and civilians who had fled were sheltering.

SHAMIMA'S INTERVIEW WITH THE BRITISH journalist from *The Times* was not unsympathetic, but like many that followed, it gave her ample rope with which to fashion her own noose. When asked if she had witnessed executions, she said no, but added that she once saw a severed head in a bin on the street: "It didn't faze me at all," she said. The remark was blasted on most every radio and television news broadcast across the United Kingdom.

THE FACT THAT SHE HAD been groomed and recruited as a fifteen-year-old, primed and indoctrinated by the Islamic State, evaporated from the national conversation about her. That she had been a child bride, married before legal age, that two of her children had recently died, did not deter reporters from interrogating her for dispatches read voraciously back home. Did she realize, they asked her, that the public questioned whether she could ever be rehabilitated? "I'm still kind of in the mentality of having planes over my head and an emergency backpack and starving, all these things," she said. What did Shamima say to the head of UK intelligence, who had said that women like her were a danger? Would she accept it if the British authorities took her child away, in the event they were admitted back to the UK? What did being "British" mean to her? Would she raise her son as a British boy? Did she accept British democracy and rights for women and homo-sexuals? Shamima gamely answered these questions, professing in a sometimes shaky voice that she could be rehabilitated, that she didn't even know what her options would be, and didn't feel it was appropriate to demand any particular course for herself; sounding more naïve and confused by the day, precisely like the traumatized, indoctrinated nineteen-year-old that she was. "I think a lot of people should have, like, sympathy towards me for everything I've been through."

BUT SYMPATHY WAS NOT WHERE public sentiment was headed. Short days after Shamima surfaced and asked for help to be brought home, the UK Home Secretary ordered her to be stripped of British citizen-ship. The legal basis was that Shamima, because of her Bangladeshi origin, was eligible for citizenship of a second country. Bangladesh quickly said it wanted nothing to do with her; Shamima had never even visited the country, how was she to become their problem? Rac-ist memes began proliferating and spreading, a whole Facebook page sprang up to curate them: Shamima likened to a black umbrella tent, Shamima in a hospital giving birth to a ticking bomb, Shamima's severed head superimposed onto porn sites and Mother's Day cards. Many of the images bled into a generalized creepy far-right disgust for Muslims, mocking her covering, her brown skin, and physical ap-pearance; her name itself became a racist slur, something British Muslim girls found themselves being called on the street in London: "*Shamima Begum,*" a new gender-sensitive incarnation of "Paki."

SHAMIMA GAVE BIRTH TO A boy in mid-February. She named him Jar-rah, and posed for a photographer, standing in the camp with a sea of white tents in the background, holding the infant in a blue-and-white-striped blanket. Three weeks later, Jarrah died of pneumonia.

. . .

OUTSIDE, NEAR THE KIOSKS THAT sell tea where people gather to smoke or chat as the sky darkens, there are tales traded about the outlandish stories circulating in the camp, stories that fleeing ISIS members will tell as they try to hide what they have done: there is the man who says he came to the caliphate as a *simit* seller and stayed to write short stories; there is a sudden profusion of cooks and clerical assistants.

All through 2017 and into 2019, camps in Syria and Iraq swelled with thousands of ISIS women and children, whose husbands and fathers were either dead or detained by Iraqi or U.S.-allied Kurdish forces. Courts in Baghdad began sentencing many of the foreign women to death. The trials often lasted only ten minutes, and the courts kept evidence, if there was any, secret; defense lawyers were paid next to nothing. Speed was the only incentive.

The Office of the UN High Commissioner for Human Rights warned these trials would lead to "irreversible miscarriages of justice," but for the Iraqi state, the summary trials were retribution for the extreme savagery ISIS and its predecessors had shown toward Shia Iraqis. The judicial authorities were also pragmatic: if most of these women's countries of origin refused to take them back, what was to be done? Who knew whether they had peeled potatoes in the caliphate, or committed atrocities? What if they still believed that everyone who wasn't affiliated with ISIS was an enemy of God who deserved death? Did you want women like that walking around your country?

In Europe, Britain and France led the way in stripping the nationality of their citizens who had joined ISIS. The UK Home Office argued this was "in the public good" and that citizenship was "a privilege, not a right," even as it rendered these individuals stateless, leaving them without the recourse or oversight of *any* state's legal process or rules. As a security measure intended simply to block the return of European citizens who had fought in Syria, it worked. But it was an approach bound to fuel more conflict and more resentment.

After 9/11, in the netherworld of the War on Terror, Western security states set down a dark path; they began rejecting the very idea that war had rules, that prisoners were still humans with rights. America's

War on Terror had created an enduring, transnational third dimension, a lethal space of limbo, untethered from the rules-based international order, in which suspects were passed around, held indefinitely, tortured, and executed. The West had become more extreme, and professed confusion at the extremism that arose in response.

THE ISLAMIC STATE WAS NOW vanquished as a military force. Over late 2018 its army dwindled down to a few thousand men in the desert hinterlands of Syria; in March 2019, the Syrian Defense Forces overran Baguz, the group's final stronghold, raised their flags and declared victory. The leaders of countries whose citizens had flocked to join the Islamic State, from Morocco to Saudi Arabia, pretended to recognize the need for changing the conditions that had propelled their young women and men to "Syria's field of jihads." But virtually many of their failed policies remained in place. So too did the dysfunctional American system of patronage of these troubled Arab regimes, which enabled their failures and protected them from their own dissenting populations.

In Tunisia, where Nour was raising her daughter alone in a country where she had been unable to get an education because of her faith, there was at least a glimmer of change. The economy still kept her family at borderline poverty, most encounters with the police still ended with a bribe, and her brand of Salafi activism was banned. But there was a democratic transition under way, powerful enough that the old regime's ambassadors and torturers went on television at night and confessed. Perhaps this transition was thin and fragile, and to Nour, who had endured much hardship, it was meaningless. Rahma, speaking to journalists from her detention in Libya, made it clear she felt the same way.

But to a great many Tunisians, their fumbling, more inclusive government—the only state in the whole of the region where the pre–Arab Spring opposition was still in the political game, and the old elites had met some semblance of justice—was something to value. The new Tunisia faced powerful regional foes, particularly Saudi Arabia and the United Arab Emirates, who chafed at seeing a country where moderate Islamists had prevailed. But at the very least, its fate was still unwritten. In 2011, a senior female politician from Ennahda served as deputy president of the country's Constituent Assembly, one of the highest political offices held by a woman in the whole of the Middle East. In the spring of 2018, Tunis elected the Arab world's first woman mayor, affiliated with the Ennahda party. Nour's daughter would grow up in a country where such things were possible.

For Asma, Aws, and Dua, the young Syrian women of Raqqa, the seeming impermanence of living as a refugee in Turkey soon became their everyday. For Asma and Aws, who once had promising futures as educated women, poised to achieve more independence than any generation of Syrian women before them, the war had blighted any such prospects. They were survival seekers now. Dua, who had only ever wanted a simple life of dignity, was stranded in a foreign country, with no skills or education, separated from her family, alone with the memory that her Saudi husband had died killing other Muslims.

In government-controlled Syria, the broken land over which Bashar al-Assad presided as nominal victor, there was no sign that the regime would cease the policies of repression and violence that had provoked the original uprising. In July 2018, the government issued death certificates for sixty thousand people who had simply disappeared in government detention. Those who remained in Syria, on both sides of the regime/opposition divide, found themselves corrupted and straining for basic subsistence amid the lawlessness and insecurity of seven years of war. Reopening a shop, procuring a death certificate, requesting information about disappeared relatives: every small act required exorbitant payments to either local militias, predatory lawyers, or bureaucrats. Nothing was normal. Reconstruction seemed a hallucination. The cost aside, who was physically left to rebuild the country? The war had decimated much of the country's male population; millions had fled, and of those who had stayed, a great many had been maimed or killed.

For Dunya, still marooned in the small Syrian village near the Turkish border, a life back in Germany held some appeal, if only she could get there. The far right were ascendant, the right wing of Angela Merkel's party agitated for the upper hand, and the everyday racism and exclusion she had seen Muslim-born Germans endure in her youth were only exacerbated by the influx of Syrian refugees. But she would take her old life back in a second. Whether the next generation of Muslims in Germany took a similar path, if they felt global injustice acutely enough to be led down the dark hole of militancy, only God could know.

In London, Sabira continued to grieve for her brother Soheil and often still struggled with the confusing, contradictory rules those close to her maintained for good Muslim women.

IN BRITAIN, RELATIONS BETWEEN MUSLIM Britons and the government continued deteriorating. In the summer of 2018, Boris Johnson, a leading Conservative politician with ambitions of becoming prime minister, said Muslim women who wore the face veil looked like bank robbers and postboxes. Street harassment and physical attacks on Muslim women spiked in the wake of his comments. In the spring of 2019, the Conservative MP Jacob Rees Mogg nodded at a German far-right group on Twitter, signaling that a party that explicitly seeks to rid Germany of Muslims was worth British attention. Bigotry against Muslims had become the crudest but surest way to politically ascend in the contemporary United Kingdom.

Under Donald Trump, the United States dropped even the pretense of supporting Arab democracy or self-determination. In the fall of 2018, the president openly described the U.S. relationship with Saudi Arabia as a protection racket, declaring that the Saudis couldn't "last two weeks" without American protection. The U.S. military, for its part, refused to count the civilians it had killed in the blitz-style final assault against ISIS. "No one will ever know how many died," a Defense Department spokesman admitted. Washington said it would pay nothing for the reconstruction of Syria unless Assad and Iran agreed to certain terms, which they would inevitably refuse. Had such terms been achievable, the war would likely not have dragged on for seven years, defying any resolution in the first place.

• • •

I INITIALLY SET OUT TO write this book because I was disturbed by media accounts of the Bethnal Green girls' disappearance, and the special culpability that was assigned to them as consorts of evil, despite their very evident youth. I was struck by how the most noxious things said about these girls were said by other women, in fact women who would otherwise identify as liberal feminists.

To the public, they were either naïve jihadi brides or calculating monsters. But most of the women in this book were neither passive nor predatory, and trying to pin down their degree of agency seemed to be only one line of inquiry, and certainly not the most revealing. Some collaborated or acted knowingly; some were so young that, despite the outward appearance of deliberate choice, they were not mature enough to exercise anything approaching adult judgment.

Most policy papers, public discussions, and security initiatives dealing with gender and extremism seem wholly disconnected from the lived experiences of women in the Middle East. This is largely because the counterterrorism discourses, from the United Nations and across national governments, seek to discuss and craft policies targeting women across a vast range of political and social contexts— from the hipster neighborhoods of peaceful East London to the collapsed, war-torn cities of Syria and Iraq to the battlefields of Somalia and Nigeria, where unpopular, weak, or corrupt states confront armed and popular opponents.

In 2017, the European Parliament's Committee on Women's Rights and Gender Equality released a report on women and violent extremism. The report speaks of the first jihad, the early-seventh-century conquest of Islam on the Arabian subcontinent, as though it were an event that happened last year. It includes the word "ideology" forty-two times, and argues that women undergo a "process of radicalisation" through a number of "push and pull factors," and then go on to "form an integral part of jihad."

Honestly dealing with problems of modern conflicts involves acknowledging awkward truths about how we have ended up with such violence in the first place. But this 2017 report locates itself in history most strangely. It begins in the seventh century, as if there were more clues about ISIS to be gleaned from A.D. 622 than from the 1990s, the years when Iraq's long history of totalitarianism and institutionalized cruelty peaked with the crushing of Shia and Kurd rebellions, or even than from 2003, the year that the United States, with the support of European allies—against the wishes of millions of people who marched across the world against this intention—invaded and occupied Iraq and set in motion the conflict that would eventually help produce the group.

When the report describes the context in which young European women have been attracted to ISIS militancy, it hedges its language in a manner that seems suspicious of factual realities: the 2003 invasion of Iraq and the atrocities committed by Syrian president Bashar al-Assad are *"perceived* injustices" (emphasis mine). The post-9/11 rise in Islamophobia has *"incited feelings* of social and cultural exclusion and marginalization." The report aims to counter gender stereotypes, but its approach is much like Victorian writing on hysteria—there are things in women's heads, *incited feelings* and *perceptions,* and there are the things the good doctors conclude are actually wrong with them. The latter are diagnosed unequivocally: "a sense of adventure," the "desire to be part of something bigger and divine," the "aspiration to build a utopian caliphate."

The authors write that in the ISIS narrative, "Western feminism is portrayed as imperialist and exclusively advantageous to white women, leaving little to no room for Islamic women and their values." But this is not simply cunning ISIS propaganda; it is something a whole generation of Muslim women across the world say readily and regularly in books, articles, dissertations, and on social media.

This perspective reminds me again of Victorian medics diagnosing hysteria as a peculiarly female condition. The report understands the extremism of the Muslim woman as a gendered pathology: the affliction of a woman who has internalized male patriarchy so assiduously that she, delusionally, seeks agency within its very strictures. Doctors in the nineteenth century believed women "hysterics" were possessed by demons and deviant sexual desires; in the twenty-first century, professional "deradicalizers" believe women militants are consumed by wicked religious ideologies and sexual repression.

The comparison is useful mainly for the sake of identifying the power of the diagnostician in relation to the subject: hysteria was a made-up disease, constructed by medical forces in a culture that prized female docility and purity. Militancy certainly isn't made up. But it is more politically expedient to suggest that women have been bewitched than to acknowledge the overarching wars, conflicts, and authoritarian repression that have created the grievances and space for extremism to thrive.

The 2010s have been the decade of feminist reading of militancy, based on the laudable aim of being less sexist and stereotypical in assessing Muslim women's involvement in supporting, developing, and sustaining jihadist groups. But this effort has not involved a great willingness to examine old beliefs about the causes and roots of violent conflicts, or dualistic certainties about enlightened secular liberalism versus regressive patriarchal Islam. Progressive analysis certainly helps us see how women distinctly experience repressive political orders, where they are marginalized and disempowered by their social status, religious sect, political affiliation, or identity mosaics of all these things. But the focus seems to dwell excessively on *the manner of their experience* rather than confronting the wider structural causes and realities that brought about that experience in the first place. What I mean to say, more simply, is that I hope the events recounted in this book will show the crucial importance of context: understanding how Nour experienced Ben Ali–era Tunisia as a woman is crucial to the arc of her life, but ultimately her story is embedded in a world she shares with Walid and Karim, her fellow Tunisians.

Social and political specificity is essential to understanding any conflict, and policies that seek to deal with extremism in toto by imposing generic language and policy ideas on a range of societies are deeply misguided. They will at best fail and waste resources, and at worst may aggravate conditions by imposing punitive and wrong-minded solutions. I hope, after having spent time in the lives of these women, you will understand instinctively why this is the case.

There is a shortage of accounts that consider how ordinary women in the Middle East are drawn to militancy as a last resort—after having sought peaceful, civic, alternative ways to negotiate themselves out of circumstances of poverty, instability, lawlessness, discrimination, corruption, state repression, and abuse. While recognizing how their gender shaped their choices, I do not see how we can disentangle their circumstances from the society around them, and indeed, from the condition of the states they lived under, and how those states interacted with the global order and marketplace, dominated still by the United States.

Women may certainly experience wars, volatility, and state repression differently than men. But ultimately gender does not define their experience, it simply particularizes it; the women of this book have far more in common with the men around them than they do with women of wholly different countries.

LATE ONE AFTERNOON, ASMA, AWS, and Dua gather for lunch in an anonymous second-floor flat in the narrow back alleys of Urfa. A sour, salty smell wafts up from the sheep's brain-and-tripe restaurant on the ground floor of the building. Asma and Dua haven't seen Aws for a while, and she shows them a new butterfly necklace she had bought at the bazaar. None of them is working, because there were no jobs available in Urfa that even a semi-respectable Syrian woman could contemplate. For men, it wasn't so bad to wash dishes in a restaurant or service cars; they were still bringing in some income, providing for the family.

For women, such menial work clung to you somehow, and sullied you in the eyes of your fellow Syrians. Five years later, no one would remember what a man had had to do to get by, but they would remember forever if a woman had entered a Turkish family's home to work as a cleaner. It was partly why the three of them thought constantly about leaving this world of Syrian refugees behind, to try to slip into some European city where they could start over again. In Europe there would be work that didn't steal your honor; women wouldn't stare at you viciously as some cheap prospect luring away their husband; and you could try to avoid other Arabs and Syrians and begin to forget what had been done to your country.

It was striking, Asma thinks, how in Syria itself so much of that old clinging shame culture had started to ebb; women in cafés, women in universities, women inhabiting the public sphere as if they had a right to be there and had been there all along, all that had been becoming more commonplace in their lives. But here, in Urfa, it was as if a generation's progress had been washed away overnight; everyone's circumstances so reduced that all those more decent ways of being active, present, involved in life were once more out of reach; amid all the strain and dislocation, the old taboos were somehow rejuvenated and in the ascendant, even though women worked harder—as everyone was working harder—just to get by. It is said that war transforms women's status in a society faster than any other sort of change. But it was not clear such a force would exert itself on the refugee diaspora that was now their home.

With distance, they could see that they had participated in that regressive destruction themselves. Asma says she could not forgive the foreigners who had shown up in Syria, disrupting the revolution with their own designs. She moves closer to the window, though it offered no breeze to soften the heat. Aws shakes her head, disagreeing and recalling the black flags draped across Raqqa so shortly after the opposition took the city. She is still stunned that many in her community, the boys she had grown up with, had wanted a future like that, so inward-turning and orthodox, an Islam of *sharia* and little more. "The point is, all the sides who fought in Syria were Syrian. It was a fight amongst ourselves. No one was really a stranger."

But it was almost as if all the mistakes had long been written in advance. What strong, bright current could really have emerged from a murky sinister rule like that of the Assads, distinct and untouched by the industrial-scale brutality, ready to take a different course? There was no faction in the Syrian conflict that had ennobled itself, that hadn't descended into a raw craving for power and had refrained from hurting others.

That is what the girls tell themselves, at least, even though they know they could never look their Raqqa neighbors in the face again. Who could forget what had been done to their loved ones, and who was responsible? That community that had existed before the war, so humdrum in its habits, but in hindsight so innocent, was destroyed now, and irretrievable. People carried war wounds into their old age, handed memories and enmities down from generation to generation. Who could even think their little world could begin to recover now, when the suffering was so fresh? There was a slow trickle of Syrians heading back to their home cities and villages, but the very idea of normality, whatever that was, felt like a grand aspiration that would now forever be denied them. "Even if one day things are all right, I will never return," says Aws. "Too much blood has been spilled on all sides. I'm not talking just about ISIS, but among everyone."

In the European cities that beckon in the distance, promising some better days on this earth, there remains an enduring fear of precisely this: that women like Asma, Aws, and Dua, as well as men who carried guns in Syria, would arrive as refugees and walk the streets, awaiting residency. It was said that an entire local command of Nusra, Syria's al-Qaeda faction, were now gathered in the same German town.

This residual fear is all that lingered of the Islamic State caliphate in the eyes of those who had never longed for one. For Sabira in London, reflecting on all that had transpired since the fateful day her brother stopped at the *dawah* stand on the high street so many years ago, the experience had left some part of her permanently adrift. Some people who had lost sisters and daughters to al-Baghdadi's project mocked it caustically. "Land of borrow someone else's car. Land of loser dying as a *shaheed*." She still chafed at those who sweepingly described the brothers who had gone to fight as zombies; for some, her own, had been propelled by valor and principle, and though she herself had been young and foolish, and would live with the consequences forever, she would maintain that forever too.

No one even said the words anymore—caliphate, *khilafa*, the abode of the faith, the land of Allah and his Prophet, Dar al-Islam— terms that had entered their conversation for a time like precious jewels. It had been enchanting just to have cause to say them, as though some window had opened up in the middle of their twenty-first-century lives, offering a glimpse of a way out, a glimpse of some kind of homeland, a future, a nation, a realm that fit. What to do now with all the hope and longing those words had held within them? Sabira imagined it would all just recede, back into whatever recess had existed before.

That darkness had held much inchoate pain and longing, emotions much easier to bear when they were blunted and in the shadows. More than any, disappointment: Was this bleak present, this civilization, this fate, their only inheritance? To live as perpetual others within the West, within it but never of it, part of it; increasingly reviled; marked as different by their religion, even if that religion was only one thread of their identities; disconnected from any power; obliged to watch one Middle Eastern state fall after another. What has it to do with you? she had asked her brother again and again, before he left. He had tried to explain, but eventually gave up. As it said in Sura al-Baqarah of the Holy Quran, "But perhaps you hate a thing and it is good for you; and perhaps you love a thing and it is bad for you. And Allah Knows, while you know not."

NOTE TO READERS

All of the women in this book are singular, real people. I have changed the names and some minor biographical details of some, in order to ensure their privacy and security. The majority of their stories are drawn from extended in-person interviews conducted between 2015 and 2018 in the United Kingdom, Turkey, Tunisia, and Syria. In some cases, I sketched accounts and scenes based on conversations over the phone and in text messages with family members, friends, and other associates, and drew on reporting in the public domain. Where possible, I consulted as many sources as possible surrounding these stories and events as well as alternative perspectives, in an attempt to verify the truthfulness of the accounts.

I spoke to more than twenty women associated with ISIS in the course of my reporting, and the families of several more. It was challenging to decide whose stories to include, because the women whose experiences most neatly reflected distinct aspects of ISIS's appeal and recruitment weren't necessarily the women to whom I had strong or consistent access. At the time I began my research, anyone touched by this subject was wildly skittish. It could take weeks to persuade even distant friends and relatives to talk, who then needed weeks of persuading to consider making further connections. The women themselves, regardless of place, were understandably frightened; they knew they were closely watched by security services and had little incentive to call attention to themselves. Some met with me once, got spooked, and then refused to meet a second time. Some simply disappeared. There was the Tunisian beaux arts student with the Communist tattoo who had fallen into what I can only describe as a subculture

of Salafi hedonism; the London girl who grew enamored of the decidedly wrong footballer; the Iranian woman from a Kurdish village who
claimed to have wandered into the caliphate in pursuit of IVF. If I had
written a play, I would have sent them onstage in cameo roles, but on
the page the already crowded cast of characters seemed to demand
enough of the reader.

In sections where I portray a wider social and political context in
significant detail, I spent months and years, in some cases, reporting
the background story myself. In Tunisia, for example, I interviewed
imams, lawyers, jurists, activists, journalists, Western diplomats, academics, politicians, militants of various backgrounds, trying to re-
create the recent past and assess the present context, as it was
recounted to me. I spent time in the neighborhoods that became characters themselves, and lingered for hours in people's living rooms. I
watched video footage of protests and demonstrations that arose in
people's stories, and looked through many cellphone photo albums,
catching glimpses of moments and people that my characters had described. In London, I spent years investigating and writing about the
complex backstory to the Bethnal Green girls' disappearance, which is
foregrounded by the evolution of the British Muslim community itself
and its increasingly tense relationship with a political and media establishment sympathetic and tilting to the far right.

The intimacy of some of the accounts reflects two things. First,
the closeness I felt to the places, characters, and story. Sitting with a
Tunisian mother railing against her loose daughters, an impulsive
British Pakistani girl railing against her stuffy parents, sitting with
young Syrian women negotiating marriage demands amidst a dark
new order that had descended overnight, the seductive appeal of political radicalism brewed together with religion, the disdain of the
educated Tunisian liberal for the veiled or bearded opponent, all of
these dynamics felt deeply familiar to me. While I don't appear in this
narrative at all, I could hear my adolescence, my mother, our family
and national history, echoing through all of it.

Second, though I often relied on a translator, given the range of
Arabic dialects and social backgrounds I was working across, I conducted interviews that touched on intimate matters alone with

sources, without the awkward presence of a man or any third party in the room.

The question may arise as to whether my Iranian background might have complicated my research. I was heartened that it did not. Like any reporter, I judged when to share personal information based on the relationship and degree of rapport and trust I established with sources. Being able to blend in physically and sharing a basic religious literacy certainly helped.

I am acutely aware that these stories do not tell the comprehensive story of all ISIS women, and that many engaged in atrocities that amounted to war crimes. That fact stands starkly as its own truth. I have tried to write most closely from the perspective of the women themselves, while providing background that might make their actions intelligible. The context is there to illuminate not to justify, and judgment remains the prerogative of the reader.

Ethical considerations matter, even with ISIS suspects. I will state openly, and wish more colleagues would do the same, that women associated with ISIS being held by Kurdish or Iraqi security forces consent to interviews in the context of civilian detention, but detention nonetheless. They may not feel safe disclosing their real views about anything, from ISIS itself to the conditions in which they are being held. The things they say, whether truthful, false, or simply coerced, may put them at risk of abuse. This must be acknowledged when writing and reporting about them, along with the ethical and legal concerns it raises. Journalists dart back to the safety of Western capitals, their front-page stories or podcast material in hand, rarely thinking about the fate of the female sources they leave behind, whether they are now more vulnerable to abuse or wrongful prosecution because of things they have said, their identities almost never protected. I elected not to include the experience of at least one interviewee in the narrative, because I felt the conditions of her detention were too securitized to consider her nominal consent freely given.

I relied on a number of publications by academics, journalists, and researchers in the course of my writing, including work by Nadia Marzouki, Hamza Meddeb, Fabio Marone, Rory McCarthy, Youssef Cherif, Habib Sayah, Darryl Li, Thomas Hegghammer, Shadi Hamid,

Max Weiss, Stéphane Lacroix, Shiraz Maher, Joas Wagemakers, Guido Steinberg, Madawi al-Rasheed, Michael Ayari, Sam Heller, and Richard Atwood, as well as the following books: Arun Kundnani, *The Muslims Are Coming: Islamophobia, Extremism, and the Domestic War on Terror*; Lisa Wedeen, *Ambiguities of Domination: Politics, Rhetoric, and Symbols in Contemporary Syria*; Hanna Batatu, *Syria's Peasantry, the Descendants of Its Lesser Rural Notables, and Their Politics*; Lisa Stampnitzky, *Disciplining Terror: How Experts Invented "Terrorism"*; Mohammad Abu Rumman, Hasssan Abu Hanieh, *Infatuated with Martyrdom: Female Jihadism from al-Qaeda to the "Islamic State"*; Mohammad-Mahmoud Ould Mohamedou, *A Theory of ISIS: Political Violence and the Transformation of Global Order, Global Salafism: Islam's New Religious Movement*, edited by Roel Meijer; Rania Abouzeid, *No Turning Back: Life, Loss, and Hope in Wartime Syria*.

ACKNOWLEDGMENTS

This book originated in a story for *The New York Times,* and for that I owe thanks to Terry McDermott, Dean Baquet, Michael Slackman, and Doug Schorzman. Also to Tara Tadros-Whitehill, for her images.

Thank you to Ann Pitoniak, my editor, who brought such keen intellect, vision, and devotion to this book. Also at Random House, thanks to my shepherding editor Hilary Redmon, and to Molly Turpin and London King. Thank you to my agent, Natasha Fairweather. I am grateful to the support of the New America Fellows program, as well as to Arizona State University: Awista Ayoub, Peter Bergen, and Daniel Rothman.

In Germany, Turkey, and Syria, thank you to Yasser al-Hajji. Also, Björn Stritzel and Abu Ibrahim Raqqawi of Raqqa Silently Slaughtered. I am indebted to Mahmoud Sheikh Ibrahim, for his integrity and for keeping us safe. Thank you to the Ain Issa/Raqqa command of the Syrian Democratic Forces. In Iraq and the KRG, thanks to Shilan Dosky and Aziz Ahmed.

In Tunis, thanks to Habib Sayah, Youssef el-Sharif, Seifeddine Farjani, Laryssa Chomiak, and Moenes Sboui. I am grateful to Hassan Moraja. To the encampment of Naveena Kottoor, Joachim Paul, and Magda Elhaitem, for offering me space, and later for being readers. For Rad Addala, who opened all the doors—I cannot begin to gather all the thanks I need.

Thank you to a great many people in London: Salman Farsi, Ben Ferguson, Fatima Saleria, Yasminara Khan, Tam Hussein, Sajid Iqbal,

338 ACKNOWLEDGMENTS

Jemima Khan, Moazzam Begg, Ibrahim Mohamoud, Mohammed Rabbani, Asim Qureshi. Thank you to Melanie Smith and the Institute for Strategic Dialogue for access to their archive. Special thanks to Tasnime Akunjee, for updates over the years. At the Kingston University Department of Journalism, for support and great encouragement, thanks to Beth Brewster, Maria Ahmed, Fiona O'Brien, and especially Brian Cathcart. Thanks to Dan Townend, for help finding things. At the Foreign and Commonwealth Office, thanks to Simon Shercliff and Jenny Pearce. And to GR, for a religious education of sorts and patient answers to many questions.

Thanks to reporter friends for operational advice: Lindsey Hilsum, Owen Bennet Jones, Richard Spencer, Jim Muir, Lyse Doucet, and Leena Saeedi.

For research help, thanks to Alice Wojcik, Ameet Ubhi, Lindsey Allemang, and Asha Hussein.

Thanks to the editors I have worked with along the way: Alicia Wittmeyer, McKenna Stayner, David Shariatmadari, Jonathan Landman, Joanna Biggs, and Toby Lichtig.

Thank you to friends who read early and late: Joseph Logan, Mohammed Bazzi, Rifat Siddiqui, Lisa Beyer, Adam Shatz, Kareem Fahim, Zahra Hankir, Scheherezade Faramarzi, and especially Bassem Mroue. Thank you to Rozita Riazati and Sarah Weigel. Extremely belatedly, thanks to Khaled Dawoud.

Thanks to Farzaneh Katouzi.

My precious Hourmazd and Siavash, for wily humor and productive needling. Most of all, Nader Nezam-mafi, my home across time and space—with love and gratitude for everything.